A FIRE
AT THE
CENTER

A FIRE
AT THE
CENTER

SOLIDARITY, WHITENESS, AND BECOMING A WATER PROTECTOR

A MEMOIR

KAREN VAN FOSSAN

SKINNER HOUSE BOOKS

BOSTON

www.skinnerhouse.org

Printed in the United States

Cover design by Andrea Guinn
Text design by Jeff Miller

print ISBN: 978-1-55896-910-0
eBook ISBN: 978-1-55896-911-7

6 5 4 3 2 1
27 26 25 24 23

Names: Van Fossan, Karen I. (Karen Irene), author.
Title: A fire at the center : solidarity, whiteness, and becoming a water protector / Karen Van Fossan.
Other titles: Collective liberation and the uneasy question of Whiteness
Description: Boston, MA : Skinner House Books, [2023] | Includes bibliographical references.
Identifiers: LCCN 2023001597 (print) | LCCN 2023001598 (ebook) | ISBN 9781558969100 (print) | ISBN 9781558969117 (ebook)
Subjects: LCSH: Van Fossan, Karen I. (Karen Irene)--Political activity--Standing Rock Indian Reservation (N.D. and S.D.) | Women, White--Political activity--Standing Rock Indian Reservation (N.D. and S.D.) | White people--Political activity Standing Rock Indian Reservation (N.D. and S.D.) | White people--Race identity--North Dakota--Bismarck. | Women--North Dakota--Bismarck--Biography. | Bismarck (N.D.)--Biography.
Classification: LCC E99.D1 V24 2023 (print) | LCC E99.D1 (ebook) | DDC 305.809/073 [B]--dc23/eng/20230201
LC record available at https://lccn.loc.gov/2023001597
LC ebook record available at https://lccn.loc.gov/2023001598

Chapter eight, "Incarcerated Bodies," was originally published as "The Incarcerated Body and Mutual Liberation" in the August 2020 issue of the North Dakota Humanities Council journal, *On Second Thought*.

For Water Protectors—
past, present, and yet to come.

For Oceti Sakowin Camp and the
resistance at Standing Rock.

For everybody everywhere who longs for
or remembers another way.

CONTENTS

FOREWORD

We all know what it's like to meet someone we feel we have known forever. Karen is one of those people for me. I can't positively identify when we first met, but she probably remembers; her memory is incredible. One day she was just suddenly a big part of my life.

One evening we were meeting at my office in Bismarck when she pulled up outside and got out of her car. I thought to myself, "Oh my goodness, Jackie Kennedy is here!" She blew into the room with a huge smile, laughing at the outrageous North Dakota wind. She brought happiness and love in with her. Truth be told, I had heard of Karen long before we met and I remember feeling sort of starstruck. She is extraordinarily beautiful inside and out.

Fast forward a couple of years to the Dakota Access Pipeline debacle and the Water Is Life movement. I like to say that my family and I participated even before Sacred Stone Camp became a camp. My cousin Miles Allard and his beautiful wife LaDonna Brave Bull Allard asked people to gather on the lawn of the Capitol in Bismarck in April of 2016 to protest the pipeline. I went with my sweetheart Rick and two of our grandchildren. Rick sang. We stood there with a huge banner illuminated by tiny portable lights. My grandkids are in that picture—how I wish I could find a copy. We tell them they were all a part of history.

I met Rissa Williams that night, another ally in the NoDAPL movement. She too had brought a drum. Little did we know then where this movement would take us and what a roller coaster ride it would be!

By the end of April, LaDonna and Miles had Sacred Stone Camp up and running. Soon the urgency of the situation compelled people to move closer to the "Black Snake," the actual pipeline site. The second encampment was called Red Warrior Camp, which evolved into Oceti Sakowin or Seven Council Fires.

Everything progressed very fast. It was Creator-driven work, and for many of us it was the only place we could imagine being. We were drawn into a sacred community living in sacred space; by doing so we became protectors of the water, the prairie, our community, and each other.

At its peak there were over 18,000 people living at Oceti Sakowin, encamped along the beautiful Missouri River. All of whom needed food, warm clothes, blankets, shelter, and everything else human beings need to survive. That's where Karen—and our many other wonderful volunteers—came in.

In a circle of like-minded relatives is a sisterhood that includes Ronya Hoblit, Bonnie Palecek, Karen, and I. Karen called me and asked if I thought it would be okay for her to put up a sign to solicit donations at the local Unitarian Universalist congregation where she pastored. I said, "Heck yeah!" Though I practice my traditional Indigenous ways as deeply as I can, I love this little UU church.

They have accepted, truly accepted, all; their hearts and generosity speak volumes.

Karen's efforts started simply and grew from there. I felt Karen had found her place, found where she belonged. A place where color did not matter. It had never mattered to her, I think.

As the spiritual leader of the Bismarck UU congregation, Karen was an essential part of bringing together volunteers and supplies, performing daily tasks to keep things moving in a good way. So many phone calls and texts! She wrote grants, gathered surveys, and engaged in creative problem solving. Most of all, she gave herself fully to Oceti Sakowin. Even when we were in different places, we were together as one in spirit and heart—as we continue to be.

This book brought back so many memories. The dust. The police. The love. The flags. The enormity of a human movement that I had never witnessed before and probably won't witness again. Seeing it anew through Karen's eyes was wondrous.

The book goes beyond the final heartbreaking days of camp to the incarceration of Water Protectors and the fight against Line 3. Although Oceti Sakowin was shut down on a cold winter day in 2017, Water Protectors will be here as long as there is water to protect. Karen became a fierce Water Protector.

To address what one might see as the elephant in the room, Karen is non-Native. Should that matter? It might matter to some. It does not matter to me. Karen's commitment to humanity probably started when her umbilical cord was cut, and it continues to this day. She was arrested protecting water at Line 3. I was watching a video clip taken by someone in a helicopter and there was Karen, still reminding me of Jackie O, still striking even covered by the flying dust and debris. I was so dang proud!

To me, she has become my sister. My heart sister. Family that I chose. In writing this book she is bringing her world, my world, and your world closer to being one, to being a collective.

We are all related.

Water is life.

We stand.

With deepest love and respect,

Sandra Bercier

Keeper of the Medicine

Enrolled member of the Turtle Mountain Band of Chippewa

WELCOME

Is it about Standing Rock?

I have been asked this question when a loved one or colleague hears about this book and generously wonders what it's about. Each time, the answer gets caught in my throat.

In this moment, the words seem to be caught in my throat again. The truest answer might go like this: *Not exactly. And also yes.*

Standing Rock showed me how to live.

At Oceti Sakowin Camp, the largest Camp within the Standing Rock movement, I was welcomed as a relative, one of a hundred thousand relatives who had gathered there from everywhere. In 2016, when the Indigenous-led uprising to protect the Missouri River roused the human family, it became my fondest wish to live as a good relative with people and all beings who comprise the Earth. When the colonial state forcibly closed the camps in collusion with the colonial extractive industry, thousands of people, including myself, lost their sense of home.

Many within our community lost their home altogether.

This book was born from that loss and longing, and also from an ever-deepening gratitude toward Oceti Sakowin Camp and the world I inhabited there. As far as I can tell, the way of life at Camp was a way of life that human beings were made for. I certainly felt more like a human being, an embodied member of the intricate web of life, than I ever had before.

Speaking of *before*—

Way back before my ancestors crossed the Atlantic Ocean, hungry for nourishment of many kinds, most of them lived in the Celtic Sea and North Sea regions of the world, landmasses that are now called the British Isles, northern Europe, and, as my mom and I were stunned to learn through DNA testing, the Baltic Sea region.

Guided by the Water Protector movement, I have begun to understand my heritage, as well as my own life's story, not only in terms of culture and land but also in terms of water. Maybe this long-ago sea connection, this abiding presence of water in my own ancestral homelands, has remained within my bones.

From my earliest years, I have always rushed to the rivers—

The Kankakee River of my childhood.

The Missouri River of much of my adulthood.

The Red River of today.

As a child and grandchild of ministers, I grew up with epic stories about the watery beginnings of creation, the presence of God— or Goddess, or Great Mystery, or Spirit of Life, or Manifestation of Love—dwelling in all peoples, places, and creatures. This heritage has nourished me with an abiding sense of Spirit.

At the same time, I also descend from the very white settler colonialism that has sought to destroy both the Indigenous-led

Water Protector movement and, for more than five hundred years, Indigenous peoples as a whole.

Though it's painful to acknowledge, the same culture and system that raised and formed me has also enacted unthinkable acts of violence as a way of life. In this dissonant context, it seems this system of violence must have something to do with who we white people are, as well as who I am as a white person. Entrained by a system based on violence, it seems I must be touched by it, shaped by it, possibly even run by it.

Today, thanks to Oceti Sakowin Camp, as well as many Water Protector events and reunions that have followed, I have a visceral sense of how and what transformation can feel like. Still, as a white person, I have come to understand that this process is not only about experiencing the great blessings or even the basic human struggles of participation in Indigenous-led, intercultural resistance movements.

When my culture has located itself in direct opposition to Indigenous ways of life—and when I as a white person seek to oppose this very opposition—my life can seem to move in two directions at once.

In order to bring my own fullness, my own wholeness, to this work of liberation, I need a genuine understanding of the situation at hand, which calls for a genuine understanding of my own culture. Through this process of unfolding, this ever-deepening sense of who I am and who I come from, I believe I can participate with more energy and integrity in decolonizing movements that have nourished my body and my spirit, guiding the course of my life.

So what might (my) white identity mean? How might (my) whiteness relate to—and not relate to—the lifelong project of becoming a human being?

In the movement for collective liberation, how might (my) whiteness both complicate and mandate the role of allyship or even accompliceship, a mutual role that happens, according to Indigenous Action Media, "when we fight back or forward, together, becoming complicit in a struggle towards liberation"?

These are some of the questions that have shaped this memoir of heart, mind, body, and soul. It is a narrative of moments, a recollection of challenges and revelations, as I have gone from unquestioning allegiance to the colonial criminal justice system in 1987 to sitting in a jail cell on a Water Protector charge in 2021, and plenty of places both before and since.

In other words, this book is a memoir of practicing—of learning, moment by moment, to be more fully human, to live in more life-embracing ways. In this story, I hope you will find something you can relate to, whether it's a lesson learned, a mistake made, or, here and there, a little bit of satire on colonial ways of life, which I have shared because, as the adage goes, sometimes satire is the only thing that makes any sense.

As you read, you may sometimes feel that parts of the story are missing, and it's true. While I am honored to have any place at all in this collective conversation, I seek to tell only the portion of the story that is mine to share.

As I reflect and learn, I intend to honor the people who have taught me, which is why you will find lots of names within these pages. Most of my loved ones and colleagues have agreed to be named, while some have opted for pseudonyms or anonymity. Out of respect for the contexts and the teachers of my teachers, I have often (and to the best of my ability) included people's cultural identities and ancestries in words that I understand them to use.

At first, I was inclined to follow Black scholars Ibram X. Kendi and Eve Ewing in capitalizing all racial designations. As Eve Ewing writes, when we capitalize some racial designations but not white, we run "the risk of reinforcing the dangerous myth that White people in America do not have a racial identity." By capitalizing white, I hoped to undermine the presumed neutrality of whiteness and invite white people—including myself—to see ourselves as a racialized group, rather than a collection of self-made individuals who transcend racialization.

But among white people, it is primarily white supremacists who insist on capitalizing white. As a white person, considering this association between white supremacy and capitalization, I have chosen to go small rather than big, believing my intention to address harm might be better served by using lowercase. As the public conversation continues, and more white people contend with our own racialization, new spellings, new forms, and new words may emerge. As Eve Ewing has said on just this topic, "Ultimately, it's good that we're having this public conversation. . . . I changed my mind. I might change my mind again."

As I write about my experiences of the Indigenous-led Water Protector movement, I sincerely hope not to act like some kind of self-proclaimed white authority. The last thing anybody needs is another report by another European descendant on the customs and cultures of other peoples.

In other words, besides being a story of my life, this book is also a story of my white settler colonial culture as I seek to understand it, grieve it, and, as a participant in movements of resistance, ultimately dismantle it.

But what is *it* exactly? What role does whiteness play in the colonial project of European imperialism? And where do I fit in?

When I look at the sweep of human history, I realize whiteness is a relatively new organizing strategy. Having been invented only a few hundred years ago, whiteness isn't that much older than the settler colonialism from which it has arisen. While different people see different relationships among European imperialism, settler colonialism, and whiteness, I see the connections in this way: Imperialism, through the Roman Empire, various European empires, and the US Empire of today, has everything to do with expansion. By increasing its territories and holdings, an empire can increase its wealth and power, particularly for the already wealthy and powerful.

For the sake of this expansion, empires sometimes engage in a project of settler colonialism, recruiting or mandating—as in the state of Georgia, which was formed as a penal colony—everyday settlers to inhabit imperial colonies. These settlers are there to displace, disturb, destroy, or, by a series of synaptic leaps, even claim to own other peoples, beings, and lands. From here, those who descend from European peoples become racialized as white in order to better serve the empire of the United States. In this hyperracialized system, we white people, in exchange for our loyalty to the empire, receive colonial privileges that tend to be violently denied to everybody else, making whiteness a tool of settler colonialism, just as settler colonialism is a tool of imperialism.

For these reasons, when I talk about whiteness in the US, I mean to talk about whiteness as a direct and deliberate function of the empire—as its functionary and even its uniform.

This is not the way I wish to live.

I wish for a way of being that I have witnessed and lived within the Water Protector movement, an Indigenous-led revolution that makes space for people of many ancestries, including mine.

Still, since colonialism is the culture into which I was born, present in the very room where I took my first breath, I am sure unexamined colonialism will be embedded in these pages. For the colonial assumptions that elude me now yet are sure to be resoundingly clear later, I am sorry. In spite of my limitations, I hope this book may play some role in a conversation about what it means to be white within white settler colonialism, what it means to be human, and, for those of us enrolled into whiteness, what we may be called to do about it now.

For many generations, Indigenous people, Black people, and people of color at large have called for an interrogation of white settler colonialism by those of us who hail from within it. Indeed, at Oceti Sakowin Camp, all people, including white-settler-colonial people, were called as well as invited into another way of life.

This memoir is part of my best, most honest effort to heed that call.

ONE

THE SPARK, THE FLAME

It is both true and untrue that for me, it began with a flame.

Even before the flame, Sandra Bercier, sister-friend and Anishinaabe tradition keeper, gave me some news:

1. There was a pipeline.
2. There was a Camp at Standing Rock to stop the pipeline.
3. The Camp would welcome gifts of supplies.

Somehow, in April 2016, word of a pipeline had escaped me, though I'm usually a newsy type. When I listened to Sandra's voice in those earliest of days, gathered around the heavy, thick table in her office, dreaming together about a project and grant, the Standing Rock resistance didn't seem to have much to do with my daily life. I didn't see a place for myself, as much as I might have longed for one. In fact, being white, a settler, and a descendant of colonialism, I figured my best place was out of the way.

Sometimes that turned out to be true.

Sometimes it didn't—or, at least, not in the way I first understood it.

We were at one of our many meetings for an unnamed entity whose intention was to dismantle racism through outspoken friendship and whose membership included two Indigenous people, two Black people, and two white people. I sat across from Sandra, facing the inner wall—the one with the three-paneled series of maps depicting the loss of Indigenous lands from the arrival of European settlers to more recent times.

In the midst of our conversation, Sandra asked us white folks a powerful question: "What happened in your lives that you're here?"

More questions, though not a lot of answers, jumped into my throat. *Where is* here? *What is* here? *And mostly, am I* here?

Here, she clarified, meant seated at the table, both literally and metaphorically.

Had Sandra asked us *if* we were here, I could have answered, *I hope so. I truly hope so.* Had Sandra asked us *why* we were here, I could have answered, *Because you matter to me, and I matter to me, and my whiteness feels like a prison in which I am both jailer and jailed, with my skin itself as a uniform of oppression.*

But Sandra didn't ask that question, not exactly. Instead, she asked what had happened to us. What shaped us? Who shaped us? Who were the ancestors of our resistance?

To that, I had little to say. Was I actually someone with a narrative of resistance—someone whose own story might belong to the story of liberation?

At the time, I was painfully unfamiliar with stories of mutual resistance. I knew nothing of the Wobblies, the Industrial Workers of the World, founded in 1905 as a global union for all peoples of all colors and lands. I knew little of John Brown, a white abolitionist who had organized an interracial raid in 1859 and plotted to overthrow the enslavement of Black peoples. I had never heard of Anne McCarty Braden, a white Southern woman who was indicted on charges of sedition twice for participating in antiracist work, first in the 1950s and again in the 1960s. There was much I didn't know.

Mostly, I knew that I was white, which meant that I was a member of the oppressing class, the villain in the antiracist plotline—the very thing that James H. Cone, a Black minister and liberation theologian, had urged us white folks to stop being.

But how? In my world at the time, there weren't a whole lot of encouraging storylines to choose from on this topic. As far as I knew, there were only three options for being white and also conscious of that whiteness: white supremacist, denier of liberation; white savior, self-deluded bestower of liberation; and white apologist, dealer in guilt regarding the very need for liberation.

I didn't want to be the first type of white, particularly after what had happened in Leith, North Dakota, population: 17. In 2013, well-armed white supremacists from out of state had tried to buy the town—literally. They hoped to build a base for white power operations. Thanks to resistance by people of many cultures, the white supremacist group never did secure ownership of Leith, but the presence of white supremacy was all too clear.

I also didn't want to be the second type of white, especially considering a job I had held relatively briefly a few years earlier in Chicago. The program, which was designed for families facing economic injustice, provided GED preparation and access to other human supports that the colonial system had generally denied to them. Adults and their young children, almost everyone Black, would come for family literacy experiences. The program staff, also Black, taught reading, encouraged healthy parent-child relationships, and more. Often, I was the only white person there. I was also one of the bosses, which was nothing I wanted to be or really could be. After a year, as much as I loved the work, I decided to transition out of the position and the agency.

The final type of white, though harder to avoid, didn't speak to me either. Surely liberation was bigger than my own feelings about it, guilt or otherwise. I wanted to be so committed to liberation that my own guilt, my own longing for absolution, would be neither my intrinsic motivation nor my chronic state of being.

Indeed, somewhere in the midst of receiving those federal charges of sedition, Anne McCarty Braden had spoken of white guilt: "I never knew anybody who really got active because of guilt. . . . Everybody white that I know that's gotten involved in this struggle, got into it because they glimpsed a different world to live in."

I really wanted to live in a different world—or, at least, I wanted to live in this world in a very different way.

So, with all of this content knocking around inside me, I did my best to respond to Sandra's question. What *had* happened to me that brought me to the table? Growing up amid endless fields of corn and soy in the heartland of Illinois, I had learned a gospel of liberation. From a mother at the piano, a father at the pulpit, and a Bible at the ready, the gospel of liberation taught me this:

1. The empire tried to kill God (in the crucifixion).
2. God rose (in the resurrection).

3. The empire was perpetually trying to overpower God (in the legacy of Christendom).

When Constantine made Christianity the official Roman religion, thus establishing Christendom as the organizing principle in thousands of people's lives, the gospel of liberation became a gospel of the empire, from Roman, to British, to Spanish, to US, to multinational and corporate.

In the fall of 2015, when I responded to Sandra's question, I had just become a minister, still yearning for a gospel, a story of liberation that I had lost. I served my home church, the Unitarian Universalist Congregation of Bismarck-Mandan, North Dakota—my adopted place of residence for two decades. Then and now, I am drawn to the UU tradition, as imperfect as it may be, for its reverence for the breadth of life. As Unitarian Universalists, we are multifaith (including no faith) by design, trusting that the universe is so vast and magnificent that many traditions and ways are needed to approach it. We are connected through shared values, like inherent human dignity and the interconnectedness of all life, with less emphasis on sharing particular beliefs or belief systems. In principle, this means that we support people to practice their Atheist, Hindu, Humanist, Indigenous, and Pagan traditions, as well as a wide breadth of other understandings, including my own Old Catholicism, an affirming Christian tradition I was grateful to find during my seminary years. All of these traditions, rooted in congregants' personal and cultural heritages, were respected and sustained.

Meanwhile, as the Standing Rock resistance gathered power and Sandra's question continued to stir within me, I started asking around, paying real attention.

I got caught up on the news about the pipeline and the resistance:

The Dakota Access Pipeline (abbreviated as DAPL, which rhymes with *apple*) was slated to cross beneath the Missouri River just a handful of miles north of Standing Rock, within the homelands of the Lakota-Dakota people. The Missouri River was and is the sole source of drinking water for Standing Rock Sioux Tribe, Cheyenne River Sioux Tribe, and numerous Indigenous communities downstream, as well as residents of many US states. What's more, Energy Transfer Partners, the pipeline company, had a steady record of environmental contamination.

From the moment they learned of the pipeline project, the Standing Rock Sioux Tribe, with then-chairperson David Archambault II, Lakota elder Phyllis Young, and many others, opposed DAPL—on the grounds that it threatened drinking water supplies, tribal sovereignty, and the Fort Laramie Treaties of 1851 and 1868. Together, four tribes within the Ochethi Šakowiŋ nation— Standing Rock Sioux Tribe, Cheyenne River Sioux Tribe, Oglala Sioux Tribe, and Yankton Sioux Tribe—filed suit against Energy Transfer Partners in 2016, objecting to the pipeline's river crossing.

As part of the resistance, Sacred Stone Camp was cofounded at Standing Rock by many collaborators, including Lakota organizer Joye Braun, with the support of—and on the family lands of— LaDonna Brave Bull Allard, a beloved Lakota elder. From the beginning, the Water Protector movement at Standing Rock was guided by elders who insisted that the resistance be rooted in prayer.

It was also inspired by youth who ran vast distances—twice— to oppose construction of the pipeline. They ran first from Sacred

Stone Camp to the US Army Corps of Engineers central office in Omaha, Nebraska. Later, they ran from Sacred Stone to the White House to address President Barack Obama, who took no action at the time but had visited Standing Rock in 2014 and pledged to honor the sovereignty of Indigenous nations and the promise of Indigenous youth.

Sacred Stone was the first Camp—and, in April 2016, the only Camp. It became a major gathering place for Water Protectors, so named because of traditions that call upon Lakota-Dakota-Nakota people, and women in particular, to protect the waters. To the best of my understanding, Sacred Stone Camp, which was nestled between the river bluffs and the wide Missouri, welcomed anyone and everyone. If you could bring a tipi, great. If you could bring a camera drone, also great. If you could get your hands on a few supplies, bring supplies. My friend Darren Renville, a Dakota writer from Sisseton Wahpeton Oyate, called Sacred Stone Camp "the most peaceful place he'd ever been," a place where he and his young son thrived. Having met Darren in 2007, at an artist event where he delightfully spent the evening wearing my boa-like scarf, I took his words to heart.

Meanwhile, Energy Transfer Partners insisted that the pipeline project was not blatantly unjust, because it was not slated to cross lands that are technically called the Standing Rock Sioux Reservation. Yet Standing Rock is just one part of the vast Lakota-Dakota-Nakota Nation, which the Fort Laramie Treaty of 1851 calls the "Sioux or Dahcotah Nation." Since 1851, the colonial state has vastly diminished these lands, which means that even though DAPL was drawn a few miles north of Standing Rock, it crossed right through the Lakota-Dakota-Nakota Nation.

Like most white people in Bismarck, progressive, conservative, or otherwise, I wasn't certain how to take all this news. As recently as 2008, North Dakota had been featured in a *National Geographic* piece called "The Emptied Prairie," replete with photos and anecdotes about abandonment, desolation, and ghost towns—very controversial among descendants of colonialism, not unlike myself, who considered the piece an insult to our vibrancy, or at least to the I'm-not-dead-yet-ness of our lives.

But privately, we had to admit, we weren't in a place where news typically *happened*. During the early 1900s, we'd had some major news coverage with the rise of the left-wing Nonpartisan League, the entity that ultimately created North Dakota's state bank, the only bank of its kind in the US. Then, in the 1980s, we'd had some more major coverage with the rise of the right-wing Posse Comitatus, which had gotten into a famous shootout with the FBI.

Still, that *National Geographic* article had put us into the public eye precisely because, according to its authors, there was so little for the public eye to see. I'm embarrassed to admit that when I relocated from Illinois to North Dakota in 1991 in a cross-country carpool at the earnest age of twenty-one, I made sure to pack a book about edible wild plants of the northern plains. After all, I wanted to have *something* to eat.

As it turned out, I was never too far from a grocery store.

In 2016, I was also never too far from Sitting Bull's grave. Or the United Tribes Technical College International Powwow. Or the reconstructed earth lodges of Nueta, Hidatsa, and Sahnish traditions. Or the site of the Battle of Greasy Grass, also known as the Battle of the Little Bighorn. Or treaty violations by a government that, through its taxes and benefits, claimed me as its own.

As I heard about DAPL in fits and starts, I took a moment.

A pipeline being pushed through Lakota-Dakota-Nakota treaty lands? Not shocking. This was, after all, the world of Custer House, Custer Elementary School, Custer Family Planning, and Custer Park—a name that Melanie Angel Moniz, a Nueta-Hidatsa community organizer, and other Indigenous community members have long been leading an effort to change.

A prayer Camp where Water Protectors intended to stop the pipeline? Exhilarating, but certainly not shocking. If there was a way to stop a pipeline, descendants of those who had stopped Custer in the first place—warriors like Sitting Bull, Crazy Horse, and others—could figure it out.

A chance to participate, given the color of my skin and the history of my people? Exhilarating. And shocking. There was something for me to do besides colonize, someone for me to be besides colonizer. Suddenly, I had a chance to do something which, as far as I could tell, few of my ancestors had done: arrive on Indigenous lands in a good way. Or at least, I hoped, in an okay way.

Self-conscious about my white identity for much of my life, I had understood myself to be not just a beneficiary of colonialism and the white supremacy that maintains it, but also an intended beneficiary, a beneficiary by design. It was as if I had imagined that European enslavers in the 1400s, equally interested in enslaving their neighbors from Slovakia as their neighbors from Africa and the Caribbean, were somehow looking out for me.

This concept of colonialism—that it existed for my pleasure— plagued me. White guilt was nothing next to my well-honed white shame. As a child, each time fundraising ads came on TV about famines in Cambodia and Ethiopia, I threw myself into despair for the children on the other side of the world as well as for myself, for my own implication. I remember one evening, my mother desperately held me from behind as I wailed that I was ugly, ugly, ugly. In my blood and bones, I sensed the ugly connection between my way of life and theirs; what had been taken from them had been given to me.

Decades later, the Dakota Access Pipeline came, another ugly thing.

At the hands of Energy Transfer Partners and Kelcy Warren, its white CEO, the Dakota Access Pipeline would be forced beneath the water, tear through sacred sites, and decimate the lands in its pathway.

I didn't know it yet, but there had been another route, earlier in the planning. That route had never made the news or gotten off the proverbial drawing board. The original route would have sent the pipeline north of Bismarck, putting us residents of Bismarck downstream from the pipeline and any breakage.

Though it's been said that we locals blocked the original plan, we didn't. We never had to protest in the first place. As a *Bismarck Tribune* article revealed, the pipeline route was redrawn internally, as a corporate decision to protect the water quality of a city that was 94 percent white. I'll never forget the moment when, as we were standing side by side at her kitchen counter, an old friend put this stunning article in front of my face. Thanks to her newspaper-clipping ability, Carol Jean Larsen was a key reason I was generally so good at keeping up with the news.

Certainly, this redirection of the pipeline was better for the mostly white residents of Bismarck like Carol Jean and myself—to be upstream of a pipeline, above the flow of water and, in the case of a pipeline breach, above the gushing of crude oil. With poverty rates for white people in North Dakota at a quarter the level of poverty rates for Indigenous people, there is little disagreement that being from a colonizing nation is materially better than coming from a nation that's being colonized.

But is it *good?* Is colonialism, this system of perpetual extraction, *good?*

Honestly, who wants to be within five planets of a pipeline break in the water?

In my experience, this is one of the slipperiest lies of white colonialism for us white people. We come to believe that just because we are favored by colonialism, we should favor colonialism in return. We come to believe that colonialism as a system, a way of life, is the best way for us white people to be. We come to believe, in the win-lose system of colonialism, that since we are the so-called winners in this system, we would be so-called losers in any other paradigm. Sometimes, in the long-term colonization of our own imaginations, we even come to believe that there is no other paradigm.

Andy Fisher, a white ecopsychologist who participates in Indigenous-led solidarity work, has said this about settler-colonial life: "We settle for partial, secondary, or substitutive gratifications—we do the best we can, even when our best still has much pain and destructiveness in it."

For tens of thousands of years, long before the invention of colonialism, human beings thrived on this planet. The planet even thrived in the presence of human beings.

In my experience, even those of us who are white—and have carried colonialism clear around the world—can still remember this ancient way of being, this ancient stirring in our bones. The more I am shown more holistic ways of being, including more Indigenous ways of being, the more I have come to understand that even we, the carriers of colonialism, would be better off without this colonial system.

In 2016 and beyond, as I have reflected and sometimes perseverated on colonialism, I have realized that just because colonialism gives me material benefits, it's nothing personal. The more I learn from writers and historians of various cultural identities like Theodore Allen, Nell Irvin Painter, and Ibram X. Kendi, the more I understand that my usefulness to colonialism has little to do with me. I now see my beneficiary status as tactical and circumstantial, created by the intended beneficiaries—those who, across generations and distances, extended to me, a daughter of the working and middle classes, a sense of white identity and thus of white entitlement, so that I could protect and even mask the behavior of the very rich and the (almost always very) white.

For the originators and purveyors of a political and cultural system called colonialism, the material benefits to myself, real and grievous as they may be, have everything to do with the role I can play in a system that cultivates white identity as social protection of, and collusion with, those who really stand to gain. As Colette Pichon Battle, a Black community organizer and environmental climate lawyer, has said, "It's not just hate. This is not just Black and white. It's green. It's about money."

When the Standing Rock movement arose, was money-hungry colonialism my friend? No.

Was the pipeline my friend? No.

Was Sandra my friend? Yes, absolutely.

So, in my first act of Water Protector solidarity—almost as much with Sandra as with a Camp I could barely conceptualize—I went to the store for paper towels and toilet paper.

The flame came shortly thereafter.

In the Bismarck-Mandan Unitarian Universalist congregation, just forty-five miles north of Standing Rock, it was our custom to give voice to our sorrows and joys by lighting candles on Sunday mornings.

This ritualized practice of compassion and connection was crucial for us, as our sense of isolation could be deep. We were a small congregation located about two hundred miles from the nearest UU congregation to the east and situated many hundreds of miles from the nearest UU congregation in Montana.

Still, one spring morning, there was a flame lit by Ronya Galligo-Hoblit, a Lakota artist, longtime congregation member, and participant in that purposeful group with Sandra. With her hands before her heart, Ronya told the congregation about the pipeline. She said that there was a Camp at Standing Rock and that people there would welcome gifts of supplies.

With the cash she received at the close of the service, Ronya and I drove to the nearest grocery store.

Peanut butter? Bread? Water? Soup?

Again, as always, paper towels.

Again, as always, toilet paper.

I had become a participant in the uprising at Standing Rock via paper products.

Later that day, I would make my first visit to Sacred Stone. As I look back, I keep remembering a quote shared with me by Chris

Casuccio, a white organizer and former staffer from the UU College of Social Justice: "It's not that difficult. When you come over, just don't act weird." Chris had been cofacilitating an antiracism workshop on another part of the continent. The white people group was about to join the people of color group for a shared discussion about oppression; the advice "just don't act weird" was given by a participant in the people of color group reflecting on how white people should make their approach.

The trouble is, acting weird around Black people, Indigenous people, and people of color in general is one of the main expressions of whiteness. We white people often ignore white identity until we encounter those who don't share it, inciting us to act all the weirder.

By weird, I mean uneasy.

By weird, I mean self-conscious.

By weird, I mean uncomfortable in our literal skin.

But who is this white-identified self we are so self-conscious of, anyway? No doubt, white people are those who hail, either recently or long ago, from a continent called Europe. But if *European, European American, European Canadian,* or *European Australian* were adequate terms to describe the phenomenon of whiteness, the term *white* would not exist. White doesn't just mean "of European descent." It means a whole host of things and people that we are not.

To be white means not-African, not-Asian, not-Indigenous, not-Aboriginal, and more. To be white requires a *them* in order to be an *us*. Philip Cushman, a white psychologist and author of *Constructing the Self, Constructing America,* speaks of this phenomenon as a negative identity among the first colonists, in which colonists understood themselves in opposition to the Indigenous people they encountered on these lands.

Certainly, cultures and communities across time have given different names to other groups of people. What's unique about white identity, though, is how consistently it defines itself in opposition to other cultural groups—for the distinct purpose of harming them.

When cultures across history have given names to other groups, there's evidence that their own sense of cultural identity was long-standing and thus preceded making contact with, and then naming, these others. On this note, Pawnee people have historically called themselves Pawnee and called the Sahnish people Arikara. The Pawnee word for Sahnish people, Arikara, was based on the way Sahnish people typically wore their hair. The Pawnee cultural identity was already in place and was conceptualized in its very origins as Pawnee, rather than as not-Arikara.

In contrast, white identity depends for its sense of self upon the very groups it is not, even as it seeks to destroy—or at least significantly capitalize upon—these others. The formation of white identity followed contact with those defined as *other* hundreds of years ago, making white identity a sort of double negative in which whiteness is a state of *not* being them, a *not*-otherness, a not-*not*-us-ness.

In the mathematics of double negatives, though, who *are* we? More to the point, since who we say we are is based primarily on who and how we are not, how can we stand it? How can we cope with our whiteness?

In my experience, we can't.

Since whiteness requires the oppression of other identities in order to understand itself, and those-who-oppress is impossible to sustain as an identity for people with any conscience, we remain unable to understand ourselves, which is why we sometimes have to be asked just not to act weird. And it's why that request can be so tough to meet.

Did I relish my first trip to Sacred Stone? Yes and no. In theory, I was in love with it. In practice, I was giving *just don't act weird* everything I had.

What I witnessed there was a circle of people from many backgrounds. A place for children to play, a swing among the trees. A kitchen tent made of tarps. Tipis going up. Cars, but not too many. A drone to take our picture, a friendly one back then. Scraggly trees. The river, always the river. And the sun. The prairie sun.

Soon, I couldn't stay away.

My mom came to visit, and we helped build a shelving unit. Beloved friends and congregants came along, and we helped sort supplies together. I brought my daughter, Michaela, to visit not long before her twenty-third birthday. "I'm bringing you for two reasons," I said. "I want you, in your life, to have an experience of this place. And I want you to have been here when you hear what's going to be said."

By now, our church had become a drop-off location and transportation hub for even more supplies: tents, tarps, coats, shoes, propane heaters, children's books, and food and water, food and water, food and water.

Noodles. Rice. Beans. Meat.

Popcorn and more popcorn.

Everything seemed possible then, before the dogs were brought out on Labor Day weekend, before the water cannons were sprayed on November 20, 2016, even before the arrests. And more arrests.

Early on, the days were mostly sweet.

The *Bismarck Tribune* ran a human interest story on our congregation's position of solidarity as reflected in two banners, each one saying STANDING WITH STANDING ROCK. We attached one banner to the outside bricks of the church building; the other, we fastened to the fence along Highway 1806, among countless other banners that announced the way to Camp, as we were pummeled by the mighty western winds.

In the article, Ronya was poignantly quoted as saying, "I want clean water for my granddaughter and her descendants that I will never meet." The image showed a line of us hauling supplies from the church.

Of course, we had just taken a run to Camp that morning, so we didn't have the visuals for an impressive photo shoot. We conjured what we could: the blanket from my car, fabric scraps from Ronya's, the donation bin (100 percent empty beneath the well-fitting lid), and one cardboard file box from the administrator's office.

At first, this was who I was called to be: someone who could get her hands not so much on collective liberation, but on supplies. Back then, I heard myself saying again and again, "Standing Rock is the center of the world right now. It's an honor to be perched at the edge of the center of the world."

In those days, I had no idea who and what would come. And who wouldn't.

But still, there was that spark, that flame.

TWO

WELCOME HOME

In August 2016, there was much I didn't know about the central fire. There is much I will never know. But as the rains came down that day, chilly and unlikely, I was grateful for the flame.

We activists of many cultures gathered there, huddled under shared umbrellas and perched beside simmering kettles that bubbled on the grates. With mud below, water above, and fire at the center, I had found myself in a circle where soon I would find everything: Meaning. Connection. Transformation. A taste of liberation.

I stood at the heart of Oceti Sakowin Camp, the new Camp, soon to be called *the big Camp*. As a beginning Lakota language learner, I miss much of the nuance, but I pronounce it *oh-CHE-tee shah-KOH-wee* Camp. To the best of my understanding, these words translate into English as *the seven council fires*, for the seven age-old councils of Lakota-Dakota-Nakota people.

On that rainy, spluttery morning, our carpool arrived with another load of supplies—bottled water, garden produce, summer clothes, camping gear. In those days, there were always people volunteering in the supply tent, usually dressed to honor the Indigenous traditions from which they came, in earrings and maybe a ribbon skirt, asking you to write your name here, list your supplies over here.

"Thank you," they'd say.

"Thank *you*," those of us bringing supplies would say.

Usually, someone would declare, and someone else would repeat, "Mni Wiconi!"

I have learned to pronounce it *mi-NEE wee-CHO-nee*. To the best of my understanding, these words translate into English as *water is life*.

Soon people made summertime awnings out of tarps and sturdy logs, where elders would come to sit in power and presence. The first kitchen tent would go up at the edge of the central fire, along with wooden racks for drying sweet corn and, not too far away, a message board for finding rides, or sometimes one another. The open-air volunteer tent would become a spot for many connections—where to find clothing, where an empty pop-tent might be waiting, what kinds of help might be needed with chopping wood, prepping meals, assembling the children's library, or sharing skills as a practitioner of various healing arts. The medic and healer tents would provide everything from medical care to massage to chiropractic to herbal remedies, all as a gift. Up on Facebook Hill, so named because of the satellite reception you couldn't get anywhere else, people would make calls, stop by the legal tent for court support, or visit the media tent for a media pass, required for anyone with a camera.

At the arrival of hundreds and then thousands of people, thoroughfares would be designated, crisscrossing in the dirt. In the sandy soil down by the Missouri, the famous signpost (which is now housed at the Smithsonian's National Museum of the American Indian) went up, featuring tacked-on markers in all directions: Fort Buffalo, 500 yards; Mississippi River, 837 miles; Detroit, MI, 1607 miles; Six Nations, 2165 kilometers; Sápmi Arctic, 3917 miles; and more. Security sheds would be built where Camp security with neither guns nor uniforms would greet everyone who arrived, often holding a wire-handled coffee can with sage smoke drifting up. Handmade posters and banners appeared all over Camp, part reminder, part encouragement, part movement art:

NO DAPL.

WE ARE UNARMED.

NO DRUGS ALLOWED.

DEFEND THE SACRED.

PEOPLE OVER PIPELINES.

NO SPIRITUAL SURRENDER.

THIS IS A NONVIOLENT CAMP.

OIL IS BANKRUPTING OUR FUTURE.

INDIGENOUS SOVEREIGNTY PROTECTS LAND—AIR—WATER.

MNI WICONI!

But in those early moments in August, most of this hadn't yet happened. The prairie grasses still grew long and tall, sodden that day, clinging to my ankles.

I had heard from friends that Oceti Sakowin Camp had all the purpose of Sacred Stone Camp with a smattering of the supplies. So I arrived on that watery morning. Still, I wasn't sure what to make of this new Camp. As usual, a group of us from the congregation had carpooled. Carol Jean Larsen took a break from newspaper clipping to offer her sparkling blue car. Wayde Schafer, a white environmental organizer for the Sierra Club, had been determined to get us there as fast as time would allow. Ronya Galligo-Hoblit, not a major fan of Wayde's velocity, sat eagle-eyeing the road from the jostling seat beside me.

By now, four months after its inception, Sacred Stone had filled to overflowing. Another place was needed, while the nations, as invited, continued to answer the call. Thanks to a vision of Dakota-Lakota-Nakota elders, Oceti Sakowin Camp had been born. While this vision isn't mine to share, I am grateful to Tim Mentz, a Dakota historian who was born and raised in the town of Cannonball on the Standing Rock reservation, for teaching me something about it over the years.

The location, a convergence place, was found through elders' prayers—west of the wide Missouri, north of the Cannonball River, east of scrappy buttes, and south of a sacred place that Water Protectors soon named Turtle Hill. According to the Fort Laramie Treaty of 1851, the grounds belonged to the "Sioux or Dahcotah Nation," more aptly described as the Lakota-Dakota-Nakota Nation. According to the US government, the lands belonged to the US Army Corps of Engineers. According to Indigenous oral histories, they belonged to many peoples and nations—and also to no peoples and no nations, as lands themselves cannot be owned.

This was a place where, generations ago, Indigenous ancestors had put medicines in the ground because this very gathering, this historic coming together, had been foreseen. Tim Mentz tells it from his Dakota tradition, environmental activist Kandi Mossett White tells it from her Nueta-Hidatsa-Sahnish tradition, and others speak of it too.

Even so, over at Sacred Stone Camp, in between sorting donations and visiting under the trees, I heard a rumor of the new Oceti
Sakowin Camp. A strong Indigenous woman had told me that they
disrespected women.

Stepping among the sideways-leaning grasses, I wondered how
disrespect would look here at this new Camp, compared to back
home in Bismarck.

Earlier in my ministry, just the year before, I had tried to find my
footing in this male-dominated field. In a town of one hundred-plus
churches, I could count the number of women ministers—most of
us white—on one hand.

After making my way onto a mailing list of the hundred
churches, I boldly attended the next ecumenical gathering, held in
the best meeting spot at the University of Mary, with two walls
made of windows and the Missouri River just outside.

On that day, I wasn't yet familiar with the labyrinthine route to
the Harold Schafer Leadership Center. I certainly wasn't familiar
with the elaborate array of hexagon-shaped cubby holes stocked
with copious memorabilia to commemorate the center's namesake,
Harold Schafer, a white entrepreneur sometimes known as Mr.
Bubble, after the bubble bath he had made and sold. Unfamiliar as
I was, I bustled from my car to the wrong building, past the wrong
chapel, down the wrong hall, and so on.

Finally, I burst in without a minute to spare. And there they
were—eleven men, most of them white, getting into their seats
around a U-shaped array of tables.

They looked at one another. At me. Then back at one another.

"Here's a woman!" one of them said in a princely tone.

As quickly as I'd burst in, I longed to back away to that labyrinthine hallway behind me.

But it was time for the scriptural passage of the day. One male pastor gave his interpretation, followed by another male pastor.

Boldly, I burst in again with my own interpretation—something about the presence of God and God's suffering with our suffering.

The group paused, suspended. Then resumed.

Until this moment, I had never understood the concept of *going over like a lead balloon*. But just in case, I tried again. The entire scene repeated itself, as if I had arrived with a clanking lunch tray, but no one much cared for my lunch.

Laura Bates, a white author and feminist from England, would call this occurrence *everyday sexism*. Needless to say, I have never been a fan of everyday sexism.

Years earlier, I had become cochair of the Women's Alliance, a scrappy, exhausted group on the sprawling university I had attended in Illinois. In that role, I had been stunned to learn of another group on campus: the Black Women's Alliance.

"Why do they need their own alliance?" one of our members asked.

Secretly, I was asking the same thing.

A couple of our members, who were white, met with a couple of their members, who were Black. Our members came back with a shocking report:

1. The Black Women's Alliance didn't care to work with us.
2. Our proposal for a joint Take Back the Night March didn't speak to them.
3. One of their stated purposes was lifting up Black men.

In the privacy of my own mind, I struggled to make sense of this new knowledge. I considered the possibilities:

1. Maybe white women have a complicated history of working with Black women.
2. Maybe women from different cultures sometimes have different sets of priorities.
3. Maybe things I thought I knew, I don't.

By declining to collaborate, members of the Black Women's Alliance prepared me for perspectives on gender and culture that would shape the rest of my life. As the work of Kimberlé Crenshaw, leading scholar of critical race theory and Black attorney who coined the term *intersectionality*, later taught me—differing realities could be possible at once, even and especially among women.

Ultimately, at Oceti Sakowin Camp, I felt respected as a woman.

Well, there was one time during a Camp meeting when a Lakota-Dakota elder repeatedly shared his delight that, in his words, "We have a pastor with us today!" In fact, we had two pastors—a white male clergyperson from miles away, and me.

More and more, though, I came to confront sexism—the abiding disrespect for women—as a defining characteristic of my own culture. The founding artifact of my own nation, the US Constitution, had not even included people like me.

For decades, I had been part of North Dakota's movement for women's freedom from family violence; that was why I had moved to Bismarck in the first place, having been lovingly recruited by Bonnie Palecek. As cofounder of the statewide domestic violence coalition, Bonnie soon became my lifelong mentor and sister-friend.

Years later, she became the other white member of the very group who met around Sandra Bercier's formidable table.

In my years with the coalition, I had repeatedly heard Indigenous men, as well as Indigenous people of various genders, proclaim, "Violence against women is not traditional."

What did it mean for me, then, to belong to a culture where it *is*? Where there's little remembered past, or even a collective narrative, to call upon and prove this aberration? In my culture, I have been told it's always been this way, that to be sexist is to be human. In fact, according to the mythological origins of my culture, represented in memes, jokes, and other images, human beings emerged from the primordial cave in full patriarchal form, men first and women second, dragged along by their hair, born to be subservient to men's wants. In a phrase coined by English author Rudyard Kipling, sex work by women is often called "the oldest profession in the world," as if a profession that is often rooted in human trafficking is inherent not only to human nature, but to every human culture.

Julia Brown Wolf, a Lakota elder, taught me that European women were the first colonized people "placed beneath the white man's feet." She said that when Lakota men put women beneath their feet, they defy their own tradition.

In intercultural women's spaces, Melanie Angel Moniz has declared, "We weren't feminists. We didn't need to be."

Lyla June, a musician from Diné, Tsétsêhéstâhese, and European cultures, has released a healing song in order to honor the millions of women who were persecuted as witches in Europe. Lyla June sings, "The first colonization of the human race didn't happen in America. It happened in the place of mamwlad."

Mamwlad translates to *motherland* in Indigenous Welsh.

Indeed, I had cast my first vote in a presidential election before I learned that the earliest human cultures were actually matrifocal, even in the complicated place we now call Europe. As a young woman learning this history from various descendants of that challenging European land—Merlin Stone, Riane Eisler, Marija Gimbutas, and many others—I had been both exhilarated and shocked.

Somehow, though the archaeological evidence is consistent, the news that even my well-traveled European ancestors used to honor women and girls continues to escape mainstream recognition. It seems that subjugating women was part of the colonial project from the beginning.

Here's a horrifying piece of history shared by Jessie Little Doe Baird, a Wampanoag linguist who has been at the heart of language reclamation:

In 1676, English colonizers beheaded Wetamoo, a powerful Wampanoag woman sachem (leader), and displayed her disembodied skull on a pike on Taunton Green for the distinct purpose of terrorizing women and girls of both Indigenous and settler backgrounds. People of all genders undoubtedly would have been terrorized by this spectacle, as they would have been terrorized by the spectacles that Julia Brown Wolf and Lyla June have described.

Surely, the millions of women lost as witches were beloved by someone who survived, even in the earliest days of colonization.

Today, Indigenous women and girls, like other women and girls of color, are the first to call out violence against them, whether from within or beyond their own communities. As I call out sexism and violence in my community, what's different for me is that in the absence of shared memory and history of another way, my call can only be aspirational—how the future *could* be. By and large, the call of Indigenous women can be aspirational *and* historical—how the future could be. How the past reminds people who they are.

I don't precisely know what my Indigenous friend from Sacred Stone experienced at Oceti Sakowin Camp, but of any place I ever slept, walked, or lived, I felt safest when I was at Camp. At least among my own neighbors. Many people I met there said the same, calling the place a homecoming, an awakening, a source of cultural renewal, and, often enough, lifesaving.

I heard numerous declarations like these in the early days of Oceti Sakowin Camp, when the Native American Training Institute received a grant from the North Dakota Humanities Council to ask Indigenous people at Oceti Sakowin Camp how being a part of Camp had changed their lives. At that time, Ronya Galligo-Hoblit was on staff. Stephanie DeCoteau, an Ojibwe/Michif social worker, was an intern. And I was in a collaborative role that the Humanities Council calls a *humanities scholar*. Ultimately, Justin Deegan, a Nueta-Hidatsa-Sahnish-Lakota artist from Thunder Revolution Studio, would become the filmmaker.

Before Justin was a part of the project, Ronya, Stephanie, and I set up a four-post tent at Camp, complete with rose-colored streamers, in order to catch the attention of potential interviewees. Soon, to our raucous amusement, the three of us realized that our arrangement had the distinct atmosphere of a red-light district.

In spite of our unintended messaging, a number of people did consent to be interviewed, including Kandi Mossett White, who shared stories of the medicines her ancestors had placed in the ground years before. Even in the earliest days of Camp, many people could sense its healing power. It was as if folks already knew, no matter whether they had been told, that people had prepared this place long ago, believing the coming generations might gather here.

And they had. And we did.

In tipis. Tents. Yurts. Cars. Campers. Remade buses.

The first kitchen tent went up fast, part army tent, part tarp invention. Summer tents became storage sheds, one for packages of noodles, one for packages of rice, one for packages of beans of many kinds. Soon more kitchen tents were needed, close to the center of Camp as well as spread throughout. Each kitchen, with its spontaneous volunteers and floors of tramped-down dirt, had counters for serving, stoves for cooking, and later, in the winter months, often even a warming spot for eating.

When I arrived at Camp, I'd sometimes chop carrots. Fry patties. Wash dishes.

Forever, I'd wash dishes.

I was joined almost always by congregants from the church, our spirited circle of eighty-and-growing adults and children. As far as I was concerned, this Camp—this way of being, this community rooted in justice—was precisely what church was about, and congregants from various cultural identities, whether Indian American, white, Indigenous, or Black, lived into this vision. Vinod and Aruna Seth brought trays of homemade meals. Pat and Dean Conrad delighted in every Camp innovation, from silk-screening operations to pellet stove installations. Ann and Mike Knudson made regular trips, bringing people as well as supplies to various destinations. Liz Anderson could cook anything out of, well, anything. Ronya Galligo-Hoblit would keep me popping with her humor. Jeffon Seely would greet us back in Bismarck with words of poetry and courage. And so on.

Before each meal, a spirit plate would be prepared for the ancestors, a prayer would be said, and meals would be offered to elders and security. One day, as the meal began, I served rice and then more rice for hours and hours, as people of many ages and ancestries ventured through the line. "There's plenty of rice. Here's the rice. How about some rice today," I said.

After all were fed, I took a look at my serving thumb. There, along the meaty part, was one lone blister, at the place where the spoon had met flesh.

That day, I had dished a thousand plates of rice.

Later, in Grandma's Kitchen, that same dramatic thumb faced conflict with a knife. I bolted toward the medic and healer area, squeezing my gory thumb above my shoulder. After passing the holistic healing tent, animated by massage therapists and other healers, and the herbal tent, crowded with end-to-end jars of medicine—I hustled through the flaps of the medic tent.

For the first time since I could remember, I didn't have to worry whether I had enough funds or whether I had insurance in the first place. I was tended to, cared for, just because I was human.

That winter, Rosemary Bray McNatt, a Black scholar and seminary president, came to Camp as part of the UU Trauma Response Ministry. As she stepped from the car, *wham*—she hit the ice hard. Instead of volunteering all day, which was her original intention, she got to know the healing tent, a Mongolian-style yurt with soft lights, soft voices, and a circle of massage tables draped with colorful blankets, also soft.

Often, new arrivals at Camp would ask, "How much does it cost?" for a camping spot, a meal, a massage.

The best answer: "Nothing."

Or maybe everything—everything colonialism had taught about human economics, culture, life. This Camp, this village of ten thousand people at its largest, was a place I had never imagined— and also a place I had always, somewhere in my being, believed was possible.

At the heart of Camp, the central fire was always burning, a steady spot for prayer. Firekeepers tended it each moment, day and night. Not too far from the central fire, there was a long, canopied tent bursting with clothing of every size, placed on hangers and stacked in bins. That's where I got my jacket, red and plaid.

On the other side of the central fire, people often did screen printing, especially in the summer months. You could choose a piece of clothing from the newest stack of donations, visit with people from everywhere in the long, meandering line, and witness, after two quick motions of the squeegee—*whoot, whoot*—the stunning emergence of wearable movement art. My shirt, black with turquoise ink, shows a woman at the water. The words proclaim in Diné Bizaad:

TÓ ÉÍ IINÁ—WATER IS LIFE.

Many mornings at sunrise, women led a water ceremony, walking, singing, praying, pouring water out of vessels into the river and over our hands. There was a Lakota language-learning school for the children, and teachers emerged from all directions; many came from Camp, others from the Lakota Language Immersion Nest, and a few came from institutions like the North Dakota State University and the University of Mary, site of my unforgettable minister fiasco. Sometimes when the kitchens were covered, I'd help sort books in the library, an army tent adjacent to the school, which convened within another army tent. I remember children of all ages popping in, eager for this book or that book or a whole stack to balance in their arms.

Each morning, the voice of Guy Dull Knife, an early-rising Northern Cheyenne-Lakota elder, would crackle across the loud-speakers. In tents, tipis, and yurts, we would hear his chiding voice, "Wake up, Water Protectors! Time to get up. Warriors, dust off your staffs. Christians, dust off your Bibles. You're not here to sleep! You're here to protect the water!"

One morning, people slept late, late, really late. Somehow, there had been no wake-up call on the speaker. Lots of us asked around, "What happened to Guy Dull Knife?"

It turned out he was fine. Hoping for a decent rest, someone had hidden the mic.

The first night I slept there, I sensed the absolute presence and wholeness of the Earth against my back. I loved the cozy spot that I called home that night, a tent borrowed from Carol Jean Larsen, kindly set up for me by Steve Crane, descendant of German-Russian immigrants, when I was away at an action. Of anywhere in the entire world, I was exactly where I longed to be. Underneath my prayers, I could hear the whispered voices of friends, so tired and yet so awakened, as they prepared for sleep nearby.

Thanks to Camp life, I met people from many traditions— Lakota, Dakota, Nueta, Hidatsa, Anishinaabe, Sámi, Blackfoot, Sufi, Buddhist, Humanist, Jewish, various Christian backgrounds, and more. At any given moment around the central fire, I could witness someone from, say, Turtle Mountain reservation speaking with someone from Spain, or someone from Cheyenne River reservation joking with someone who had an accent I couldn't place. Much the way I had heard others describe, a sense of Spirit called to me—a sense that this was a living moment, a vibrant and pulsating place on planet Earth.

Inspired by the thousands of people from countless different traditions, I began to wish for a yurt where we could gather in interfaith expression, as Ikce Wicasa, a Lakota organizer from Camp, had said was needed. With fundraising support from many directions, Mark Halvorson, a winter camper whose people hail from northern Europe, found exactly that: a secondhand, earthy-brown yurt, ready to be assembled. Liz Loos, my soon-to-be board president and a white activist like me, pulled together the details—and, to my extreme relief, each and every piece of material for the flooring.

Liz steered the bobbling pickup, ambling over the craggy roads of Camp on our way to put the yurt together, as I kept a hold of the flooring in back. With the wind twirling my hair and people's voices calling hello, anything and everything seemed possible. After the yurt was assembled, I tried to remember the names of all who had lent a hand. But so many people had helped, no one asking for anything in return, I couldn't do it.

As nations arrived—Aztec, Māori, Palestinian, Métis, more than three hundred Indigenous nations and more than five hundred nations in all—they often came in ceremony, bearing gifts, offering dances, and bringing songs. Often, they would also bring a flag. Along the expansive entrance from Highway 1806 to the homemade road inside the Camp, hundreds and hundreds of flags caught the breeze like a people's United Nations.

Early on, the Crow nation came despite being historical enemies of the Lakota. Part Crow and part Lakota, my friend Jeff Iron Cloud would quip that this dual heritage was why he sometimes felt so conflicted, as human beings tend to do. Raised in a Lakota community in South Dakota, he has said, "It's an honor. Over the years, I have gotten to meet my Crow relatives, and they are so beautiful. It's healing."

At Oceti Sakowin Camp, his nations joined together at the central fire.

For the water. For the people. For life.

At first, even local governments offered peace. At an outdoor rally in Bismarck, local police fell in step with a Water Protector round dance. In the heavy press of summer, the North Dakota Department of Health supplied the Camp with a water truck. The US Army Corps of Engineers even said they wouldn't hassle the Camp, though they thought the US government owned the land.

Meanwhile, there were other gestures of peace. From across the US, more than five hundred Christian, Jewish, Unitarian Universalist, and other religious leaders answered the invitation of Clergy Climate Action and John Floberg, a white minister and the presiding priest of Episcopal churches at Standing Rock. Near the central fire, the group repudiated and literally burned a copy of the Doctrine of Discovery for its continued role, since 1493, in manifest destiny and other forms of cruelty masked as faith. Essentially, the Doctrine promoted the legitimacy of Christian conquest and the annihilation of Indigenous peoples across the Earth.

In a complicated project organized by Wesley Clark, Jr., a white veteran of the US Army, over two thousand US veterans arrived. Near the central fire, many got to their knees, asking for forgiveness for the role of the US military in genocide. Lakota spiritual leader Leonard Crow Dog, Lakota elder Phyllis Young, and other

Indigenous elders from Standing Rock and elsewhere granted this forgiveness.

All told, this was who I could be there: not missionary, not soldier, not invader—but simply a human being. A person among people.

According to the Indigenous traditions I have had the honor of being taught anything about, all humanity—all of life—is related. Committed to the collective human family, my Indigenous mentors at Camp did not simply turn the table on colonialism, proclaiming themselves to be the true human beings and the descendants of settler colonialism to be less.

They dismantled the colonial table altogether.

As Indigenous Water Protectors affirmed their own humanity, they affirmed the worldview of humanity taught by their traditions. In this worldview, I was also invited to be human. After all, it wasn't just Indigenous people at Camp who declared that they had never felt so whole, so alive.

People of many backgrounds, including white people like me, often said so too.

At Camp, I began to adopt a more nuanced view of white privilege. What if whiteness wasn't only a privilege, but simultaneously a lesser state of oppression, in which those of us who are white are both oppressors *and* oppressed?

What if whiteness had managed to harm me too?

As far as I can tell, my white settler culture creates gradations of human beings from less-than-human (them) to human (us) to superhuman (the elite, the sainted, the royal, the famous, the rich). It's what Isabel Wilkerson, a Black journalist and author of *Caste:*

The Origins of Our Discontents, calls the *hierarchy of caste*. As she has said about US culture, in which caste is embedded, "No one escapes its tentacles."

In this way, my culture fosters anxiety for all who live along that spectrum from less-than-human to more-than-human. Certainly, no one's humanity is secure when one person's admittance into the category of human (or superhuman) depends upon denying that designation to others. In this system, all gradations of humanity become slippery.

Am I up? Am I down? If I'm scared as hell but I can instigate fear in others, am I secure?

How exhausting to be the bully on the playground. Or the planet. Or the psychiatric hospital.

I have spent many years working with children and adolescents in psychiatric treatment, both as a minister and as a therapist. Consistently, I have seen that those who seek to terrorize others and deny them their full humanity are the ones who experience the most profound insecurity about their own humanity and worth. Would a person try to take something they knew they already had and trusted they could keep? If you have it and you can keep it, you don't need to take it.

Aggressive behavior like this can be difficult to address in psychiatric settings precisely because it is so embedded in the larger colonial system. In the marketplace, which permeates existence in the US (and, thanks to the pervasiveness of advertising, often permeates people's thoughts and wants), there is a price tag on products, resources, human labor, even time. In this capitalist system, the best way for me to get more is by making sure others have less.

Indeed, wherever there is great wealth, there is also great injustice.

This zero-sum pursuit of wealth is why whiteness was invented in the first place, as historians of many cultures, including white authors Theodore Allen and David Roediger, have said. In the formation of the United States, as impoverished dark- and light-skinned people banded together against economic injustices proffered by wealthy European American colonists, those same wealthy landholders invented a system to split the alliances of impoverished European Americans. If we who came from Europe would see ourselves as white first and poor second, we might align with others called white and experience just enough entitlement to the privileges of whiteness to sacrifice our allegiance with others who are poor.

Today, after generations of practicing this competition in the sphere of economics, we can't help but extend it to the rest of our lives—because our economic system is foundational to our very culture, to our collective psychology. It shapes both our worldview and our view of ourselves in the world.

What, then, is the culture of whiteness—the collective psychology of white people? Do I dare ask? Do I dare face the analysis of Toni Morrison, acclaimed Black author and recipient of the Pulitzer Prize, who called us white people "terrified"? Or of Lakota elder David Swallow, Jr., who has called us white people "weak"?

When I begin to look at whiteness, especially my own whiteness, *just don't act weird* becomes a complicated task. As far as I can tell, we white people often don't know how to belong outside of whiteness, because belonging to whiteness requires us to belong to nobody else. Still, expressions of humanity are, by nature, common expressions of humanity. Humanity is a group, a collective, an *us*.

In seeking to make *others* of those who are not white, we have othered our own selves. Having split our alliances, we white people have split our own psyches. We have sacrificed our place in the larger human family and culture for the sake of a little bit more—or sometimes a lot more—economic security than Indigenous people, Black people, and people of color typically enjoy.

In 1903, Black civil rights leader and sociologist W. E. B. Du Bois spoke of the split—the *double-consciousness*, the "two souls, two thoughts, two unreconciled strivings"—of Black people in the US. For Du Bois, double-consciousness meant a "sense of always looking at one's self through the eyes of others, of measuring one's soul by the tape of a world that looks on in amused contempt and pity."

At Camp, I began to wonder about another kind of double-consciousness. Could such a thing also belong to whites? At once, we are members of the human family and, by the very definition of our constructed race, deniers of that same human family. At once, we are *us* and, by virtue of the arbitrary lines surrounding *us*-ness, perpetually at risk of becoming *them*.

As Shelly Tochluk, a white antiracism educator and author of *Witnessing Whiteness*, has said of white people, "We end up with splits in our psyche that keep us disconnected from both ourselves and other people."

Indeed, why are white people so *weird* when faced with discussions of race and culture?

The longer I have sat with this question, the more I have come to believe that this insecurity—desperation, even—when we look in the face of our whiteness arises because whiteness gives us nothing in and of itself. It gives only by taking. It was *invented* for this taking.

In spite of historical efforts by white scientists to argue for the supremacy of a white man's brain, anthropologists of various cultural identities like Audrey Smedley, a Black woman, and Ashley Montagu, a white man, have revealed that there is no genetic basis for racial designations. In fact, whiteness itself is an orchestrated illusion.

Who can live as an illusion? For how long?

By now, I am acquainted with thousands of white people. Still, I don't know any white person—not one—who is absent of discomfort or defensiveness about being white, at least not once our whiteness is the topic of discussion. As historians like Nell Irvin Painter, Black author of *The History of White People*, and David Roediger, white author of *The Wages of Whiteness*, have laid out, waves of European immigrants in the US gave up—and often still give up—their cultures of origin in order to become white and thus get jobs, lodging, and food for their hungry families. Yet what does it mean to be white when we no longer know or sense who we come from?

At the central fire at Oceti Sakowin Camp, there were often songs, prayers, and dances that all were invited to join. The prayers and prayer songs taught me words like Wakȟáŋ Tȟáŋka (Great Spirit), Tȟuŋkášila (Grandfather), and Mitákuye Oyás'iŋ (All My Relations). Even as a descendant of settler colonialism, I was welcome to drop loose tobacco into the fire and make heartfelt prayers of my own for this community, the Earth, and, as I was learning, all my relations.

Still, not everything was mine to touch. Not every act was mine to populate.

Later, I came to learn the term *third space* from Stories and Songs events organized in the Black Hills by Indigenous people and allies. To the best of my understanding, *third space* refers to the shared space—something like the central overlapping section in a Venn diagram—where two or more cultures overlap. The third space contains elements of both cultures but does not contain the entirety of either. In my view, this schema can help white people like me (or maybe any people) remember that other cultures exist in spaces beyond our reach or experience, even as we coinhabit a shared third space.

Sometimes at Camp, I felt myself pushed to the edge of the shared third space, glimpsing the sacred regions beyond my reach and experience. One dark, moonless night, a circle of Lakota, Dakota, and Nakota people moved in a dance around the central fire, praying, singing, and stepping as their traditions have taught. This time, it was just Lakota, Dakota, and Nakota people—and possibly loved ones from other Indigenous traditions—who invited one another to join the dance.

Maybe I would have been welcomed in, had I asked.

But I wasn't directly invited, and the dance, song, and language weren't mine. Had I tried, I wouldn't have even known how to join.

As the circle moved before me, a deep sense of hollowness overcame me, a palpable sense of grief. As I pulled my coat tighter and stood motionless at the edge, I allowed myself to descend into my sadness.

No such songs, dances, or shared traditions have persisted in my culture. At multiple points in history, my people had already lost or abandoned any such practices. Indeed, many of my own ancestors' Indigenous practices likely died when the women who Lyla June sings about—the six to nine million women persecuted as witches across Europe—lost their lives.

In that communal and lonesome moment around the fire, I came to wonder: Could cultural misappropriation sometimes serve as a displacement, an avoidance, of this grief? Could it stem from a longing for something that we white people sense but can't for the life of us remember?

I realize that to be an ally and an accomplice, which I very much long to be, I need to hold my own grief, letting it be mine rather than someone else's problem to repair. As Indigenous people have generously taught me about their cultures, I have come to understand that for those of us who are white, sometimes our cultural inheritance is this very lack of cultural inheritance.

Indeed, sometimes we have a cultural inheritance we *wish* were not our own.

It wasn't uncommon at Camp to hear Indigenous people decrying white people, sometimes termed *the white man*, for generations of cruelties past and present. In my experience, creating the internal capacity to witness statements like these is one of the basic practices of being a white ally or accomplice. If we are going to know ourselves, if we are going to be freed from the same colonialism that has thrust whiteness upon us in the place of common humanity, we need to understand to the best of our ability how others have experienced that whiteness. If I accept that whiteness isn't so good for me, either, then I have little to lose in facing the wrongs of whiteness.

Or maybe I have much to lose. Maybe it's just what I need to lose.

At Camp, I experienced what has often been called the gift economy, as compared to the capitalizing economy I had been raised in. This ad hoc village was able to feed, clothe, lodge, and support ten thousand people at its height and one hundred thousand across its duration, because of the gifts it both gave and received: food, work, funds, supplies, time, and Spirit.

As I reflected on Camp life after it was over, grieving the loss of that place, I often found myself saying, "It wasn't perfect. It was better. It was real life."

By fall of 2016, whenever I would cross the threshold back to Camp in a carpool or on my own, Camp security people burning sage and wearing jeans would tell me, "Welcome home."

Home was what I found there, in the presence of the fire, the commitment to the water, and people made of both. At any given moment, a voice might call across Camp, "Mni Wiconi!" From the kitchens, the central fire, the camps within the Camp, the Rosebud Camp south of the Cannonball River, and every and all directions, voices would echo back, "Mni Wiconi!"

In the beginning, my place was to be backup in the kitchens. There was community in the kitchens. There was dignity and purpose.

But not all offers of peace would persist in being peaceful.

Other actions, other means of solidarity, would soon come.

THREE

BRIDGE TO SOMEWHERE

I will never know for sure, but I imagine it went like this—

Late in the summer of 2016, at the Dallas headquarters of Energy Transfer Partners, executives in tailored Brooks Brothers suits and the occasional Gucci dress gather around a forbidding marble table, nary a hair nor seam out of place, looking like the cinematic gentry of our time, seasoned actors on a real-life stage.

The emergency meeting is called to order. The coffee stops pouring. The chatter stops flowing. Finally, the oaken gavel stops pounding. CEO Kelcy Warren takes the floor. "We got a PR problem, folks."

A cheeky, longtime staffer asks, "What do you mean, Kelcy? You got so many North Dakota leaders on your team, you could pretty much build your own organized baseball league."

Kelcy Warren replies, "Trust me, I don't get it either. North Dakotans are supposed to love oil. Absolutely love it. There's even a monument to oil in Crosby, North Dakota, of all places. It has this giant quote from Harold Hamm of Continental Resources, that blowhard. Why didn't one of you buy me a monument? Oh, well. That's the least of our worries. The stuff that's going down right now, it's enough to make you question the meaning of life."

The cheeky staffer retorts, "Get a grip, boss. DAPL is going to make you a billionaire seven times over. Wait, aren't you already a billionaire seven times over?"

Kelcy Warren responds, "You can joke all you want, but we are in serious trouble. Those so-called 'Water Protectors' [doing air quotes here] insist on being peaceful. And nonviolent! And unarmed! There's not a weapon on them anyplace. Not a rifle, not a handgun, not even an AR-15! Frankly, it's un-American. They say they're armed with prayer. Prayer! You know where this is going, don't you? They're making us look like greedy, self-serving capitalists!"

One of the newest staffers (who always wanted to make a living as a singer-songwriter but, for now, plays in a 1980s hair band on alternate weekends) thinks to themselves, *Are we greedy, self-serving capitalists?*

Having just listened to a TED Talk on self-compassion, the singer-songwriter readjusts their thinking.

No, of course we're not greedy, self-serving capitalists. We're just— we're just—we're afraid. We're afraid of—what are we afraid of? Nonviolence. That's right. We're just afraid of nonviolence because . . . um . . .

Kelcy interrupts the singer-songwriter's thoughts. "Did you catch what I just said? Water Protectors say they're inviting every-one. They say they're protecting the water . . . for everyone! They invited the cops to lay down their badges and join them. They invited the workers to lay down their tools and join them. Some of them even invited us to lay down our portfolios and join them! They say there's a place for everyone, because we're all related! What kind of hooey is that? I don't buy it. Do you buy it?"

Just about everyone, including the cheeky, established staffer, hollers, "No!"

Of course, the budding singer-songwriter doesn't holler, "No!" The budding singer-songwriter hums a fresh little tune in their mind while plotting how to catch a ride to Camp.

Meanwhile, the charts come out. The whiteboard comes out. The fancy bullet points come out. The lists, rows, and categories of numbers all come out—with dollar signs before them. In just one afternoon, with the Texas sun hissing against the protectively tinted windows, the problem is solved.

Energy Transfer Partners hires TigerSwan.

Of course, if you were to ask the singer-songwriter, TigerSwan would make a way better song title than the name of a private security company with a stunning capacity for human rights abuses. But the singer-songwriter isn't in charge.

TigerSwan is in charge.

Of course, I will never know precisely what was said in that upscale corporate boardroom on Westchester Drive in Dallas, Texas. But the reality of what came next was so staggering, so disturbing, it makes my satirical imaginings seem mild.

As soon as TigerSwan got hired, Water Protectors were attacked by dogs at sacred sites along the pipeline route. Water Protectors were brutalized by authorities when marching in prayer and ceremony. Water Protectors were arrested in numbers so large, the prosecutor's office in Mandan couldn't process them all—and ulti-mately dropped more than half the charges. Water Protectors were targeted with water cannons and other "less-than-lethal weaponry" on the evening of November 20, 2016, in the dead of northern win-tertime in subfreezing temperatures. Some ended up with bone frac-tures and vision impairment. Most ended up with hypothermia.

And more.

Sadly, then-governor Jack Dalrymple, a white agribusiness-person and descendant of bonanza farms, probably didn't need TigerSwan or even Energy Transfer Partners to tell him how to (try to) bust a movement. In October, along with other state leaders, Dalrymple had the Backwater Bridge shut down, claiming it had sustained structural damage caused by—as you could probably guess—Water Protectors.

From Standing Rock's location, to have the Backwater Bridge shut down would be something like having the George Washing-ton Bridge, which connects New Jersey to New York, shut down. Then-chair of Standing Rock Sioux Tribe David Archambault II said at the time, "This blockade has been a serious issue for our people, as it cuts us off from the shortest route to major hospitals and other emergency services. The closure has also substantially damaged our reservation economy."

By late 2016, profits from Prairie Knights Casino, a major source of income for Standing Rock, had plummeted. Due in part to the bridge closure, the casino became markedly less accessible to its formerly loyal, mostly white clientele in Bismarck-Mandan, nearly doubling the forty-five-minute drive and creating a wintertime maze of back-road inconvenience. Not only that, but the closure of the bridge helped to foster a sense of menace, an aura of danger, around the Camps for those very residents of Bismarck-Mandan.

I never experienced this sense of menace at Camp, not at the hands of Water Protectors. But when low-flying, unmarked helicopters buzzed relentlessly over our ears, I felt a sense of menace. When a mysterious, thin line of prairie fire advanced down the hill toward our sleeping places in the middle of the night, I felt a sense of menace. When the National Guard stopped our vehicles at military-style checkpoints along Highway 1806, I felt a sense of menace.

In later months, as I attended hearing after hearing, bench trial after bench trial, at the Morton County courthouse, I heard law enforcement officers take the stand and admit in various cross-examinations that they often didn't know who in particular had issued the orders they were following. Under oath, they shared that they were not certain who had ordered them to advance, make arrests, and unleash midnight firehoses in the dead of winter.

Even so, the efforts to portray nonviolent Water Protectors as the exact opposite of nonviolent were so thorough, so complete, that many schools in Bismarck-Mandan went on lockdown whenever a Water Protector rally took place within city limits.

Speaking of which, I fondly remember a rally outside the Morton County courthouse in Mandan, where about a hundred Water Protectors, from children to elders, called for Morton County to drop the charges against the newest arrestees, which Morton County ultimately did. Amy Goodman, a white journalist and host of *Democracy Now!*, was one of these arrestees, having recently received a warrant for entering private property to cover the dog attacks.

At this particular rally, Water Protectors from one of the Camps offered to run and get crackers and other snacks for those who were hungry. This kind of generosity was commonplace at Water Protector actions, part of the world being cocreated in the movement.

On another day, everyone was offered fresh, homemade tamales.

On yet another day, it was macadamia nuts, sent with love from Hawai'i.

As I remember all the delicious faraway snacks people received at action after action, I can imagine a devotee of the oil industry saying, *Well, see? You need oil too. How else did those treats arrive?* No doubt, those treats did arrive thanks to the development and use of petroleum. I don't know anyone who denies a certain amount of shared complicity in the overproduction of oil and the consequences for the planet and all of life. To the best of my understanding, the Water Protector movement acknowledges this shared responsibility and has consistently called for a full public conversation, as well as full Indigenous participation in that conversation.

On this particular day, Water Protectors shared a marvelous food called goji berries in between chanting, visiting, seeking some kind of public conversation. By this point, I knew exactly what goji berries were, since I was always coming face-to-face with open-hearted people offering them as a tasty gift, whether at events outside the courthouse or at actions closer to Standing Rock, south of town.

In Bismarck later that night, it was time to watch the evening news in the living room of my daughter's trailer. The goji berry-inspired rally was about to be on TV.

And here it came.

The headline: RIOT? NOT A RIOT? YOU DECIDE.

"Riot?" I exclaimed. "Riot?! See what they're doing? That's the power of suggestion! Have we ever been polled about whether the classic car show or the family golf clinic or the Capital Quilters Guild was turning into a riot? No, we have not!"

It was like that thought experiment where a person tries *not* to see a pink elephant. But just the words *pink elephant* evoke one, regardless whether we're trying to see a pink elephant.

Or a riot.

That was frustrating enough, but what really got under my skin was the headline YOU DECIDE.

Who was YOU? And how was YOU to decide?

The headline reminded me how self-reflexive, how self-referencing, my settler colonial culture can be. The longer I sat with the headline, the more it seemed to say, HEY, 90-PLUS PERCENT WHITE POPULATION OF NORTH DAKOTA, WAS THIS INDIGENOUS-LED EXPERIENCE A RIOT? OR NOT A RIOT? YOU, AS USUAL, GET TO DECIDE.

I couldn't sit still.

Why was a prominent local news station telling a (settler) public, which mostly wasn't at the rally in the first place, that they could, on the basis of a three-minute news blurb, determine the nature of an hours-long event which took place within a months-long struggle—or, actually, a centuries-long resistance?

How did distant, mostly white observers get to be the deciders?

Couldn't Indigenous nations be the deciders?

About a rally.

About a Camp.

About a pipeline.

In early 2016, when DAPL received the blessing of the North Dakota Public Service Commission, the North Dakota Industrial Commission, the US Army Corps of Engineers, and more, the news was full of much colonial headshaking about Standing Rock.

"If only they'd shown up at the public meetings," the shaking heads said. "But they didn't bother to show. Sad to say, our hands are tied." According to the official word, Standing Rock had had a chance to object but didn't until it was too late. Until their resistance made no difference.

In reality, during a public meeting on September 30, 2014, two years prior to the project, Standing Rock Tribal Council members stated, in no uncertain terms, that they objected to the pipeline, they would always object to the pipeline, and they would resist the over-reach onto treaty lands.

While I wasn't at the meeting myself, I listened to the recording, which the Tribal Council has since posted on the Standing Rock website. The meeting was real. The recording was real. The concerns were genuine and real.

But in a colonial worldview, the concerns of Indigenous peoples can't be real. Not *really*. If Indigenous peoples' concerns were real, then pipelines—and dams, and uranium mining, and fracking, and man camps, and boarding schools, and so on—could all become problematic.

Besides, people who have real concerns are probably real people. But the "Vanishing Indian" myth persists yet today.

According to this myth, Indigenous people used to be real, used to exist, used to inhabit reality—but not anymore. As explained by Dina Gilio-Whitaker, an author and historian from the Colville Confederated Tribes, this myth gained fluency as soon as European settlers arrived and maybe even sooner. Because settlers "wanted the land," as Gilio-Whitaker says, "they narrated the reality they wanted to see."

In 1620, the reality they wanted to see was a vast and empty landscape. In 2016, it was a pipeline.

Steven T. Newcomb, a Shawnee-Lenape scholar best known for his work on the Doctrine of Discovery, calls this phenomenon "a mental process of negation." In this process, then and now, "the original rights and existence of the Indians were imaginatively diminished and, to that extent, mentally negated."

Today, if Indigenous peoples were not mentally negated in the colonial mindset, if Indigenous peoples were *really* real, then the real concerns of Indigenous nations would be central to colonial decision-making processes. In fact, these real concerns would likely be conveyed by real, designated spokespeople. Leaders, even— with power.

But in September 2016, law enforcement officers from Morton County arrested David Archambault II, Standing Rock tribal chairperson, for crossing a police line. On Lakota-Dakota-Nakota treaty lands. Not only that, but the Morton County prosecutor took him to trial.

Ultimately, a jury found Archambault not guilty. But I can't imagine anyone arresting, say, Prime Minister Justin Trudeau for crossing a police line on Canadian soil. In a colonial worldview, Trudeau really exists, and the leaders of people who exist *also* really exist. They can't be put on trial for walking where they live.

But according to colonialism, Indigenous people's concerns can't *really* be real, and neither can Indigenous leaders or Indigenous people at large.

So white people get to decide about a riot. About a pipeline. About everything.

From the earliest days of European exploration and colonization—the days of Christopher Columbus, Amerigo Vespucci, Ferdinand Magellan, William Bradford, Pope Nicholas V, Pope Alexander VI, and so on—this worldview has persisted. Today, colonialism no longer claims discovery of Indigenous lands. Just ownership. Management. Power.

And so descendants of settler-colonialism, from governors to pipeline owners to nightly news watchers, come to believe that they (or we) can ascertain the truth among ourselves.

Lately, as I look at human history, I can't help wondering, what *is* the nature of truth within settler colonialism? Where does truth in colonialism come from? Where does it go?

While imagining a post-imperial, postcolonial world, Sharon D. Welch, a contemporary white theologian, has said, "To engage in this work with courage, creativity, and persistence, it is essential that we tell the truth." Yet across this sweep of human history, there seem to be colonial claims of truth. And then, well, truth itself.

Colonialism teaches that Columbus discovered America. Truth teaches that Columbus landed in exactly the wrong place in 1492 and, with support of the crown, immediately set about colonizing the Taíno people.

Colonialism teaches that Thanksgiving was a joyful celebration among "Pilgrims" and "Indians." Truth teaches that a day of giving thanks was first honored in 1637, when the governor of Massachusetts Bay Colony, John Winthrop, an English Puritan, declared a day of celebration following the massacre of seven hundred Pequot people.

Colonialism teaches that General George Custer was a positive local figure, a military hero, and a reputable namesake for a public park in Bismarck, an elementary school in Mandan, and so on. Truth teaches that Custer, while acting on behalf of the colonial government, not only broke the Fort Laramie Treaty by instigating the gold rush in the Black Hills but he also worked as a so-called "Indian fighter." He entered Indigenous lands for the purpose of murdering Indigenous people, including Indigenous children, for pay.

In 2016, side by side with my daughter on her sofa, I asked myself, were settler-colonial decisions regarding the Indigenous-led Water Protector movement just another example of the conflict between colonialism and truth?

That next year, the Water Protector Legal Collective commissioned a survey of residents of Bismarck-Mandan. The purpose was to ascertain whether the local jury pool could provide NoDAPL defendants with a jury of their peers. According to the survey, upward of 85 percent of local residents already believed that Water Protectors were guilty.

Meanwhile, the Lakota People's Law Project (LPLP) got curious: What were these local perceptions based upon, besides generations of settler-colonialism in the first place?

As later shared with me by Danny Sheehan, a white attorney with the Project, LPLP studied footage, communications, police reports, and so on. Thanks to investigative journalism by *The Intercept*, they also paid a lot of attention to TigerSwan, the private security company hired in a pinch by Energy Transfer Partners. According to their findings, TigerSwan was determined to paint Water Protectors as terrorists and even jihadists. Apparently, the anti-Indigenous, anti-Muslim fervor that swept across Europe centuries ago is still creeping across the United States today.

TigerSwan, along with other private security companies, even went so far as to bring in infiltrators—fake Water Protectors—whose role was to instigate violent confrontations if they could, ensuring that Water Protectors would be seen as terrorists by a mostly white public that was already predisposed to such a view. After all, in the presence of terrorists, jihadists, and other violent actors, private security companies like TigerSwan would become crucial to public safety. Not to mention their employer's bankroll.

Still, how could all these machinations come to influence the public? In the findings of LPLP, the flow of information went like this:

1. Energy Transfer Partners hired TigerSwan, a private security company founded by the former head of worldwide antiterrorist operations for Blackwater, a private military firm that had botched its operations in Iraq.

2. From here, TigerSwan convinced the National Sheriffs' Association to hire Behind the Scenes, a PR firm founded by the designer, fifteen years prior, of the misinformation campaign about weapons of mass destruction in Iraq.

3. Through regular briefings, Behind the Scenes fed misinformation about Water Protectors to local sheriffs and state police.

4. Through public statements and news conferences, local sheriffs and state police then fed this misinformation to media venues.

5. Finally, through the nightly news and daily newspapers, media venues fed this same misinformation to the public.

In other words, through a calculated chain of communications, Energy Transfer Partners, TigerSwan, and Behind the Scenes ultimately fed calculated and deeply damaging misinformation to the public.

All the while, TigerSwan held meetings every evening at its headquarters at the Bismarck Municipal Airport. These "order of battle" meetings, as they were called, involved briefings with sheriffs' departments, police departments, and state police, during which TigerSwan presented further false information, laid out current strategies, and ultimately called the proverbial shots.

As concerning as all of this may be, I no longer see it as some kind of aberration in an otherwise just and workable system. I see it as colonialism doing what colonialism does.

Years ago, before I had any understanding of the colonial worldview at hand, my brother and I grew up on a steady diet of *Perry Mason* reruns—versions of truth, reality, even justice, that were unmoving and unmovable. There were crimes, motives, consequences. Period.

According to the show, the colonial justice system was a genuine justice system, and that system could reliably, possibly with the help of a brilliant attorney, ascertain the truth.

Literally, each and every story ended with *the truth*.

This was so much the case, I would turn our family's little digital clock toward the wall at about 9:50 p.m., ten minutes before the end. I was such a fan of the show, I had ascertained that at about 9:56 p.m., the truth would be revealed. On the stand, the guilty party would make a spectacularly delicious confession. But it was more fun to solve the mystery through my own devices, not through the timekeeping device on the ledge by the TV. So, to better support my own capacity for truth finding, I hid the clock.

By the time I became a part of the Water Protector movement as a distinctly lapsed fan of *Perry Mason*, I began to notice the leaders of my culture manufacturing truth about, well, just about everything.

To name a few instances: In 2002, President George W. Bush falsely claimed, with the help of Behind the Scenes, that Iraq possessed weapons of mass destruction. In 2007, Goldman Sachs falsely claimed that its mortgage-backed securities were trustworthy and safe. In 2017, Governor Doug Burgum falsely claimed that an ecological disaster was about to emanate from the Camps.

Meanwhile, I found myself wondering, could colonialism exist at all without this erasure of truth? Was colonialism inherently a system of falsehood and erasure?

Far from being the justice bearers of *Perry Mason* fame, colonial courts have consistently encoded such erasure into the very law of the land. An example from 1835, which I learned about from Steven T. Newcomb's work, really gets to me. While writing for the Tennessee Supreme Court, Judge John Catron, a white jurist, suggested that even if the colonial government had been established on a falsehood, that falsehood must be maintained in perpetuity. Catron wrote at the time:

> We maintain, that the principle declared in the fifteenth century as
> the law of Christendom, that discovery gave title to assume sover-
> eignty over and to govern the unconverted natives of Africa, Asia,

and North and South America, has been recognized as a part of the national law, for nearly four centuries, and that it is now so recognized by every Christian power. . . .

Aware of challenges to his view, Catron went on:

The claim may be denounced by the moralist. We answer, it is the law of the land. Without its assertion and vigorous execution, this continent could never have been inhabited by our ancestors. To abandon the principle now, is to assert that they were unjust usurpers; and that we, succeeding to their usurped authority and void claims to possess and govern the country, should in honesty abandon it, return to Europe, and let the subdued parts again become a wilderness and hunting ground.

In other words, colonial wrongdoing in the present can be justified by colonial wrongdoing in the past.

As a person born into colonialism, into whiteness, all of this leads me to wonder: What would settler colonialism become if we who have inherited it were to genuinely absorb the truth of this very system?

After all, a portion of Mandan, the town in which that so-called riot occurred, sits firmly within unceded Lakota-Dakota-Nakota treaty lands —lands that the Lakota-Dakota-Nakota Nation has not given away or ceded to the colonial US government. The entire forty-mile distance from Mandan to Standing Rock sits firmly within unceded Lakota-Dakota-Nakota treaty lands. In fact, a stretch of the Dakota Access Pipeline now sits firmly within unceded Lakota-Dakota-Nakota treaty lands.

For all the colonial preoccupation with truth and justice that TV

shows like *Perry Mason*, *FBI: Most Wanted*, *NCIS*, *Chicago P.D.*,
and countless others suggest, there is little truth, little justice, in the
colonial disregard for mutually held treaties. In fact, even the
numerous treaties written by the US government to designate
boundaries with Indigenous nations aren't absolute paragons of
justice. They have never fully represented the relationships between
Indigenous peoples and the land.

In one example of many, in the Fort Laramie Treaty of 1851, the
US recognizes particular lands as *territories* of various tribal nations.
Yet it does not explicitly acknowledge that the territory—which
it describes as the homelands of the Sioux or Dahcotah Nation—
also includes ancestral homelands of Nueta, Hidatsa, and Sahnish
peoples, as well as many others.

In other words, even to honor the treaties would be a beginning,
not an ending place.

Sometimes, at actions along the pipeline route as well as in-town
rallies, Water Protectors of many cultures would shout with powerful voices for the end of the police state. For the coming generations. For land back. For water. For life.

Ironically, the police, who often characterized the raised voices
of Water Protectors as violent, were consistently the only people on
the scene who were armed—often with literal weapons of war,
thanks to the US Department of Defense. Because of two federal
programs, the 1033 and 1122 initiatives, the Department of Defense
can donate its excess (and excessive) military equipment to local law
enforcement agencies—for free. All law enforcement has to do is
come up with the money to have it shipped.

Still, as a local North Dakotan, I have heard plenty of stories.

It has been said that Water Protectors, or at least apparent Water Protectors, sometimes threatened to use violence against supporters of the pipeline, usually by phone. In late 2016, I heard this concern shared by an attendee at a teach-in at the public library, hosted by the Dakota Resource Council, a local sustainability organization that was largely in solidarity with Standing Rock.

I have no personal knowledge of such incidents of harassment. But I can accept the possibility that an occasional Water Protector of one cultural identity or another may have made an occasional phone call, threatening an occasional act of retaliation. Such phone calls undoubtedly would have been in direct contradiction of the wishes of Lakota-Dakota-Nakota elders, who insisted that the movement remain both nonviolent and prayerful.

But there's more to this issue than that.

The Fort Laramie Treaties of 1851 and 1868 are international documents, pieces of international law. Violations of these treaties are blatant, if habitual, invasions into Indigenous peoples' homelands, particularly when sacred sites are destroyed, access to drinking water is compromised, and two North Dakota governors send in the National Guard.

This makes the occasional unsettling phone call, even if made by an actual Water Protector, little more than—well, an unsettling phone call.

A phone call can absolutely be disturbing; I have had more than my own share of personal dramas over challenging communications on email, social media, my cell phone, you name it.

But in colonial America, all things are not equal. Even though feelings matter, and even though hurt feelings matter, this is an issue of scale; the feelings of one human being are not of greater relevance than the basic human rights of entire peoples.

As the cliché goes, I learned this lesson the hard way.

When I was about fifteen years old, I had what I considered an amicable rivalry with a peer who was of Asian American/Pacific Islander (AAPI) identity. I don't remember all the things we said to each other, but, with much regret, I do remember making fun of each other's surnames. He would add or change a letter or two to mine, making it sound like *Van Flossin* or *Van Faucet*, which hurt my feelings.

I'm sure I hurt his feelings too when I made fun of his name, which sounded unfamiliar to my white ears. But I didn't just hurt his feelings with my comments. I contributed to a context that regularly denied or at least challenged his basic human rights, in reaction to that very unfamiliarity.

According to Ian Shin, an AAPI scholar and professor, people of Asian American/Pacific Islander identity are seen as "'forever foreigners' who never truly belong in the US." This othering of AAPI people has had real consequences, from driving AAPI people out of their homes in the 1800s, to the Chinese Exclusion Act of 1882, to anti-immigrant attacks of the 1980s and today.

This is some of the context, the bigger picture, in which my teasing took place.

By the time I glimpsed my mistake, my friend-and-rival had already left our mostly white high school and transferred someplace else. It turned out that he had faced harassment daily at the hands of other students.

If I could change any actions in my life, I would honor and respect his name, his absolute personhood.

If I could change any actions in the life of my culture, I would honor and respect all names—the absolute and undeniable personhood of all people.

Which brings me back to treaties.

Not only does the United Nations insist that treaties are binding pieces of international law, which the US Constitution supports, but white citizens of the colonial US expect nothing less when our own sense of nationhood is at stake. If, say, the government and corporations of Mexico were to disregard the 1848 Treaty of Guadalupe Hidalgo and send a pipeline backed by tanks through Prescott National Cemetery, it's hard to imagine the Arizona Minutemen simply making a phone call—even one that hurts.

At this point in history, I have no idea how many colonial infractions and transgressions there have been on treaty lands.

The Backwater Bridge, north of Standing Rock, was just one of many.

In January 2017, roughly four months after the bridge was shut down, the North Dakota Joint Information Center published a not-so-shocking revelation: The Backwater Bridge was structurally sound—and had been all along. But due to the governor's orders, the Backwater Bridge, which sat firmly within unceded treaty lands, stayed closed. In fact, it stayed closed until March 2017, when the last Water Protector from the last Water Protector Camp had been evicted and removed.

As far as I can tell, it wasn't the soundness of the bridge that was the problem.

The problem was the presence of Water Protectors.

Back in October 2016, in the days preceding shutdown of the bridge, Water Protectors had created a new Camp, sometimes called Sacred Ground Camp and sometimes called the Treaty Camp, just north of the Backwater Bridge. This Camp, which sat within unceded Lakota-Dakota-Nakota treaty lands, was established with tipis, tents, and prayers along the would-be pathway of the pipeline. According to international law, also known as the Fort Laramie Treaty, Lakota-Dakota-Nakota peoples and their invited guests had every right to be, pray, and camp there. And they did.

Temporary barriers went up, made of old fencing, wood, and tires. Armed with prayer, Water Protectors stalled construction of the pipeline for more than two days.

It was a difficult, promising time.

As I chewed on a nourishing gift of goji berries, I walked with Carol Jean Larsen from the big Camp toward the Treaty Camp, sensing a tense electricity in the air. I felt as if the whole place was somehow louder, while also holding its breath.

Up ahead, we approached Kandi Mossett White of the Indigenous Environmental Network.

"Karen?" she said.

"Hi, Kandi."

She replied with something like, "Here we are in this war zone."

I didn't know what she meant until we moved on.

"Get back, get back!" a voice cried. "There's a gunman. Stay on the other side of the road!"

There he was.

The gunman.

I didn't know his name at the time, or how he got there. All I knew was that he held a machine gun. He was maybe thirty feet away, within shooting range of the crowd.

Four Water Protectors stood between him and the rest of us, facing him straight on.

Later, I learned those same Water Protectors had just shepherded him into the knee-high backwaters, not too far from the Backwater Bridge.

Like the rest of the crowd, Carol Jean and I were careful to stay on the far side of the road, our hearts—and probably all of our vital organs—in our throats. We heard that the Bureau of Indian Affairs had been called, but they said this wasn't their jurisdiction, this complicated stretch of land between Standing Rock and Mandan.

Like I was watching a silent movie, I could tell that the four Water Protectors were talking to the gunman, beseeching him, by the way their heads moved and their hands shifted. All the while, that weapon didn't budge. The gunman faced it away from the crowd, but he kept it. I was keenly aware that he kept it.

Then, at last, at last, at last—here came the BIA in a row of shiny cars!

One, two, three, four. Was that five?

Soon, the BIA apprehended the gunman and the gun. The crowd erupted in cheers.

Once the BIA left the scene, they released the gunman to the FBI. Who released him to Morton County. Who released him, period.

As the gunman, who claims both white and Indigenous identities, would later tell the public, he had been hired by a private security company (not TigerSwan, but another) to infiltrate the movement. He had even arrived wearing Water Protector fashion on his head—with a pickup, machine gun, *and* a handgun. Later, Morton County questioned him, seeking testimony against—as you might have guessed—Water Protectors.

In the colonial worldview, resisters of that worldview were the threat. So the state's attorney, along with the federal prosecutor, sought evidence against those who'd kept us safe that day.

Meanwhile, while the gunman was never charged, a group of Indigenous Water Protectors ended up doing time—years of time— in real, colonial prison for allegedly burning a barricade on that same Backwater Bridge.

A bridge that was structurally sound. A bridge that could have been traveled. A bridge that sat on Indigenous treaty lands all along.

FOUR

CARRYING

A lot took place at Camp meetings, just in my life alone.

Every morning and many afternoons, Water Protectors would gather for community-wide meetings at Oceti Sakowin Camp. At first, they were held in the long, green army tent, up by Hunkpapa Hill. Later, when Camp grew to the size of the fifth-largest city in North Dakota, the meetings moved to the dome—a fancy geodesic structure that looked like a mythical crystal ball, lit as if by magic from within.

But first, the meetings were held in that tent.

Ikce Wicasa would make sure the meetings began with the burning of sage, an offering of prayers. Then he would facilitate. The practice was to move around the circle— of thirty people or, later, into the hundreds—giving each of us a chance to speak and share an idea, a concern, an invitation. We would go in clockwise order as often as necessary for each of us to have a voice.

At that point in my life, I had probably heard the chant, "This is what democracy looks like!" hundreds of times at hundreds of rallies. Though I never heard this chant uttered at Camp meetings, it seemed pretty true to me.

Because democracy takes energy as well as time, we were given a few caveats:

1. If you don't have anything new to add, please don't.
2. If just one person from your smaller camp could speak, thank you for that.
3. If you have come late to the meeting, please consider that your idea might have been shared already, in which case you wouldn't have anything new to add, so please don't.

People from many backgrounds spoke of areas where help was needed, issues with police outside of Camp, what to do if you were catching a cold, and so on.

Sometimes literally hours into the meeting, when we would be almost-*almost* done, hoping against hope that we could get back to cooking or chopping wood or heading out to actions, there would be someone—a latecomer—addressing, say, areas where help was needed, issues with police outside of Camp, what to do if you were catching a cold, and so on.

In one collective breath, the place would groan. Then, as was the practice, we would move around the circle again.

If, on the other side of the circle, another latecomer had arrived, and *they* felt inspired to share something about, say, areas where help was needed, issues with police outside of Camp, or what to do if you were catching a cold, I'm pretty sure the groan could be heard forty-five miles north, in Bismarck.

How I wished all of Camp could be heard in Bismarck!

Even more, I wished all of Bismarck would heed the call from Lakota-Dakota-Nakota elders and visit us at Camp. I figured they would see, as I had seen, a way of life that defied the presumptions of Bismarck.

Not that I had a bad life back in Bismarck. Over the years, I had found a vibrant subculture, a countercultural network that insisted as best we could on ways of life that truly felt like life. There was the Pinwheel Modern Dance Company, where we brought the shapes and forms of our names, embodied, to the stage. There was Dragon Jane Performance Art Company, where we raucously performed, with props, as a menstruating football team. There was the truth-telling, teen-centered writers' group, which I got to cofacilitate, where the members challenged the public silence about everything they could think of.

Still, Bismarck was rarely easy.

Ever since 1991, when I moved nine hundred miles from central Illinois to North Dakota's capital, I had wanted to belong. As soon as I arrived, I delighted in the ways people said things, the unfamiliar music of daily speech. A couch was a *davenport*. A car was a *vehicle*. Gums was said like *gooms*. Tour was said like *terr*. The lilt of people's speech sounded Canadian to my ears. With one Canadian grandparent—my grandpa Zurbrigg on my mother's side—I took it as a sign, a source of comfort.

From the start, I loved the river, the prairie, the sunsets, the sky that never quit. Across the wide Missouri, I might spot a stretch of eagles in flight, a pack of chatty coyotes, a storm of downy cottonwood seeds, a shock of wild strawberries on the riverbank. And the sun—the glorious sun, the color of peaches and eggplants and pumpkins—was delicious enough to eat.

I felt at peace with the land, but not all the time with the people.

In 2016, my sense of out-of-placeness wasn't exactly new.

Still, by fall, after being so much at Camp, I began to feel more and more out of sorts, both in Bismarck and, descendant of colonialism though I was, in colonial culture anywhere.

Over the years, in Bismarck and other colonial towns, I would sometimes get harassed just for moving along the sidewalk. Maybe because I was female. Maybe because I was different. Maybe because I was there.

Once, as I waited to cross Sixteenth Street near Hillside Park, a masculine-sounding voice called from a passing car, "Nice scarf, bitch!" and then broke into laughter.

Another time, as I strolled across River Road using the crosswalk, another masculine-sounding voice called from a passing truck, "Hey, you! [Garble, garble, garble.]" And then, again, came laughter.

These forms of harassment—sometimes heckling, sometimes leering—had become commonplace.

At Camp, the only time strangers called out to me was to declare, "Mni Wiconi!"

There seemed to be a place for everyone, including many LGBTQAI+ people who cocreated the Two Spirit Camp within the larger Camp. While not all people may have felt welcomed all the time, the aspiration, at least, was to be welcoming, to hold all people in community together.

What a visceral relief it was, seeing LGBTQAI+ people in central Camp roles, even honored roles, especially given the history of homophobia, transphobia, and related forms of prejudice that I had long witnessed in North Dakota.

In the mid-1990s, a group of North Dakota legislators put forth legislation proclaiming that only one man and one woman could legally get married. Certainly, North Dakota already had a similar law on the books. But this one went further, proclaiming that North Dakota no longer had to accept the legality of marriages performed in other jurisdictions. Rumors and news stories abounded about the much-touted possibility that same-sex marriage was on the brink of legality in Hawai'i. Like legislatures in too many other states, North Dakota acted fast, lest any show of extravagant humanity in the Aloha State be binding here at home.

Though I had never had my heart set on getting all-out legally married with the rings and the towering cake, I wanted to know that I could, no matter who I was dating—a woman, a man, a genderqueer person, or any combination thereof.

In the colonial US in the 1990s, those of us in same-sex relationships had essentially been told two things: Your relationship isn't valid, so you aren't allowed to get married; you aren't allowed to get married, so your relationship isn't valid.

Without the sanction of the state, we LGBTQAI+ people somehow became more beholden to that same state, with our way of loving weaponized against us. In our longing to love and be loved, it was said that we threatened the very sanctity of marriage, the institution of loving, just by wanting in—or by pointing out that we couldn't get there.

Naturally, I wanted to decide for myself if I would get married, or if I wouldn't.

So, knees buckling, I testified against the marriage bill before the North Dakota legislature. I had been invited by Lola Huwe—beloved Mama Lola, maker of delicious homemade lefse from her Norwegian American tradition and founder of the statewide PFLAG chapter, a uniquely courageous and supportive entity at the time. At age twenty-five, I had no idea I was about to be outed on the front page of the *Bismarck Tribune*, which would ultimately lead to further isolation at my white, female-dominated workplace, white and female though I am.

At this point, all I knew was that a self-proclaimed cowboy from western North Dakota, an avowed white, male heterosexual, wanted to speak next. For those of us in the LGBTQAI+ community, this was hard to believe. A bona fide cowboy in blue jeans and hat—on our side?

Still, in spite of his cowboy allyship, the anti-same-sex marriage bill became law.

Just six legislators, out of a total of 141, voted on our side. When Mama Lola asked us activists to send thank-you notes to those six gutsy legislators, it took almost no time at all, yet plenty of energy.

As if the law wasn't convincing and binding enough, there soon came a proposed amendment to the North Dakota Constitution, redundantly saying that only one man and one woman could be married in our state, even if they had gotten married elsewhere. In North Dakota in 2004, the voting-age populace passed it by a landslide.

A landslide.

Nearly three out of every four voters.

As I walked the city, passing people here and there, I couldn't help but wonder, *Which three out of four? Which sixty out of eighty?*

Extrapolating to North Dakota's adult population, which 480,000 out of the rest?

Even as I grieved these losses, I wasn't exactly convinced about the sanctity of the colonial institution of marriage. As a minister's daughter and granddaughter, I had read the Bible closely enough to realize that marriage, in this historical context, wasn't so great for women. In the world of the Bible, it seemed we women either had to share a man we didn't entirely care for, or worse, get stoned to death for loving the one we did. If we did.

And if we didn't? That was rarely spoken of.

Though I might have appreciated the economic privileges of marriage—tax breaks, insurance benefits, emergency-room access, occasional anniversary cards from my family, occasional noncontroversial hand-holding in public—I was mostly A-OK without them.

But, as it turned out, in a colonial system so unlike the way of life I later experienced at Camp, there were consequences that weren't so A-OK.

In 2007 or so, I got a call—my first call on my first flip phone.

This phone call would put me on the pathway of becoming a mom, a dream I had been watering and seeding since my own childhood. From the age of twelve or so, I had been taking notes on being parented and schooled: what I was going to do (and not), how I would raise my children (and not), who my children might become if they so chose (and not).

Chose was the point. That would be our way. My children would be entrusted to help me make the rules. My children would be trusted, period. They would have freedom. They would live their lives to the fullest, with joy, curiosity, and cooperation across the generations.

Naturally, as the mom-making call came in, my own mother was with me.

Or, more aptly, I was with her. We were shopping for shoes, coats, and tops at my favorite thrift store in northern Illinois. The phone rang, or probably dinged.

With a startle, I flipped the cover. I pressed a button—too many buttons. I asked, as if I wasn't exactly sure, "Hello?"

The caller was Kathy Blohm, a white psychologist back in Bismarck. She had read an article in the *Bismarck Tribune* announcing that I had received a two-year Bush Artist Fellowship as a writer—specifically, a performing writer. Meanwhile, she had been looking for a writer, even a performing one.

She knew a number of young women who were creative, vibrant, powerful. They were world changers, yet each one spoke of loneliness, out-of-placeness, in Bismarck-Mandan. Incidentally, each one liked to write.

Which was where I came in.

"How about a six-week group?" she asked me.

To myself, I couldn't help thinking, *Teenagers? Did she say teenagers?*

To Kathy, I said, "I'd love to."

I talked her down from six weeks to three.

Then as soon as I got back to Bismarck, we began. A group of five young women gathered together, as vibrant and world changing as Kathy had described. We met for one week. Then two. Then three.

Around about week two, they said, "Wait. This group isn't almost over, isn't it?"

I looked around the circle. "It doesn't have to be," I said.

Affectionately, they called themselves The Group That Opened the Box. True to their name, they opened the box on just about everything: racism, climate change, sexual assault, birth control, genuine human desire. This was exactly the place where a scrappy young woman with a penchant for rants and ruckus-making would find herself.

On week four, Michaela blazed through the door in a firestorm of poetry.

This descendant of German-Russian immigrants was every bit as powerful as my steely Grandma Van had been. I should have known right then and there that this girl, quick to laugh and slow to smile, would change me.

In the meantime, the group wrote, performed, traveled, did a radio play for Prairie Public Radio, was featured in a film by Kyja Kristjansson-Nelson (an Icelandic American artist who had just returned from Iceland), and more.

One day, at the start of a regular session, out of no place on Earth, this scrappy young woman named Michaela looked across the table and said, "I want *you* to be my mom."

I stammered, "Uh—let's talk about this . . . after."

Immediately after the session, Michaela rushed to stand beside me. She put her head on my shoulder. And that was that.

In private, Kathy Blohm had made the same point. Michaela had sat too long—many months too long—in a group home, awaiting placement in a loving foster home, or even a less-than-loving foster home. But there were none to be found, especially not for a scrappy teenage girl with a penchant for rants and ruckus-making.

I was in.

In fact, I had already started the paperwork, even before Michaela had asked me to. The trouble was, I was in a same-sex relationship.

Up until that moment, the state had told same-sex couples who wanted to be foster parents that only married people get to be parents—a requirement that automatically ruled all of us out.

But there had recently been a rule change, based on the shortage of foster parents in North Dakota. So my partner and I became the first same-sex couple even allowed to begin the lengthy application process in Burleigh County. For months, while Michaela waited and continued to wait for a home that felt like home, the social services office shelved our paperwork, rejected my phone calls, and issued a disapproving assessment of the seriousness of my relationship with my partner. After all, we weren't legally married, so how valid could our ten-year-plus relationship be? In the end, we were together for nearly twenty years, during which time we ran a private animal sanctuary together and also coparented.

For me, the issue wasn't just my right to be a mom or our right to be parents. It was Michaela's right to have a mom, to have parents, when she needed them.

When an attorney from my church put the kind of pressure on an agency that only an attorney can give, unbeknownst to me, the agency moved the paperwork along.

At last! Michaela was coming home!

But now that my partner and I were licensed, the county changed the plan. Instead of foster care, it was suddenly time—right that minute—to attempt reunification with Michaela's not-super-enthusiastic dad in a town ninety miles away.

Well, okay. Reunification was good. I didn't need or want my partner and me to be the only parents to raise her. I figured we were there to fill in any gaps, not to replace the people who already loved her and had raised her, people who had already given her life.

There were plenty of ways to be the mom Michaela had asked me to be. It didn't need to look the way US colonial culture often says it does, with a pink bedroom, two dogs, a tree to climb—though, as I look back, all of that was possible.

In any case, I believed in family reunification. Most of the time, families shouldn't be pulled apart in the first place, making *re*unification necessary. We need to be with—to be claimed by—the ones we come from. With a genuine, organic circle of support, the ones we come from can almost always give us the love we need.

But the staff within the colonial system didn't see this circle of support. Worse, they disrupted Michaela's efforts to make her own. They ended up pulling, pushing, and placing her from group home to group home, place to place, setting to setting. It was as if checking the boxes—group home number one, group home number two, family reunification—was the point.

When the final box was checked and reunification was the word of the day, the system made little preparation for that much-lauded reunification. At whiplash speed, Michaela was sent to Minot, a ninety-minute car ride from Bismarck, which had been her long-time home.

Meanwhile, she asked me to drive her back and forth. She stayed with my partner and me for weekends and the occasional week. As imperfect a mom as I will always be, I was with her when she had her wisdom teeth out, when she spoke poetry to adoring crowds, when she pushed herself toward high school graduation.

All along, the county had a program for licensed foster parents like me to be reimbursed for this kind of care, or at least this kind of mileage. I asked the system to place me on the program but, as part of the first same-sex couple to be licensed in Burleigh County, I never was. Though Michaela plainly stated that I was her chosen mother, I was rarely invited to meetings. I showed up when I knew of them, but the meetings generally progressed as if I wasn't there, either in the room or in Michaela's life.

Once, when I was certain that Michaela was being hurt by a family friend—and she was—I asked the social worker to schedule a meeting with Michaela's team. Before we could have the meeting, the social worker insisted that I share my concerns. After exacting a promise that I would be allowed to attend the meeting, I told her what I knew.

Later, Michaela called to inform me that she had been sent to an emergency meeting that day. Without me.

By now, I realized I probably went too far, expecting to be included in that conversation.

All along, my instincts said I shouldn't act all that involved, all that concerned, all that loving, lest I be labeled, well, a deviant and a pervert out loud. When all was said and done, the system pushed Michaela into a scene where she would be harmed—for the third time in her young life, by a third abuser—rather than let her get too close to her chosen maternal figure, a person who happened to be queer.

Still, in that space between truth and state, I knew who my daughter was.

She called me Mama K, sometimes Momma K. And that's who I had to be—not a replacement for other mamas, other papas, or other parents. Just a mama in the mix.

Blood is thicker than water, it has been said.

By this point, Michaela and I were even thicker than blood.

But the system had no way to understand this, to ascertain that family structures are wider and more organic than the nuclear family model, as instituted by colonialism, would have us believe. In those early years of becoming Michaela's mama, I began to glimpse my inherited colonial system for what it was—or at least for what it wasn't.

Today, I have a wide, diverse family, full of loved ones I can't categorize.

Again, Michaela has been the mover. When her spirit sister, a young white woman named Raquel, gave birth to Chaz, her second child, Michaela was there in the apartment, in the hospital, in the neonatal ICU. Just as Michaela had looked at me seven years prior and made me a mom, she now saw promise in me that I had not yet seen: Grandma Karen.

With those two words, Michaela opened up worlds of love and duty.

These worlds included Nevajeh, Chaz's older sister, and ultimately Eri, the youngest. Then, through another twist of good fortune in another part of the extended family, Brynlee, about the same age as Chaz, also became my beloved grandchild.

I love them all deeply: my daughter, my grandkids, their mothers. Yet not one of them is understood by colonialism, not one is sanctioned or approved by the colonial state, not one has all the requisite paperwork.

But why would so much paperwork be needed? Why, in a nation that proclaims its family values, would so many limits be placed on how family is defined?

So far, the best answer I can come up with is property, private property—who gets what, and when, and why, and who doesn't. In the original form of the US Constitution, even white men were denied the right to vote unless they were property owners.

To have a voice, you had to have stuff. And this view persists today.

If I had paperwork for Michaela, Nevajeh, Brynlee, Chaz, or Eri, they would get my stuff, and that would make them my family—my daughter and grandkids. Since my parents have paperwork for my brother, in the form of a birth certificate with their names in key locations, he has a right to their stuff; any other brotherlike men in my life are only *like* my brothers. And on and on.

When Michaela first became my daughter, I hadn't heard much about Indigenous or noncolonial family constellations. I had no idea that most—maybe all—Indigenous traditions here on the Great Plains make grandmothers and aunties out of every elder woman, much like the way that many Black cultures, AAPI cultures, and cultures of color around the globe have cultivated practices to honor the wisdom of elders.

In my colonial context, such practices and honors mostly don't exist. A person can be loved *like* a mother, *like* a sister, *like* a daughter, but not *as* such. By the rules of colonialism, a person's bloodline—the people you come from or don't come from—has everything to do with the rights you get to exercise.

In colonialism, based on your bloodline, you may have the right to claim land as property, or not, due to the Homestead Act and the Alien Land Laws; you may be deemed more than three-fifths of a person, or not—due to article 1, section 2, of the US Constitution; you may be considered human at all, or not—due to the Doctrine of Discovery and the Indian Removal Act.

In colonialism, blood rules.

Indeed, as recently as the early 1900s, whiteness in the US was codified into law based on this very notion of blood. According to Virginia's Racial Integrity Act, which became a template for other states, a white person was someone who had "no trace whatsoever of any blood other than Caucasian." To access the privileges and rights reserved exclusively for white people, particularly white men, a person could not possess even one drop of so-called non-Caucasian blood.

Even today, the US government tracks percentages of "Indian blood" contained within the populace. Based on various blood quantum laws introduced in the 1700s, the US Bureau of Indian Affairs assigns Certificates of Degree of Indian Blood. These certificates are used to determine rights of citizenship and impose a colonial worldview based primarily on blood relationships.

According to my mentor, Clyde Grubbs, a Western Cherokee minister and community organizer, this preoccupation with blood quantum is antithetical to traditional Indigenous ways of understanding identity, relationships, and culture. The community as a whole, not an individual's blood quantum, determines a person's belonging.

Certainly, even within colonialism, people still have direct, organic experiences.

Bismarck-Mandan itself, like any other settler colonial area, has always been more layered and complex than one uniform, colonial worldview can describe. Having lived most of my life in the Missouri River Valley, I have delighted in hand-picked juneberries for sale on Mandan's Main Street. I have caught music for free at the city parks in Bismarck. In recent years, I have even danced in those same parks—at Pride Fest, no less. I have seen loved ones find their way, thanks to WIC, public housing, and Medicaid expansion. What's more, I have never, in all the winters I have lived in North Dakota, had to push my car through the snow alone. I have never left a stranger to push their car alone either.

All these experiences are signs of humanity, community, aliveness. Even within a colonial paradigm, people still insist on being human.

This sustains my hope, but it doesn't make colonialism a hope-sustaining system.

These deeply human moments are like delicate saplings rising from a felled tree. In spite of improbable circumstances, life yearns to be life.

At the same time, colonialism continues to level the saplings—literally.

Before colonialism invaded, redwood forests in California, tropical forests in Southeast Asia, and rainforests in the Amazon were all thriving and teeming with life. Before colonialism reinvaded, Oceti Sakowin Camp was certainly thriving and teeming with life. On any given day at Camp, I was also thriving and teeming with life.

I could mosey out of the kitchen, stroll past the central fire, cross the main dirt road, wander by the medic and healer tents, venture out to the famous signpost down by the river, and back again, without an intrusive word.

Only "Hello."

Or sometimes, "Have you seen so-and-so?"

Or certainly, "Mni Wiconi!"

As a descendant of settler colonialism, I began to sense how much I had lost. I had learned to tighten my body and restrict my range of motion every time I crossed the street or even approached a street, a meeting, an event, or an otherwise lighthearted party.

At Camp, for the first time in decades, I could stop tightening and restricting. I could stop lifting my soles from the earth, my stomach from my intestines, my shoulders from my heart.

The closest I had come to this sustained sensation in mainstream Bismarck was during the early 2000s, when a bill was introduced to include sexual orientation as a protected category in the state's non-discrimination laws. Thanks to the work of many, the North Dakota Senate managed to pass the bill.

In those days, as I strolled along my gritty, tree-lined street, the air itself felt sweeter, almost kind. With every step, the barrier I felt between myself and the rest of the town seemed to loosen and diffuse.

But then the bill died in the North Dakota House of Representatives.

For all these reasons and more, I longed for a place to call home.

In the fall of 2016, I found one. As Phyllis Young, Oceti Sakowin Camp cofounder, later said to a small crowd at the Human Rights Film Festival in Fargo, "We created a new threshold for humanity at Standing Rock."

Though I never pitched a tent at the Two-Spirit Camp, I loved to know it was there. So much of life was there within Oceti Sakowin Camp: Community cooking. Respect for the web of life. Women's long-held traditions, like understanding moon time to be a powerful time—and the water ceremony where women were the first to receive and give the blessing. Even today, the sound of healing waters falling from the vessel into the Missouri River has still not left my memory. Or my longing.

Even wearing a skirt was a sign of women's power, of women's distinguished-yet-equal role in the larger community. Lakota-Dakota-Nakota women asked all women to wear skirts at Camp, since Camp was a place of ceremony and, traditionally, Lakota-Dakota-Nakota women wear skirts in ceremony.

Time and again, when men or teenage boys would offer to help me carry something (usually supplies I was carting in from Bismarck), I would receive the help as a gift, rather than as an infringement on my power. Each time, it was as if the men and boys were saying, *You carry plenty already. I got this.*

I can scarcely express how much all of this meant in my life—to feel like a human being, an actual human being who could breathe, and live, and be. Borrowing the words of Louise M. Paré, a Ukranian American women's spirituality scholar, I was "coming home to my body."

By comparison, whenever I was back in Bismarck-Mandan, working, walking, or tooling around, I wondered where the full, vibrant humanness was hiding. All those separate yards. The frequent fences. The very wealthy and the very not. Plastic bags clogging the various ditches along the roadways. Big-box stores blaring their neon signs and endless products. The ever-increasing collusion with a political and economic system that was fracking the very lifeblood out of the land, as well as the people. The "Nice scarf, bitch!" blurted from passing cars. The falsehoods and misunderstandings about the realities of Camp.

Not all the time, but often, I experienced Bismarck and Mandan as empty, isolating, sometimes even hopeless.

As a therapist, I had been taught to look for exactly these characteristics and factors when helping people assess whether they may be facing depression. If individuals could feel depressed, it seemed groups of individuals could also feel depressed.

And it wasn't just Bismarck-Mandan; it was any settler colonial city or town. I didn't know this at the time, but according to the American Psychiatric Association, rates of depression are extremely high among white people.

For these same white people, the effects of depression, as well as other behavioral health challenges, are often mitigated by greater access to mental healthcare and other supports. This makes health disparities very real for Black people, Indigenous people, and people of color overall.

Still, for all its economic advantages, whiteness itself is no protection from despair. According to the Suicide Prevention Resource Center, suicide rates are higher among white people than any other cultural group.

All things considered, it seems that Bismarck and Mandan, two overwhelmingly white cities, *could* collectively feel something like depression. It also seems possible that other colonial towns with the same yards, plastic bags, and misunderstandings could also feel something like depression.

I realize my wonderings could sound unnecessarily judgmental or disparaging. Yet I am trying to understand. I am trying to wrap my mind and heart around what it means to be a settler in a settler colonial paradigm.

In this paradigm, Bismarck and Mandan are border towns. They are settler towns on the edge of Indigenous nations, which makes border towns the vanguard of the colonial project. Often, Indigenous people say border towns are a prime location for racism. In fact, border towns have so long been sites of anti-Indigenous racism that the US Commission on Civil Rights continues to study it.

Today, considering the preponderance of Indigenous reservations contained within the boundaries of North Dakota, maybe every town and city in this state is essentially a border town. A town on the front(ier) line. A town that exists to maintain—and sometimes advance—the colonial state.

It can be exhausting, even depressing, to hold a border. As Lillian Smith said in 1949 about the borders of whiteness in her own white Southern context:

> Something was wrong with a world that tells you that love is good and people are important and then forces you to deny love and to humiliate people. I knew . . . that in trying to shut the Negro race away from us, we have shut ourselves away from so many good, creative, honest, deeply human things in life.

Indeed, young people of many ancestries in North Dakota often seem to want nothing more than to find those good, creative, honest, deeply human things. They often leave to find them. "Outmigration of young people" is a phrase I have heard as often as "Go, Bison!"

And it's not just young people. I have had so many openhearted friends move to other places, I don't even complain or rail against it anymore. I just lower my shoulders and say to the ground, "Oh, okay."

In North Dakota, we often hear that fracking is—or will be—good for our state, providing jobs and thus creating incentives for young folks to stay in the area. As it turns out, fracking has attracted hundreds of job seekers from out of state—usually solo men, ready to head out when the job is over. Unlike the Camps at Standing Rock, fracking hasn't brought us community, and it hasn't helped our young ones (or other earnest ones) feel assured that they will have community if they stay.

In 2021, as if to make staying all the more complicated, the North Dakota legislature rescinded the Equal Rights Amendment. The stated reasons for rescinding the ERA, as shared by the white Republican women who led the effort, included "not needing it anymore." At the same time, the local feminist analysis suggested that the real motivations were anti-abortion and anti-trans. After all, in the recent past, protections against discrimination on the basis of sex had been extended to include women's rights to reproductive freedom, as well as nonbinary people's right to be.

During that same legislative session, many of the same legislators also introduced anti-trans legislation, banning trans athletes in schools from participating in their actual gender category, which would have ensured that most trans students wouldn't participate at all. I was grateful to be one of many people who provided testimony against the bill. I was also grateful to see that the legislation ultimately failed. Because anti-trans legislation isn't good for business, the governor vetoed the bill. Then the Republican-dominated legislature was unable to override the veto.

At an equal rights rally during the 2021 legislative session, those of us gathered on that blustery day kept calling, "We're not going anywhere! We're not going anywhere!"

All the while, I realized that many of us were. Or could. Or might.

Even I might. For thirty years, I had been leaving and returning, leaving and returning. By this point, I had even relocated from
Bismarck to Fargo, perched at the more progressive edge of the
state.

In my rally speech, I had beseeched the crowd to stay in North
Dakota. I wanted—and still want—to stay. Never more than in
2016. At Camp.

At Camp, I began to experience new ways of being human, person-
ally and communally.

In fall of 2016, Liz Loos and I huddled in our mittens, hats, and
layers, as another Camp meeting began. At the end of the meeting,
we would leave that long, green tent and head back to the kitchen.
But we weren't in the kitchen yet.

At this point, I hadn't directly met Ikce Wicasa. I had also never
announced either my presence as a minister or my congregation's
presence as a congregation. Since it wasn't about us, I had never
uttered a word in the meetings. As was often said at meetings, *If you
don't have anything new to add, please don't.* So I didn't.

In those days, I didn't always know—and I still don't always
know—when I should have voice and when not. When is being
silent a means of respecting others? When is being silent a means of
disrespecting myself? Or even disrespecting others?

On that chilly morning at Oceti Sakowin Camp, all I knew was
that I was a guest on Indigenous lands. As at home as I felt, as at
home as I was invited to be, my settler colonial people had rarely
made a mutual sense of home possible in Indigenous space, so I kept
quiet. Besides, as a queer girl and then a queer woman within colo-

nialism, I was accustomed to being seen rather than heard. Often, in the crosswalk, legislature, and foster care licensure system, I wasn't so sure if I was truly seen either.

Meanwhile, as the Camp meeting progressed, Indigenous leaders expounded on the cultural dynamics in Bismarck-Mandan. True, there were Bismarck-Mandan people at Camp, living there every day, but, as Indigenous leaders said in that meeting, Bismarck-Mandan at large—North Dakota at large—didn't seem to notice, care, or get involved. Not when sacred sites were destroyed. Not when Indigenous people and accomplices were arrested and abused. Not when the prayerful heart of the movement continued to be missed and misrepresented.

By now, I had decades' worth of opinions, as well as feelings, about what Bismarck-Mandan and North Dakota at large did or didn't notice, care about, or get involved in. Still, *if you don't have anything new to add, please don't.* So, again, I didn't.

Then Ikce Wicasa asked this question, "Where are the Bismarck-Mandan churches?! If anyone should understand prayer, shouldn't they?!"

Well, if there was ever a time for a stage whisper, this would be it.

"Psst psst psst," Liz and I said to each other.

All the while, the focus was moving around the circle.

Closer. And closer.

"Anyone over here have something to add?" Ikce Wicasa asked.

Somewhere in my body, I found my voice.

I introduced myself. I named my congregation. Then I said something like, "We're here—in the kitchen, mostly. Our congregation in Bismarck has been here, in the kitchen, since Camp started. We'd be honored to visit more, if anyone would like."

It wasn't the most eloquent series of words I had ever spoken.

But following the meeting, visit we did.

FIVE

OUT THERE SOMEWHERE

Camp was where I wanted to live, heal, and be. Forever.

The feel of my back on the Earth—or, in colder months, on the cot—must not have been so different from the feel of my skin against my mother's arms when I was freshly born. The presence of Unci Maka, Grandmother Earth, at Oceti Sakowin Camp reminded me of that embracing sensation in long-forgotten ways.

Meanwhile, the visits before and after Camp meetings shifted my center of gravity. I had been welcomed into a placeness, a fullness, at Camp. My congregation as a whole had been welcomed. And now, out of love for that placeness and that place, it was time to pivot toward another place.

At the direction of Camp elders, as shared with me by Ikce Wicasa, it was time to turn our attention back to Bismarck and Mandan, the nearest border towns, those complicated locations I knew so well. By now, I had been involved in a number of collectives of one kind or another, where there always seemed to be more work to do than people to do it. In this context, if one scrappy entity (or another) needed to move a little metaphorical water, and I happened to be situated next to the bucket, then I would go ahead and move a little water.

Maybe I wasn't the best of all possible bucket carriers. Or web developers. Or lobbyists. Or songwriters. Or whatever various roles were needed. But I would carry water because I was there.

Following those visits at Camp, *there* became Bismarck-Mandan. Not only were Bismarck and Mandan the pass-through location for countless long-distance Water Protectors, these two towns were also the local outpost of white settler colonialism, the whereabouts of numerous colonial standard bearers, which included more than one hundred churches. My congregation and I didn't have the chance—the luxury, even—of first studying to be the best possible allies and accomplices and getting into the local action second. It was time to carry a little water, because we were there.

All in all, we did the basic, humble work of allies and accomplices. Thanks to an intricate network of activists and supporters from many directions, we helped coordinate laundry access for Camp elders; a food bank and supply hub in our building; court support for Water Protectors facing charges; media visits from places like San Francisco and Paris; interfaith and intercultural prayer gatherings in Bismarck-Mandan; transportation of people, food, and supplies to and from the Camps; rides from emergency rooms in Bismarck after acts of police aggression; collaborative, truth-telling events like the congregational Water Is Life series; homestays for hundreds of people in the sanctuary and in activists' homes; and jail support for Water Protectors being released from custody, often from jails around the state.

As we soon learned, when Morton County was beyond capacity, Water Protectors would be sent to jails over a hundred miles away, in places arrestees had never been. For unexplained reasons, the releases often seemed to happen in the middle of the night.

Around this time, I began to long for signifiers—palpable descriptors of my lived experience, a way to say what I was up to that really said what I was up to. But as much as I have always loved words, I had never been one to invent handy, mind-bending strings of them.

As a child, fitting together the elusive pieces of human language like children the world over, I had managed to coin a few haphazard signifiers: "Excorbing the whole neighborhood" meant "Making a ruckus on a scale that the neighbors would not appreciate." And so on.

But after all these early childhood efforts, I had mostly managed to get by with the words and word combinations I had already inherited: Community organizing. Logistics support. Social justice.

For the most part, those words were true. Yet I longed for one particular term to evoke what it looked like, in my life, to be welcomed as an ally and accomplice in the Water Protector movement at Standing Rock, which was different from being a leader, and also different from not being there at all.

But I didn't quite have the language to describe my daily work, these efforts to embody my deepest commitments. Much like I did as a child, matching together disparate sounds and concepts, I created a phrase. It was nothing fancy or extravagant. Simply put, it meant details, details, details, collaborations, collaborations, collaborations.

In all its obvious artlessness, the term was *logistical ministry*. Logistics plus ministry. Details plus purpose. Collaboration plus vision.

In retrospect, doing this work in Bismarck-Mandan was a lot like doing communal food preparation in the Camp kitchens. If someone had wanted to make a ratings-busting reality TV show about it, they would have had to impose a plotline. We weren't the larger story. We supported the larger story.

As a descendant of settler colonialism hoping to be a genuine ally and accomplice, I turned to Indigenous loved ones, colleagues, and elders for verbal and nonverbal cues about how to support that larger story in a good way, or at least a good-ish way.

I made missteps all the time, like the time I got interviewed for the *Huffington Post*. The reporter couldn't find the Lakota Water Protector they were also going to be interview, but I went ahead with the interview just the same, ending up looking like some kind of Camp spokesperson.

Meanwhile, I began to develop something like a new sixth sense—an instinct, almost—which would ping me whenever I was veering off the path. Any glimmer of glamour, like the *Huffington Post* situation, was a likely sign of that diversion. Amidst my mistakes, I asked myself questions like: *If I am about to enjoy a delicious dessert, did I help to prepare the metaphorical meal? Was my body involved in the sacrifice as well as the indulgence? If so, how could I know that this, right now, was the moment to indulge? To what end?*

Certainly, I had some small role in the movement. And since the movement mattered, my role in the movement likely mattered too.

But not every role that mattered was mine.

This was when I began to develop a deep and abiding longing for stories, or even fragmented anecdotes, of humble, sometimes-invisible accomplices doing humble, sometimes-invisible work. I was pretty sure these stories wouldn't be easy to find.

In colonial culture, there seemed to be plenty of stories of wannabe white saviors, like *Dances with Wolves*, a film where a white soldier protects Lakota people from other white soldiers. Or *The Help*, where a white Southerner protects Black Southerners from other white Southerners. Or *Green Book*, where a white rabble-rouser protects a Black concert pianist from other white rabble-rousers.

There even seemed to be plenty of stories where white villains showed their evil ways, like the white soldiers in *Dances with Wolves*, the white Southerners in *The Help*, and the white rabble-rousers in *Green Book*. To this day, Hollywood hasn't even begun to document all the racism and colonialism of white people across time and space, so you could say we have it coming.

Still, when it comes to stories of antiracism and anticolonialism, is this all that we, as white people, have to say about who we are? In the representational mathematics of whiteness, when we solve the equation for wannabe saviors and consummate villains, it certainly doesn't seem that there's a whole lot left to be. Who knows, maybe cinematic white saviors depend upon cinematic white villains to cocreate white space and then center it.

I keep coming back to "White Savior: The Movie Trailer" by Amber Ruffin and Seth Meyers, TV hosts and comedians of Black and white identities, respectively. In the beginning, the satirical voiceover lists the standard tropes of white savior movies: there's the bar scene, where a white person sticks up for a Black person, and the work scene, where a stunned white person learns that their Black coworker is, well, smart.

And then there's this well-known character: "That one racist who's so cartoonishly racist that other racists watch this movie and

say, 'Well, at least I'm not that racist.'" Following a string of gar-
bled insults by that same racist, the narrator goes on to say, "If
you're a Black person hoping for the catharsis of watching a Black
character punch a racist, you'll get the next best thing: the white guy
punching a racist."

Why do we as white people long to punch that racist? Who, in
particular, are we punching when we do?

The white psyche, sometimes including my white psyche,
seems animated—riveted, even—by white villains and their copious misdeeds. Not long ago, when I watched *Loving*, a movie about
a couple who challenged so-called miscegenation laws, I realized
how accustomed I had gotten to white villains appearing in certain places and ways. The film is set in Virginia and Washington,
DC, in the late 1950s and early 1960s. It tells the story of Mildred
Loving, who was Black and Indigenous, and Richard Loving, who
was white, and their struggle for the simple right to have a legal
marriage.

Out of sheer cinematic habit, I braced myself whenever a white
person other than Richard came onto the screen. Not just when a
frustrated white judge or an unwelcomed white officer entered the
picture. But every single time.

I could hardly stop bracing, even when Black people and white
people in Mildred and Richard's hometown, the relatively antiracist
town of Central Point, interacted in antiracist ways.

Considering the time and the place, I expected graphic, visceral
violence. There was plenty of systemic violence and institutional
racism depicted in the film, but there was none of the bloody cinematic violence I had come to expect, without even knowing I
expected it.

I don't mean to say that graphic racist and colonial violence or even verbal threats are somehow overrepresented in Hollywood. Over the course of history, there have been more than five hundred years' worth to document.

Yet maybe there are a few more antiracist white people than popular culture would allow. Even Richard and Mildred's hometown would suggest that.

How do we—those of us white people aspiring to be antiracist—tell stories of real, live white people in the antiracist, anticolonial struggle? Not as saviors or as villains, just as human beings.

Am I capable of telling my own story in that way? As a white person, can I tell a story that is centered in my lived experience without habitually centering whiteness? Can I trouble whiteness enough to decenter it, even a little? Or at least disrupt its centrality?

I need antiracist, anticolonial white people to learn from, to be encouraged by—just as Beverly Daniel Tatum, an African American antiracism scholar, has encouraged. As a professor who addresses the effects of racism on African American students and also teaches white educators, Tatum has offered an in-depth definition of the white ally's role—an alternative to what she calls the white supremacist model, the white guilt model, and the What whiteness? model. She suggests that those of us who are white need to know about white ally figures past and present, in order to be inspired toward our own white allyship.

The more I pay attention, the more I find that they're out there, these white allies, across time, history, and space. There's John Brown, abolitionist; Joe Hill, union organizer; Anne McCarty Braden, civil rights activist; and the countless unnamed. That's who I really long to learn about: the countless unnamed.

Still, as positive as most of my teachers were in my upbringing, I hardly learned about any of these antiracist white ancestors in my schooling. The ones I did hear about were depicted as solo actors, not members of a longtime—if perpetually interrupted—movement toward collective liberation.

In that same school system, I didn't learn much about BIPOC folks either.

Not Black people like Sojourner Truth, abolitionist and women's rights activist; Ella Baker, civil rights leader; or Alvin Ailey, choreographer and dancer.

Nor Indigenous people like Sequoyah, creator of the Cherokee syllabary; Sarah Winnemucca, Northern Paiute author and interpreter; or Leonard Peltier, Anishinaabe-Lakota American Indian Movement (AIM) activist and political prisoner.

Nor Asian American-Pacific Islander people like Anna May Wong, Chinese American film star; Frank Emi, leader of the draft resistance of interned Japanese American men; or Haunani-Kay Trask, leader of the movement for Hawaiian sovereignty.

Nor Arab American people like members of the United Automobile Workers' Arab Workers Caucus, who waged one of the first divestment campaigns; Etel Adnan, celebrated poet, essayist, and visual artist; or Rosemary Barkett, born in Mexico to a Syrian family, first woman to serve on the Florida Supreme Court.

Nor Latina-Latino-Latine people like Roberto Clemente, major-league baseball player; Sylvia Rivera, activist during the Stonewall rebellion and beyond; or Dolores Huerta, cofounder of the United Farm Workers Association.

And, of course, the countless unnamed.

Is the US colonial system almost—*almost*—as disinterested in stories of white accomplices who have genuinely disrupted racism as in stories of BIPOC folks in general? Is racism such an engine of colonialism that even white people must stay in our lane?

What does it mean to be white *and* antiracist? *And* an accomplice?

Having been in various antiracist spaces over time, I have noticed that sometimes, white allies and accomplices speak to other white people, including white allies and accomplices, with what I can only call disdain. Maybe disgust. Maybe simple frustration.

I don't exactly blame us when we do this; it's annoying to witness each other "Columbus-ing" things, like that famous College-Humor skit where white people claim places, trends, and cultural practices as our own just because we're white. Still, when we white people talk to other white people as if we ourselves aren't equal inheritors of whiteness and its problems, I wonder if we might unintentionally be engaging in another kind of cultural misappropriation.

In my experience of antiracist spaces, it is understood that Black, Indigenous, Asian American-Pacific Islander, and people of color in general have the hard-earned right to rail against white supremacy, white settler colonialism, and the white people at large who have materially benefited from these systems—including white people in the antiracist space at hand.

As Black blogger and social commentator Marley K. says regarding systemic racist violence, "Victims of crimes and atrocities have a right to feel angry, they have a right to protect themselves; they have a right to express themselves, and they have no obligation to be nice to anyone. . . . Nice is a centerpiece of White Supremacy and it needs to end."

As far as I understand, this means that full self-expression by BIPOC folks is a basic means of self-protection from racist crimes and atrocities across generations. Like Marley K., many BIPOC leaders insist that being real and authentic, not being nice, is the point. When we white people insist on niceness, we are clinging to a comfortable, disaffected sense of racial neutrality.

Here's what Michael Eric Dyson, a Black theologian and author of *Tears We Cannot Stop: A Sermon to White America*, says whiteness is really about: "Beloved, to be white is to know that you have at your own hand, or by extension, through institutionalized means, the power to take black life with impunity." According to Dyson, the declaration that Black Lives Matter is so "effortlessly revolutionary" because "it takes aim at white innocence and insists on uncovering the lie of its neutrality, its naturalness, its normalcy, its normativity."

This, in Dyson's words, is what's at stake if white people hold onto that innocence:

"You maintain power."

In other words, niceness, a practice demanded by white innocence, is at the very heart of the problem. It creates a psychic space in which we as whites behave as if whiteness isn't violently powerful—when it is.

As such, no one doing antiracist, anticolonial work is obligated to be nice—not those who are BIPOC, not those who are white, not even those who are white allies and accomplices talking to other white allies and accomplices. But we white allies and accomplices may have another obligation—another calling, even.

In antiracist spaces, BIPOC folks tend to hold a place of informed authority about race, racism, and prejudice, which is rooted in firsthand experience and understanding. This authority opens forms of speech and self-expression that grow from that lived experience. But when we white people behave as if we can speak with this experiential authority, when we copy these forms of self-expression, I wonder if we appropriate this conversational and emotional space. When we rail against other whites as if we ourselves are BIPOC folks having experiences that BIPOC folks have, maybe we enter a rhetorical and spiritual terrain that is not ours to occupy.

In this slippery appropriation, it seems that we can make ourselves look a little more antiracist than the white people around us. Energetically speaking, this trend might also be something like rushing to the Black Hills in the 1870s. For many whites in antiracist and anticolonial spaces, I wonder if BIPOC identity has started to look like gold.

But for white people, whiteness remains our inheritance—in racist, as well as antiracist, spaces.

Lena K. Gardner, cofounder of Black Lives of Unitarian Universalism and a seminary friend of mine, has taught me much about allyship and accompliceship. At a regional gathering of mostly white Unitarian Universalists, Lena spoke of followership, of taking and accepting the lead, in the case of the Movement for Black Lives, of Black people who live at the heart of the work. This teaching had everything to do with my decision to head to the kitchen and follow at Oceti Sakowin Camp.

While copresenting with Lena, Ashley Horan, a white minister, friend, and co-activist, called to mind those annoying white people in our lives, the ones who wear their white privilege like a floppy, brand-new Easter hat. Then Ashley said to the other white people in the space, "That is where our work is."

The collective—though silent—groan was palpable. Visceral. Especially within my own throat.

She didn't mean that every comfortable, privilege-flaunting white person should become our new missionary focus, making us the newest white saviors on the newest white block. As I understood it, she meant that our work and role as white people in the struggle includes one another.

In other words, in genuine decolonizing efforts, it doesn't work for white people to be the beneficiaries of white identity in mainstream white spaces—and then try to become the beneficiaries of a BIPOC-adjacent identity in BIPOC-led spaces. We keep on being white, just like the white people who enrage us.

I once heard David Swallow, Jr., call out white people as the ones who had elected President Donald Trump. In the privacy of my own mind, I took offense. I had done no such thing! But as I listened, I acclimated to the worldview he was sharing. There is a collective, a culture, a people we come from. We white people are not just a random array of random individuals doing randomly individual stuff. The people I come from have seen, been, and done many things, including get Donald Trump elected.

Mary Wilson, a white activist and a longtime sister-friend, shared this insight with me during the NoDAPL movement: "As white people in Indigenous-led work, we need to support each other—well."

I had never heard anyone make such a suggestion before. In my experience of antiracist spaces, white people don't generally talk about *supporting* one another. Holding each other accountable, yes. But being there, aspiring antiracist to aspiring antiracist, in support?

Today, I have to ask myself, what does it mean to be an accomplice collaborating with other accomplices? What might genuine solidarity among white accomplices look like? Even more, as we dismantle white colonial systems, what might it mean as white people to be in solidarity with all human beings, including those who are white?

After all, we white people are locked into the same colonial puzzle with everyone else who's white—with everyone else, period. When I fight, energetically or materially, with other whites around me to be the good one in the bunch, or the better one, or the best one, I am perpetuating the very same white supremacy culture—the very same construct of good versus bad, us versus them, white savior versus white villain—that has gotten us into trouble in the first place.

Still, even when we white people intend to be more authentic, more real, more humble than all of that, we may not always succeed. And even when we think we've succeeded, others may not agree.

In early 2021, a predominantly white Christian church in Mandan erected a full-color billboard discouraging people from participating in gossip. As far as I know, no one objected to this anti-gossip message. The objection, as shared by Melanie Angel Moniz, was that the lips of each of the people on the billboard had been sewn shut. Dramatically. Garishly, even. You could see the stitches.

Plus, the only people on the billboard were people of color.

Melanie reached out to the pastors of the church, as well as to the Mandan City Commission, calling for the billboard's removal. She urged others in the community, especially white pastors, to do the same.

In my letter to the pastors, which I shared with the city commission, I used phrases like, "I don't doubt that your intention is inclusivity," "Particularly as faith leaders, we are often under public scrutiny," "I'm under the impression that your staff and congregation, like mine, are primarily white people," and "With gratitude for your attention."

I never did hear back from the pastors. But two Mandan city commissioners replied—Amber Larson and Dennis Rohr, both of whom I believe to be white. Each one let me know that they had driven by the billboard and that the billboard was now gone, replaced by a timely Easter message. Amber Larson closed by wishing me a nice weekend.

Dennis Rohr went on to suggest this: "In reading your concerns, it appears, to me, that you may be somewhat pretentious in assessing the situation."

Well.

After getting this email, I kept forgetting, then remembering, his scathing word choice. Did he say *premature?* No. *Persnickety?* No. *Pretentious.* Ack! It's hard to imagine a word further from authenticity.

Maybe I need more practice writing letters like these, or maybe the city commissioner needs more practice reading letters like these. Or maybe both.

Meanwhile, I keep thinking about those wannabe white saviors from the movies: Tony Lip from *Green Book*, Skeeter from *The Help*, Dances with Wolves from the movie by the same name.

Could the entire white savior versus white villain trope be the seed of another story that's trying to take root? A story we white people long for but our own white culture cannot tell.

According to Tema Okun, a white scholar who studies white supremacy culture, one of white supremacy's central characteristics is either/or thinking. This binary approach means positioning or presenting options or issues as either good or bad, right or wrong, with us or against us.

Indeed, following the attacks of September 11, 2001, then-President George W. Bush said to the world, "Either you are with us, or you are with the terrorists." Being beholden, as white culture seems to be, to this binary thinking, what happens when the locus shifts? What happens when racism and colonialism are now the locus of concern? How do we white people contend with the Indian Removal Act, the Fugitive Slave Act, the Chinese Exclusion Act, the Muslim ban, and on, and on, and on?

What happens when whiteness itself shifts to a villainous role?

Maybe, under the psychic protection of the wannabe white savior, we are trying to make sense of those white villains. Maybe we are trying to understand how we, as collective white people, got here, how we became and can unbecome those famously unsavory white villains across history. It seems we are trapped in the traps that whiteness has set for others: good versus evil, white versus Black, cowboy versus Indian, cop versus robber, American versus foreigner, Christian versus Muslim, citizen versus alien.

When we are either good or bad, and white people have behaved so badly, how do we be *good*?

I believe we want to be good, we white people—or, at the very least, we want to be believe ourselves to be good, with particular definitions of *good* shifting within our contexts. Generations of lived experiences have shown us that we will be punished—by God, by the state, by parental figures—if we aren't good. The colonial US doesn't end up with the highest rate of incarceration in the entire world without a perpetual fixation on punishment (being bad) and its antidote (being good).

Thandeka, a Black theologian who has interviewed a number of white people about their childhood experiences of whiteness, even believes that the Euro American child is shaped into white identity through a process of white shame, where the child essentially comes to feel that they are flawed and bad. She considers the Euro American child to be "a racial victim of its own white community of parents, caretakers, and peers, who attack it because it does not yet have a white racial identity. Rather than continue to suffer such attacks, the Euro American child defends itself by creating a white racial identity for itself." This is when the child develops white shame, Thandeka says, which happens because "the parts of her that were not white had to be set aside as unloved and therefore unlovable."

While white guilt gets plenty of airplay, I don't hear a lot about white shame. According to Brené Brown, a well-known white scholar on the topic of shame, "Shame means 'I am bad,' while guilt means 'I did something bad.'"

In the either/or worldview of whiteness, once I am bad, that's it. Clearly, I can't be good. In fact, I may need to tell myself that other people are bad, so that I can then be good or, at least, I can be less bad.

I can't help but think of the two white children who, in the summer of 2021, flipped off a group of us Water Protectors at the Mississippi River headwaters, where we were protesting the Line 3 pipeline. How were their white identities formed? How were their parents' white identities formed? If the white adults in their lives saw the flipping-off incident, which they surely did, how did they understand the white people they were raising? In that moment, how might they have defined the word *us*, compared to *them*?

Within white setter colonialism, *us* is a complicated concept.

In my white culture, the collective is generally seen as a threat to the individual. White cultural standard bearers like Russian American philosopher Ayn Rand even proclaim, "It is man's independence, success, prosperity, and happiness that collectivists wish to destroy."

Coming from this colonial cultural background, I was stunned to find myself becoming both more selfless and more self-loving, both more independent and more interdependent, at Oceti Sakowin Camp. At Camp, independence and interdependence existed in a powerful, dynamic tension. After all, having voice and finding voice at Oceti Sakowin Camp happened much the way Al Miller, a Seminole organizer, and Stella Leach, a Colville-Lakota organizer, had described the Indigenous-led occupation of Alcatraz nearly fifty years before.

As Stella Leach said, "Here we practice the purest form of democracy. It is the people who have the final say-so."

As Al Miller said, "We've had different spokesmen from time to time, whoever was there to do the job. Every man out here's a spokesman."

At Camp, the community participated directly in decision-making. That's what daily meetings were about. That's what daily life was about. While egos would get in the way sometimes, like egos anywhere, this principle endured. Though we were not all the same, all of us were equal. The dignity of each individual enhanced the dignity of the whole. This meant we all had something to give.

As part of the Water Protector movement at Camp and even in Bismarck-Mandan, I gave everything I had—any talent, any skill, any proximity to resources or to power. And I had something real to give, small as it was, that the larger moment called for. I also received everything I genuinely needed to receive.

I had a place in human culture, in human history, where past and future animated the present, and my role as a real, living person was to be a part of the web, part of the whole, rather than denier of that web or destroyer of that whole.

Sometimes I could sense the liberation, the visceral unmooring, in my very DNA. What more could I hope to receive?

In Colorado in the late 1990s, I worked with adults and teens who had developmental disabilities. As people who were often in the position of receiving, receiving, receiving, they showed me the importance of being generous, of having the power to be generous. I learned that if I truly intended to honor the people I was working with, I needed to be willing to receive, whether it was a helping hand, a line drawing, a piece of advice, or a showstopping idea for our upcoming performance. I needed not to interrupt their capacity to give.

At Oceti Sakowin Camp, I was allowed this power, this grace, of giving. At Camp, in the movement itself, it seemed this grace was everywhere. At the earliest teach-in, held in October in our small, overpacked sanctuary, Indigenous presenters like Kandi Mossett White, Winona LaDuke, LaDonna Brave Bull Allard, and Layha Spoonhunter riveted the crowd. At the close of the event, Kandi asked me to leave my spot in the back, join her at the front, and face the crowd of Water Protectors.

As I stood beside her, Kandi asked me, "What would you like to say to your people?"

I can scarcely remember how I responded. Mostly, I just remember being asked—learning, in that moment, that the people gathered there could be my people, that I could be their people.

In November, keenly aware that the prayerful heart of the movement was being missed and misrepresented in Bismarck-Mandan and in North Dakota generally, Camp elders said it was time for an interfaith and intercultural prayer gathering in the very heart of that misunderstanding. Since our small sanctuary was indeed small, and since it was November in North Dakota, I reached out to local faith communities and institutions, including the University of Mary, which had much more spacious indoor seating space.

A handful of my ministerial colleagues expressed deep regret that their communities wouldn't get behind the event, let alone the movement. Some asked their decision-makers for space and were denied. Some felt asking would be time-sucking and counterproductive.

With an ironic plot twist brought on by global climate change, the early November weather turned out to be mild, easy enough for a gathering outdoors. Two hundred-plus people assembled on the congregation's yard, which was slightly more spacious than the sanctuary.

In the end, the event was glorious. We shared prayers from Lakota, Sufi, Hindu, Buddhist, UU, Humanist, Christian, and other spiritual and cultural traditions. We shared delicious foods in many vibrant colors—the spirit plate was prepared first, then elders and children were invited to partake, and then everyone else got in line. We shared earnest conversations about the Water Protector movement, the Fort Laramie Treaties, the reasons the Camps existed, the history behind Lakota-Dakota-Nakota-led resistance to the pipeline, and more. Privately, the two openhearted Christian leaders who gave prayers—a white Protestant minister and a white Roman Catholic scholar—let me know that they had come on their own behalf, so the name of their respective faith communities should not be stated publicly.

I had never seen the faith community of Bismarck-Mandan so reticent to pray together in public. In Bismarck-Mandan, there are Ten Commandments monuments, local groups with *Christ* prominently featured in their title, and plenty of parochial schools with Roman Catholic, Missouri Synod Lutheran, and nondenominational Christian affiliations. During each biannual session of the North Dakota Legislative Assembly, local pastors flock to the capitol day after day, one after another, to offer a morning prayer in the Senate or the House.

One year, the list was so full, I wasn't able to get on it.

Another year, a local pastor led the Senate in this impromptu call-and-response:

PASTOR: "God is good."
SENATORS: "All the time."
PASTOR: "All the time."
SENATORS: "God is good."

Though not all senators participated, most did. We white North Dakotans tend to wear our faith—and our prayers—pretty boldly on our sleeves.

Yet in relation to the Dakota Access Pipeline, what did our faith say? What were our prayers about? What would it take to pray together across cultures?

As the winter of 2016 drew closer, a special day approached: a call to interfaith prayer at the invitation of Arvol Looking Horse, keeper of the Sacred White Buffalo Calf Pipe Bundle. The December event, which was to be held at the heart of Camp, would ultimately coincide with the famous day the veterans arrived.

All would be welcome. *Thousands* would be welcome.

Ikce Wicasa told me that he would get the word out to Indigenous nations; I just needed to reach out to churches across the US.

Did he say churches *across the US*?

As much as I enjoyed his sense of humor, this wasn't that. By this point, I had adopted a working principle of movement-based accompliceship: Show up first. Sort out the details second.

As soon as I could get cell service after walking to Facebook Hill, the highest spot at Camp, I got on the phone. I talked with congregants, the UU College of Social Justice, Minnesota UU Social Justice Alliance, regional UUA offices, and on, and on, and on. Back in Bismarck, I sent a lot of emails. I reached out to the one hundred-plus pastors of the one hundred-plus churches in Bismarck-Mandan and to many faith keepers across North Dakota.

The email to local clergy went something like this:

We have received one of the most important invitations we are ever likely to receive as people of faith and conviction. Chief Arvol Looking Horse, keeper of the Sacred White Buffalo Calf

Pipe Bundle, has called upon each of us to join him at Standing Rock on Sunday, December 4th, for an Interfaith Day of Prayer. In solidarity with Indigenous people and mutual love for the water, it is my hope that you and your communities of faith will participate in this history-making day.

As those who have visited know, the nonviolent Water Protector movement at Standing Rock is deeply rooted in prayer. Each day I spend at Oceti Sakowin Camp, I feel myself challenged and inspired to live a more prayerful and faithful life. We awake with prayers, dine with prayers, go to rest with prayers, and pray continuously throughout each day.

The Camps at Standing Rock are based on the conviction that prayer, especially collective prayers, can protect our living water. Your prayers—and your presence—mean the world.

The most common response from local clergy went something like this: _____. In other words, nothing.

The second most common response: "Please remove me from your mailing list."

The third most common response was a gracious decline, considering that their faith communities would never join them at Oceti Sakowin Camp on a Sunday morning. I was happy to hear from the rabbi at Temple Beth El in Fargo, who sent an eager *yes*.

But there was also this email from a Bismarck-Mandan pastor:

I will not be participating in your prayer service. The Standing Rock Sioux and their supporters are causing division throughout North Dakota and the nation, attempting to impose their extreme and unreasonable views concerning petroleum on the rest of

America. Petroleum is a gift from God and is being used respon-
sibly in North Dakota. In addition, your movement is creating a
dangerous situation for the local community, attracting criminals
and agitators to Bismarck-Mandan from throughout the world.
Schools are being put on lockdown every day. Law enforcement is
being put in danger and race relations in North Dakota are being
greatly set back. Please reconsider your own support of this divi-
sive movement and pray for order, harmony, peace, and obedience
to authority in the days ahead.

    Yours in Christ.

Back at Camp, Ikce Wicasa asked what kind of response I was
getting from local faith keepers. When I hesitated, he interjected
with, "Let me guess—something like, 'Why are you praying with
those savages?'"

I returned to Bismarck-Mandan with a troubled heart.

Still, in spite of my uneasiness, that special day did arrive.

On December 4, thousands of people gathered around the sacred
fire, next to heaping bundles of sage and well-worn cans teeming
with tobacco. Where the Missouri and Cannonball Rivers converge,
they came to pray. They came because Chief Arvol Looking Horse
had invited them.

That same Sunday morning, at our snow-swept little church,
we made a sacred caravan. People had arrived, as people were
always arriving in those days, from miles in many directions. And
now here we were, one car after the other—after the other—after
the other—in just about every shape and size, much like the movement itself.

New snow hung above us in the clouds, waiting for release. On the roads, snow drifts reached, arced, and played like the skirts of passing ghosts. Ronya Galligo-Hoblit led the caravan with her family. Having called so many of us to the Water Protector movement months ago, she led us there again.

I was in the last car to leave for Camp. We were, in a manner of speaking, a choir of white allies—myself, Liz Anderson, Andrea Ficek Falcon, and Karen Brammer, Karen having just traveled 1,500 miles from New York to support us. At the prayer gathering, this morning's destination, we would offer the UU prayer in song. With help from Karen Larrivee, another white ally, we had sung the people on their way, as each person left the sanctuary that morning, heading out in carpool after carpool.

Now, on our journey toward the Camp, the rivers, the fire, we sang again, "As I went down to the river to pray, studying about that good ole way." We had switched up some of the words, hoping the song might carry an interfaith spirit.

Since then, I have questioned our decision—my decision, as a white minister—to change these lyrics and remove the words *robe and crown*, as well as *Lord*. I have since learned that while the origin of the song is no longer known, it has long been shared across Christian traditions, including Black Christian traditions.

We—and I—altered the lyrics specifically in preparation for this intercultural prayer event, aware that colonialism in the form of Christendom has repeatedly made *the robe and crown*, as well as the conceptualized *Lord*, into deadly weapons against Indigenous peoples. The genocidal legacy of Christian boarding schools in the US, Canada, and Australia is just one poignant example. But that's not all that Christianity has been across the centuries.

Thanks to the teachings of Glen Thomas Rideout, a Black musician and music scholar, I have come to understand the importance of retaining the original lyrics of African American spirituals, so that the original experiences of the original voices are honored and not erased in our present times and contexts.

Today, I don't quite know whether "Down to the River to Pray" is an African American spiritual, a white Appalachian song, or both. Having roots in Appalachia, I could claim the song as part of my own cultural tradition and then adapt it, much like my cultural ancestors did with songs like "In the Sweet By-and-By," "There Is Power in the Blood," and "Nearer, My God, to Thee."

Joe Hill of the Industrial Workers of the World had revised each of these songs in poignant and sometimes hilarious ways: "Pie in the Sky," "There Is Power in a Union," "Nearer, My Job, to Thee."

But in my own context, it's hard to say. Whose *robe*? Whose *crown*? Whose *Lord*? I could change mine; I could erase mine. But it wasn't upon me to alter anybody else's.

In my activist circles, it is pretty common to note differences between our intentions and our impacts. My intention to be a good ally or even a badass accomplice can sometimes have distinct and nuanced impacts.

On that day, on that glorious trip back to Camp, I was doing the best I had in me at the time to be a good and useful ally and accomplice. While I question some of my choices in retrospect, I hope I made the journey in a good-enough way.

Meanwhile, we continued to sing our revised lyrics.

Instead of *robe*, *crown*, and *Lord*, all of which surely meant love to some, we sang of *love*, *peace*, *hope*, and *strength*.

Where shall all our love be found? Oh-oh, show me the way.

———

We did love it—that song, that trip, that day, as we inched and stopped, inched and stopped, on that endless stretch of snow, road, and cars.

The trouble was, having been invited to co-organize the day's event, we were generally expected to show up on time to the day's event. But all those thousands of people, even as they carpooled, slowed us down. Inching along in our car, we spoke aloud the names of the nations—more than three hundred in all—whose flags flew at the entrance to Camp: Oglala Lakota, Cheyenne River, Omaha Tribes, Métis. All the while, I watched the minutes move faster than *we* could possibly move.

9:50. 9:52. 9:55.

10 a.m. The beginning of the interfaith day of prayer.

Where shall all our hope be found? Oh-oh, show me the way.

By luck or by chance, we made our way to the entrance gate to Camp, where we often received a blessing of sage.

"Welcome home," the security folks at the gate said.

"Good to be home," I said.

Not too far from the sledding hill, we found a spot to stash the car. Then we ran past the California kitchen. The giant dome. Tipis, tents, yurts. Porta-potties. And people, more than a thousand people, in all manner of thick winter hats.

There is a phrase I like to say sometimes: *If you see me running, you'd better start running too, because something must be on fire.*

And we were.

We made our way into the layered crowd, electric with excitement. We had just missed the opening prayer by Arvol Looking

Horse, arriving just as Ikce Wicasa announced that the other prayers would begin. Now.

This was supposed to be our cue.

But with all the glorious people in between us and the central fire, the place for sharing prayers, there was no way.

Ikce Wicasa leaned in closer to the microphone. "Karen . . . I know you're out there somewhere."

Thankfully, I actually was. Thankfully, we hadn't stopped at that long porta-potty line, as tempted as we had been. Thankfully, our group had been on fire enough to up and run.

I know you're out there somewhere.

Since this time, these words have taken on layers and layers of meaning.

This was a practice of faith, to build a prayer Camp, to hold an intercultural prayer gathering. This faith, this trust, says that how we live matters. As James Luther Adams, a white theologian and author, has taught, "Faith is not fundamentally about one's beliefs but about one's commitments." This faith, this commitment, says that we people of many identities can hold a space for what we envision, a place where human communities can be life-sustaining and where it actually means something to be alive.

Whatever the outcome, whatever the result, faith says we can hold a space now for the world we imagine. We can touch the dreamed-of future by committing to it in our time and place. This was the kind of faith that moved people to live in tipis and yurts, to share collective kitchens, to create tents solely devoted to healing of body and spirit, to pray in the morning and midday and night, to challenge ourselves to coexist across cultures.

Faith says the journey is the destination; how we live is who we are.

On that day at Oceti Sakowin Camp, around the sacred fire, I looked out at the faces without number, faces deep in prayer, flushed with Spirit and with cold, one beside another, beside another, beside another. Out in that crowd, there were people of many traditions—Indigenous traditions, Earth-based traditions, Humanist traditions, Abrahamic traditions. There were even white North Dakotans like myself who had heeded the sacred call.

I told myself that day, *Remember this. Remember everyone. A time will come when you will need this moment.*

I have needed it indeed.

Seeing so much injustice, such unrelenting injustice, at the hands of my own inherited culture, can make me prone to despair.

Where shall all our strength be found? Oh-oh, show me the way.

Whenever I can, I remind myself of the people around that fire, the faith of the people around that fire. I remind myself of their prayers.

And I remind myself of the people who are reminding themselves of us.

I know you're out there somewhere.

SIX

TRASH TALK

Not long ago, I heard a rumor I had never heard before. According to this rumor, there were underground brothels at Camp.

Literal brothels under the ground.

I tried to wrap my mind around this one, so elaborate and specific. All I could figure was that someone had seen the homemade insulation under the flooring.

When colder weather approached, many of the common areas (the kitchens, mostly) needed strong wooden floors. Meanwhile, as gifts of supplies continued stacking up, crucial items like boots, coats, and winter gear would be placed in the clothing tent. But the clothing that couldn't be used—items like the four-inch heels that had given Jeff Iron Cloud and me a hearty, headshaking laugh—ended up having a special purpose. Thanks to the resourcefulness of Camp building crews, unused clothing was repurposed as insulation—everything from ruffled tops to superfluous pants to extra bras.

That's the best sense I can make of the underground brothel rumor: those under-the-floor bras.

This rumor was shared with me over four years after Governor Doug Burgum and the US Army Corps of Engineers evicted all Water Protectors from the Camps. Up until this point, there were plenty of rumors I had already heard:

Water Protectors had drug parties at Camp. (False.)

Water Protectors had public orgies at Camp. (False.)

Water Protectors somehow had an accumulation of deceased human bodies at Camp. (Also false.)

Throughout the Camp, handmade signs let folks know that drugs, alcohol, weapons, and disrespect were not allowed. On rare occasions when people did defy Camp agreements, Camp security would intervene. According to Rattler, a Lakota activist who served as Camp security, people were generally given a choice at this point. If they could not agree to follow Camp agreements, they would be escorted out of Camp, along with any contraband. If they *could* agree to follow Camp agreements, any contraband would still be removed, but the people themselves would be allowed to stay, as long as they remained accountable to their word, and as long as the Camp community was strong enough to help hold them accountable.

Because Camp was a healing place, Camp security did their best to support people to stay and, by virtue of staying, to participate in healing activities and space.

This was true restorative justice in action.

Still, the rumors of unjust, violent actions persisted.

The local news regularly covered the rumor of deceased human bodies as if it was a credible concern—a painfully ironic preoccupation, given the often-untold story of Indigenous ancestors whose remains many colonial museums have acquired and have yet to repatriate. As Water Protectors were being forcibly evicted from the Camps, the state brought in so-called cleanup crews who bulldozed everything in the vicinity, while keeping their eyes peeled for rumor-justifying items like weapons and human remains.

They found neither, because neither was there.

Today, no one is there. No people are there, anyway. Oceti Sakowin Camp looks much the way it looked before Water Protectors got there, with wide, scruffy prairies next to wide, scruffy buttes.

The only real difference would be the gates and the official NO TRESPASSING signage.

On Fort Laramie Treaty lands.

On Lakota-Dakota-Nakota ancestral lands.

On Nueta-Hidatsa-Sahnish ancestral lands.

On lands where Indigenous peoples have gathered for generations.

Today, as official gates block access to these treaty lands, the colonial signage essentially makes the claim: *We, the colonial state, are henceforth protecting what's ours.*

But the land didn't belong to the colonial state in the first place, and there's nothing to protect *against*. Oceti Sakowin Camp never ran any underground sex-trafficking operations. Indeed, there never was any connection between the Water Protector Camps and the sex trade.

Except for one thing.

In resisting extractive industries, Water Protectors at Standing Rock also resisted the human damage caused by these extractive industries, which has everything to do with the sex trade. Specifically, sex trafficking.

On this topic, the United Nations Development Programme, which exists to end poverty and support sustainable global prosperity, has plainly stated that the extraction of nonrenewable raw materials has "triggered violent conflicts, degraded the environment, worsened gender and other inequalities, displaced communities, and undermined democratic governance."

Even the US Department of State has voiced concerns about the man camps near fracking sites: "Service providers in areas near camps surrounding large-scale oil extraction facilities, such as the Bakken oil fields in North Dakota in the United States, have reported that sex traffickers have exploited women in the area, including Native American women." What's more, "Sex trafficking related to extractive industries often occurs with impunity."

There are many ways, both judicial and extrajudicial, by which this impunity can happen.

In particular, when extractive industries and their adherents accuse Water Protectors of causing precisely the harm that extractive industries cause, those who engage in sex trafficking get to hide behind the sidetracked conversation.

In fact, by the winter of 2016, the most common slur against Water Protectors, as implied by the colonial state and openly spoken by local folks, was *hypocrites*. This slur picked up rapid speed in the complicated days between December 4, 2016, and January 24, 2017, between outgoing President Barack Obama's much-delayed dismissal of DAPL and incoming President Donald Trump's speedy resurrection of the project.

On December 4, 2016, after Donald Trump's election, the Obama administration finally denied the easement that would have permitted Energy Transfer Partners (ETP) to drill under the Missouri

River north of Standing Rock. Then, on January 24, 2017, the newly inaugurated President Trump, an investor in ETP, signed an immediate executive order that reversed Obama's decision and pushed the pipeline through.

Meanwhile, as rumors and accusations abounded about the Camps, I kept sensing an unexpected connection to some of my earlier life experiences. Years before, when Bonnie Palecek had recruited me to the statewide domestic violence coalition, I'd had enough direct experience with personal violence that I often drafted materials based on my immediate knowledge. I remember cocreating a quiz where we helped readers sort out whether they might be dealing with emotional abuse.

One question asked: *Do they accuse you of doing things they do themselves?*

In so many words, the materials explained that it's emotionally abusive for someone to shift responsibility for their own behavior onto you, acting as if you made them do it, or that you were the one who did what they've been doing. Someone might accuse you of spending too much money, lying about your whereabouts, or sleeping with somebody they don't believe you should be sleeping with, when they themselves are doing these things.

Through this rhetorical shift, the accuser claims control of the emotional space by creating blame, promoting self-doubt and shame on the part of the accused, and neutralizing behaviors they themselves are doing, such that any counter-concern simply sounds defensive.

When individuals do these things, I've often heard it called gaslighting. (This term comes from a 1930s British play where a man manipulates his spouse into doubting her own reality so he can steal from her.)

When colonial entities do these things, I've often heard it called "the way it is."

I've even been told, "It's just life."

But it isn't really life. And it isn't really living.

At best, it's living to make a living, rather than living to make a life. It's what V, a white playwright who created *The Vagina Monologues*, might call "being dead while being alive," a phrase she shared with me in the summer of 2021, as we were both knee-deep in the Shell River in northern Minnesota to resist the Line 3 pipeline.

Meanwhile, on the topic of life and death, I keep being reminded of the famous "Beyond Vietnam" speech. Cowritten by Black civil rights leaders Vincent Harding and Martin Luther King, Jr., along with white ally John Maguire, this unequivocally pro-peace speech was delivered by King on April 4, 1967, at Manhattan's Riverside Church with Rabbi Abraham Joshua Heschel, another white ally, vigorously supporting him from the chancel. After the speech, King was swiftly disinvited to the White House by then-President Lyndon B. Johnson, disavowed by many of his friends, renounced by prominent newspapers, and, exactly one year later, assassinated.

Today, this particular line keeps ringing in my ears: "A nation that continues year after year to spend more money on military defense than on programs of social uplift is approaching spiritual death."

In other words, a nation that values military prowess over the shared well-being of its people is on the brink of losing its spirit, its heart, its very essence of being.

Having witnessed the desecrations wrought by DAPL—and, more recently, Line 3—I can scarcely imagine a clearer display of spiritual death on the part of the people, the state, and the culture that has allowed them. These images, these losses, continue to haunt my nights and days.

Meanwhile, when it comes to DAPL and other extractive projects, these spiritually deadly acts have, as the "Beyond Vietnam" speech would predict, everything to do with military might.

I remember the tanks near Standing Rock.

I remember the human targets of water cannons and more.

I remember the fatigues, the guns at the ready, the orders shouted by unnamed officials.

Indeed, I have heard many Indigenous people refer to reservations, including Standing Rock reservation, as prisoner of war camps. First established in 1871 through the Indian Appropriations Act and related legislation, reservations were expressly created by the US government in order to confine Indigenous people to certain tracts of land, disallowing them from leaving except by special permission. Ultimately, these pieces of legislation prohibited further treaty-making and weakened the tribal sovereignty guaranteed by earlier treaties.

Because of this history and more, AIM organizer John Trudell often decried the connections between the colonial present and the colonial past. In 1980, his children, pregnant spouse, and mother-in-law died in a house fire, which was likely set to silence him and his family. During a Thanksgiving Day address that same year, Trudell said,

What is racism? Racism is an act of war. What is sexism? Sexism is an act of war. It's a war against our human dignity and our rights to self-respect. This is the war that they wage there. War! They are warlike. And we have to understand that the American Corporate State got to where it's at through the act of war.

On this topic, Leon Joseph Littlebird, a Diné songwriter I met around the time DAPL was completed, gets to the heart of it:

> Every treaty ever written wasn't worth the paper it was on.
> Every single promise has been broken. Only lies still live on.
> The lust for oil has replaced the lust for gold
> and repeats the saddest story ever told.
> All you sons and daughters, if you call this great land yours,
> stand with the Water Protectors, who still have to fight Indian Wars.

Once again, Lyla June's lyrics bring it home.

> It's a war,
> but we've seen it all before,
> and we know we can change it, 'cause that's why we were born.

In other words, when colonial entities intrude on Indigenous treaty lands to move gold, or oil, or even human beings, these entities are engaging in a lucrative, if stealthy, battle in a long-term war.

Still, the posture of white innocence persists. This gaslighting posture, this rhetorical device, says, "We're not weaponizing the area. *They're* weaponizing the area. We're not enabling sex trafficking. *They're* enabling sex trafficking. We're not creating ecological devastation. *They're* creating ecological devastation."

Which brings me to the most insidious of the trash talk about Camp.

On February 15, 2017, Governor Burgum issued an emergency evacuation order. In addition to concerns regarding flooding, which never manifested and which Camp organizers had thorough plans to address if they did, the executive order spoke of "months of accumulated debris," which allegedly caused "environmental hazards," which would lead to "a significant and increasing threat to the waters of the Missouri River."

This maneuver went way beyond the efforts of Jack Dalrymple, the previous governor—like the time when Dalrymple had proclaimed in the dead of winter that anyone bringing supplies to Camp would be fined $1,000. I first learned of the fine when the *Bismarck Tribune* called the church, asking if we planned to change our course of action.

We didn't. In fact, to the best of my knowledge, the thousand-dollar-fine situation turned out to be a public relations nightmare for the outgoing governor. Public opinion veered toward the Water Protectors again, which meant a new strategy would be required.

Again, I don't know for sure, but I imagine the scene unfolding in an upscale executive boardroom in Dallas, as high-backed chairs scrape the porcelain floor. Kelcy Warren, CEO, paces in his newest Diciannoveventitre dress shoes. Or maybe it's the Jason of Beverly Hills shoes.

Regardless, tension is in the air again.

For one, it's been days—weeks, even—and no one has seen that free-spirited singer-songwriter who used to run the AV. An infiltrator at Oceti Sakowin Camp sent back photos that looked distinctly familiar, but that's so ridiculous it's not even worth discussing.

For two, that cheeky, long-term staffer hasn't gone anywhere. There he is right now, sloshing his golden cappuccino dangerously close to the conference microphones.

AV equipment costs money, you know.

For three, the cheeky staffer is about to speak, which, as anyone in the conference room could attest, is no surprise.

And here he goes.

"Kelcy, come on! Who needs that AV nonsense anyway? You want to have a meeting with your cronies from North Dakota? You of all people should know where to find them! Seriously, they're never far away!"

With that advice, Kelcy finally takes control of this top-secret meeting. Meanwhile, North Dakota's most influential leaders lean in, looking a little rumpled, having just been released from the pockets of Kelcy's twill Versaces.

Naturally, the cheeky staffer pipes up again, "Get a load of this. Do I have an idea for you!" Dramatic pause. "What if the Water Protectors aren't really Water Protectors? What if the water needs to be protected *from* them?"

Suddenly remembering why he's never all-out fired this guy, Kelcy gives a slow, thoughtful nod.

Then the North Dakota governor jumps to his feet. "Wait, you mean . . . ? What if the state of North Dakota has to protect the water . . . from the Water Protectors?"

The room erupts with applause.

Everyone pats him on the back, jostling his shoulders, calling him "boss" and other encouraging terms.

Soon, there's a news release about an executive order from the governor, complete with declarations of environmental threats and the forced evacuation of all Water Protectors from all Water Protector Camps.

From here, there is much fist-bumping, high-fiving, and even the occasional pro-DAPL chant: "Gimme a D! Gimme an A!" and so on.

While I will never know if the decision to (try to) bust the Water Protector movement was made in that way exactly, the decision was certainly made.

Not only did North Dakota's new governor declare a pending ecological disaster, he also mandated that all Water Protectors either evacuate on our own or be forcibly evicted by February 22, 2017, the week following the order, because of this so-called disaster.

Like most people I knew, I was devastated. But also, like most people I knew, I was too busy gathering and hauling supplies out of Camp to process much else.

In concert with the governor's order, as well as a filmed-in-North-Dakota, pro-DAPL commercial—which ran constantly on North Dakota television at the time—another public relations strategy emerged. Energy Transfer Partners donated $15 million to the state of North Dakota and $3 million to Morton County for expenses related to pipeline protection. They even donated $5 million to the University of Mary in Bismarck.

Sometimes, pipeline companies don't even wait until the job is done.

Even before the Line 3 pipeline in Minnesota was complete, Enbridge Energy Partners, the pipeline company building Line 3, donated more than $500,000 to local law enforcement agencies to patrol Line 3 construction. Since that first donation, Enbridge has given millions of dollars to the state of Minnesota for an escrow account managed by the Minnesota Public Utilities Commission, which pays for law enforcement expenses in policing the Line 3 resistance.

In other words, when hundreds of people, including myself, were arrested by the sheriff of Hubbard County for protesting Line 3 in June 2021, Enbridge had already bankrolled the police.

And it's not just pipeline companies who figure out how to hire public agencies.

In July 2021, a major white Republican donor from Tennessee paid the state of South Dakota $1 million to deploy the National Guard to the southern border of the US for the purpose of keeping migrants, most of whom are Latine, out.

These days, a person could start wondering if TigerSwan is able to get any business anymore. After all, who needs private security when you can buy public security? Or maybe even the public.

That said, TigerSwan does still seem to be running a lucrative business.

According to court documents, as well as reporting by Unicorn Riot, TigerSwan has continued to gather intelligence about Water Protectors who have resisted DAPL, such as white ally Jessica Reznicek, who was sentenced to eight years in federal prison for her resistance. Still, despite TigerSwan's prominent role, the ETP spokesperson didn't mention TigerSwan when Energy Transfer Partners donated all those millions to the University of Mary in 2018.

Instead, he said, "I appreciate the people of the state and how you stood with us and how you stood behind us when we were trying to complete the pipeline. That will never be forgotten. For us, getting to meet the people of North Dakota, getting to spend some time here, has been a huge blessing."

A huge blessing.

As far as I can tell, this kind of quasi-religious language isn't rare in oil and gas talk. In 2021, the Associated Press picked up just this kind of language in an article about the fracking debate among New York farmers. Some farmers were worried that if New York lifted its moratorium on fracking, their dairy cows would face the same deadly consequences as dairy cows in the much-fracked state of Pennsylvania.

But then there was one farmer who wished New York would catch up with the fracking phenomenon. According to the article, when he and "others in his coalition look south" to Pennsylvania, they "see the land of milk and honey."

A huge blessing.

Land of milk and honey.

What else?

I keep thinking of Harold Hamm, a white multibillionaire and CEO of Continental Resources. In 2011, in Crosby, North Dakota, he sponsored a large stone monument to the oil industry—and to himself, as a self-described "pioneer" of that industry. While the monument was being christened, Hamm delivered a speech about the linguistic origins of the Bakken oil fields.

In that speech, he said, "The word *bakken* means *hill* in Norwegian. And sometimes you have to climb a hill to get somewhere. We did that and, today, North Dakota has become a shining place on a hill."

A huge blessing.

Land of milk and honey.

A shining place on a hill.

What's going on?

"Shining place on a hill" comes from "shining city on a hill," which comes from the Sermon on the Mount, where, according to the book of Matthew, Jesus of Nazareth says, "You are the light of the world. A city set on a hill cannot be hidden. . . . Let your light shine before others, so that they may see your good works."

As a third-generation minister, I have spent much of my life swimming in religious language. But when it comes to oil development, it's hard to know: Are people talking about religion or economics? And why is it so difficult to tell?

The Christian city-on-a-hill motif has been used by countless settler colonial leaders, from John Winthrop, English Puritan and cofounder of the Massachusetts Bay Colony, to Ronald Reagan, fortieth president of the United States. In 1630, Winthrop promised the Puritans that if they followed the will of God, "The Lord will be our God and delight to dwell among us, as his own people and will command a blessing upon us in all our ways." Thanks to this blessing, "Ten of us shall be able to resist a thousand of our enemies."

Winthrop didn't specify who the "enemies" would have been. But just six years later, the famed Pequot War began, after which he declared the first day of thanksgiving.

Around that time, Winthrop also said, "We must consider that we shall be as a City upon a Hill. The eyes of all people are upon us."

Three hundred and fifty years later, President Ronald Reagan often echoed Winthrop. In just one example, he said, "America is a shining city upon a hill whose beacon light guides freedom-loving people everywhere."

In fact, Presidents John F. Kennedy before him and Barack Obama after him did the same. In 1961, newly elected President John F. Kennedy said, "Today the eyes of all people are truly upon us—and our governments, in every branch, at every level, national, state and local, must be as a city upon a hill [. . . .] We are committing ourselves to tasks of statecraft no less awesome than that of governing the Massachusetts Bay Colony."

In 2006, when speaking in Massachusetts, US Senator Barack Obama said, "It was right here, in the waters around us, where the American experiment began. As the earliest settlers arrived on the shores of Boston and Salem and Plymouth, they dreamed of building a City upon a Hill. And the world watched, waiting to see if this improbable idea called America would succeed."

More recently, US Senator Mitt Romney picked up the lingo. In 2016, as he condemned Donald Trump's bid for the presidency, Romney said, "His personal qualities would mean that America would cease to be a shining city on a hill."

As I take all this in, I keep remembering words an old friend of mine once said as we tiptoed toward romance: "Who are we, really?"

As inheritors of the white settler colonial project called the United States of America, who *are* we, really?

Borrowing the language of Walter Wink, a white theologian and religious author, I wonder, what is the nature of our shared inner spirit, our "corporate angel," our collective being? How can we have one, retain one, nurture one, if we descendants of the settler colonial US don't know who we are—or worse, if we say we are who we are not?

I understand how comforting promises can be. But I can't take any comfort in promises God ostensibly made to the United States, when the US has behaved in such ungodly ways. Among other ungodly acts, the US has superimposed itself upon thriving Indigenous nations, kidnapped people from their homes on the African continent, and decried the presence of immigrants, especially dissenters and people of color, even while capitalizing on their labor.

I don't believe I'm speaking from a place of white guilt right now. Or settler colonial guilt. Or even imperial guilt.

Right this minute, it feels more like rage.

I keep thinking about the descendants of settler colonialism, especially the young ones, who, after learning of the legacy they have inherited, resentfully insist, "It's not fair. I didn't do it. I wasn't even born then!" When I feel resentful, I find myself resenting the people who decided my role before I was born, who perform these unjust actions in my name. Not the people who have been most harmed. Not the people who have disabused me of my illusions about my nation.

I feel angry, sometimes all-out furious, with the ones who created this system and then handed it down to me to carry forward based on the color of my skin (like theirs), the religion of my family (like theirs), and the country of my residence (also like theirs). I am mad at the ones who have promised, as John Winthrop once promised, that if we obey God's voice and continue "cleaving to him," then "we and our seed" may live in God's prosperity.

As if wealthiness is next to godliness.

As if material goods are a sign of God's favor.

As if having more means a person *is* more.

Speaking of promises, that's what the "shining city on a hill" is all about—the biblical land of milk and honey, the land that God allegedly promised to the colonists. According to the biblical book of Genesis, God once made a parallel promise to Abraham. After Abraham and his people sojourned into the land of Canaan, God said, "Unto your seed will I give this land."

Your seed meant the descendants of Abraham. *This land* meant Canaan. And *give* meant that God would help the descendants of Abraham organize an invasion.

Yet, as the authors of Genesis state, "At that time, the Canaanites were in the land."

Why were the Canaanites *in the land*? Because they were, and still are, the Indigenous peoples of the land. They belonged there when Abraham's people planned to invade. They still belong today.

In his research on the Doctrine of Discovery, Steven T. Newcomb connects the promised land of Canaan to the promised land of the US. More to the point, he identifies the self-serving connections that white settlers have made between one land grant (Canaan) and another (the US).

As Newcomb says, "This story of the Lord's land grant to the chosen people frames Abraham and the Hebrews as destined to be the subjugating masters or lords of the land of Canaan." He goes on to say, "When dominating forms of reasoning . . . found in the Old Testament narrative are unconsciously used to reason about American Indians, Indian lands metaphorically become—from the viewpoint of the United States—the promised land of the chosen people of the United States."

In other words, the story of Hebrew inevitability in the land of Canaan has long been the dubious template for white settler inevitability in the United States.

Still, as deeply disturbing as all of this is, there's a catch. According to a number of biblical scholars, including Carolyn Pressler, a white liberation-focused educator and my seminary professor, there are no apparent anthropological or genetic differences between the ancient Canaanites and the ancient Hebrews. Even the much-lyricized Battle of Jericho, the Hebrew invasion of that Canaanite city, doesn't seem to have happened in history.

This means that various stories of Hebrew land grants seem to have been what Pressler calls "legends of origins." At the time these stories were written, the Hebrew people were a struggling people, sometimes made captives and exiles, sometimes occupied by impe-rial powers. It's not hard to understand why they might create sto-ries that bestow power upon them, much in the way their power had been overcome. It's also not hard to understand why they might long to understand themselves as protected by God.

The trouble comes when stories created by people who have been disempowered get adopted by those who have a ton of power—the Roman Empire, the Spanish Empire, the Portuguese Empire, the Italian Empire, the French Empire, the Belgian Empire, the German Empire, the Dutch Empire, the British Empire. The US American empire.

The multinational, extractive, corporate empire.

When powerful people see themselves (or ourselves) as the chosen people, when they (or we) believe God has made special promises to them (or us) about a shining city on a hill, any land can become the new land of Canaan.

Unfortunately, unlike the Battle of Jericho, battles fought by the empires of Europe and the US have been very real, very lucrative, and very deadly. It's like the chosen people's business plan, a handy coupling of theology and economics.

Still, in spite of their prevalent antisemitism, the Pilgrims did have a few things in common with the ancient Hebrew people. Much like the ancient Hebrews, the Pilgrims were often on the move, escaping torture, persecution, and death based on threats from the powers that be.

Even when times and places got better, they were still tough. After fleeing England for Holland, the Pilgrims faced long hours, grueling work, ill health, and general desperation. So the Pilgrims had conversations with the Plymouth Company, which King James I had formed in 1606 for the purpose of establishing settlements along North America's East Coast. Together, they worked it out.

The seventy investors who constituted the Plymouth Company agreed to finance the Pilgrims' voyage to North America. In return, the settlers would reimburse the company by harvesting timber, animal fur, and fish, and then sending these so-called commodities back to England to be sold. In other words, the Plymouth Colony, often cited as the germ of US nationhood, was a business deal. Its very name came from the name of its financiers, the Plymouth Company.

Curiously enough, the Mayflower wasn't even built for passengers. It was a cargo ship rented for the occasion.

From my perspective as an adult, these realities aren't so mind-bending. But when I was a child, steeped in concepts like "the promised land" and "the land of milk and honey," the origin story of the United States was recited to me as a story of faith, a story of belief, with the Pilgrims even figuring in as the prophets. All along, though, that story was propelled by another story—a less laudable story about people with means, their means to certain ends, and their means of turning a profit.

Which they might have called—

A huge blessing.

The land of milk and honey.

A shining city on a hill.

Meanwhile, this story-under-the-story is everywhere.

Not only was Christopher Columbus steeped in Islamophobia, antisemitism, and Christian zealotry, and not only did he torture and oppress Taíno people, but he also did so on a business venture. *VentureBeat*, a pro-capitalist publication, has even called him "the preeminent entrepreneur."

Then there was Amerigo Vespucci. After his small company helped to outfit one of Columbus's voyages, he followed in Columbus's proverbial footsteps. As they had for Columbus, King Ferdinand and Queen Isabella once again picked up the tab. Unfortunately for their coffers, Vespucci eventually went to work for King Manuel I of Portugal, who no doubt was just as eager to maintain his monopoly as Ferdinand and Isabella had been to break it.

And then there was Ferdinand Magellan. Like Vespucci, Magellan sometimes sailed for the Portuguese Empire and sometimes for the Spanish Empire. First aligned with Portugal, he got his start with voyages and sieges that were intended, in the words of the *Encyclopedia Britannica*, "to wrest from the Arabs the key points of sea trade." In other words, much of this traveling, striving, and seeking came down to money—who had it, who didn't, and who could get more.

It's not that this is news. I've heard it said that Ferdinand and Isabella—or really, the people of Spain—picked up the tab for Columbus. I've probably heard it said that they picked up the tab for Vespucci. From there, I could probably guess that someone must have picked up the tab for Magellan.

But I have rarely heard it said *why* they picked up the tab. I have rarely heard it acknowledged, out in the open, that these royal endorsements were investments in various European empires through invasions of the Canaans of the world. Imperialists with great wealth, aided by sometimes desperate helpers with lesser wealth, amassed greater and greater wealth by grabbing everything they could—lands, goods, and bodies—from Indigenous peoples anywhere and everywhere.

That is the origin story of my country. It is the story under the story, the mover behind the motion.

Today, with American billionaires profiteering in the frontier of space, maybe the contemporary "land of Canaan" doesn't stop at the stratosphere.

When I was a child, I believed the story of my people was a story of religion.

And maybe it is. Maybe a religious framework is the best way to understand the values, practices, and beliefs of the settlers and colonizers of this contemporary Canaan land. Maybe this is a peek into our *civil religion*—a term sociologists use to define the rituals of membership in a community or a nation.

In the colonial United States, maybe God has always been about money. Maybe money has always been mixed up with God. Maybe those who make the "milk and honey" possible, those with biggest access to big money—and big oil—begin to look like emissaries of God, living saviors in the flesh.

As it turns out, the *Harvard Political Review*, in assessing North Dakota's economic past and future, puts it that way exactly: "Many North Dakotans, especially those who have been a part of the economic prosperity in recent years, see the oil boom as the state's savior."

In Christian trinitarian theology, the Savior, the Creator, and the Holy Spirit together constitute one God. While these three persons of God are distinct, they intermingle, meaning that the Savior, the Creator, and the Holy Spirit share an essence, a life force. The Savior's essence is inclusive of the Creator's essence, the Creator's essence is inclusive of the Holy Spirit's essence, and so on.

But unlike the Creator, human beings—even the wealthiest of human beings, including Harold Hamm of Continental Resources, Kelcy Warren of Energy Transfer Partners, John Hess of Hess Corporation, and Al Monaco of Enbridge Energy Partners—do not create the things they claim to own. Not the oil, the gas, the trees, the lands, or the waters.

Much like imperial families before them, they take. And because they take, they can give—just enough.

Continental Resources has donated $100,000 for a new hospital in Crosby. Hess Corporation has donated $100,000 to the Great Plains Food Bank. Energy Transfer Partners has donated $5 million to the University of Mary. Not to be outdone, the Harold Hamm Foundation and Continental Resources have donated a whopping $12 million to the University of Mary, establishing the Hamm School of Engineering.

Not unlike the historical lords of the manor, these corporations and their CEOs perform acts of largesse for the rest of us, those who have never seen the kind of money the lords see every day. Even today, *lord* is a slippery word, a slippery role. Especially when milk and honey—or bread and butter—is at stake, one kind of lord can seem much like another.

After all, that's what it means to be a lord: to provide, to have the means to provide for the people if you so choose, to be in possession of the things the people need.

Years ago, I used to believe that the established religion of settler colonialism (Christianity) had been colonized—that Christendom, then and now, was the pairing of an invasive colonial power (the Roman Empire, the US American empire) and a liberative faith.

I still do.

But today, thanks to the ways of life that were opened to me at Oceti Sakowin Camp, I no longer think that we as human beings keep these categories—religion and economics—separate. Whatever time we're in, whatever space we're in, our economic system seems to become our defining system of life. A gift economy. A capitalist/ colonial economy. A socialist economy. Each one has everything to do with who we are as human beings, as human cultures.

Our economic system is our way of life, our way of organizing relationships. Ultimately, it's our worldview.

Today, in the settler colonial framework, it's a worldview of hypocrisy.

I don't mean to say it's a hypocritical worldview, though maybe it is. I mean to say it's a worldview that understands humanity as existing in a chronic state of hypocrisy.

People who said Water Protectors were hypocrites saw the world, well, the way they saw the world. In that worldview, which is rampant in today's settler colonial culture, you should *say* you do a thing because of faith, spirit, or prayer, but underneath it all, in the story beneath the story, you should basically do it for money.

Maybe this is why descendants of settler colonialism here in North Dakota have been so ready to trust Energy Transfer Partners (which we know exists to make money) over the Water Protector movement (which inexplicably acts as if it does not). All those other rumors—that billionaire George Soros bankrolled the Camps, that Water Protectors were paid to get arrested, that Water Protectors were even out there getting rich—all fed into, and were fed by, the worldview of hypocrisy.

Because in the colonial worldview, people have to be hypocrites. There is no other way to be. No other way to survive. In the colonial economy, you have to take to give. You don't live in communion with the land. You must take from the land in order to give to your family, your community, even the local food bank.

As Roxanne Dunbar-Ortiz, an Indigenous scholar and author of *An Indigenous Peoples' History of the United States,* has said of the European past, "For the first time in human history, the majority of Europeans depended for their livelihood on a small wealthy minority, a phenomenon that capitalist-based colonialism would spread worldwide. . . . Subjugating entire societies and civilizations, enslaving whole countries, and slaughtering people village by village did not seem too high a price to pay . . ."

In other words, in colonialism, you not only have to take to give; you have to kill to live.

As John Trudell and many others have insisted, colonialism itself is a state of war.

More recently, Tania Aubid, a member of the Rice Lake Band, which is part of the Mille Lacs Band of Ojibwe, has described the Line 3-based collusion between Enbridge and law enforcement as "keeping on with the Indian Wars."

Indeed, this is not a new story. Many settler colonial ancestors themselves had already been violently overcome in Europe by the very Roman Empire that had brought them imperial Christianity. That's how they lost their original, Earth-based religions, their original, Earth-based languages. And knowledges. And names. And worldviews.

The reality of Europe-on-Europe colonialism—imperialism, even—was very real. It resulted in the horrific deaths of millions of human beings. That's how they lost their means, their structures, of survival.

In particular, such violent imperialism looked like this:

- Following the Holy Land Crusades against Muslim peoples, the Northern Crusades terrorized the Pagan peoples of the European Baltic Sea region for three hundred years. Beginning in the 1100s, these Northern Crusades consolidated land and wealth in the hands of monarchs and popes. In 1147, Pope Eugenius III even made this eerily familiar proclamation: "We utterly forbid that for any reason whatsoever a truce should be made with these tribes . . . until such time as, by God's help, they shall be either converted or wiped out."
- For about three hundred and fifty years beginning in the 1300s, the European witch hunts terrorized various peoples, particularly women and Pagans, burning roughly sixty thousand human beings at the stake and consolidating power in the hands of self-proclaimed Christians. The *Malleus Maleficarum*, written in 1486, functioned as a detailed guidebook for inquisitors about preferred methods of interrogating and sentencing those accused of witchcraft. It says: "The method of beginning an examination by torture is as follows. First, the jailers prepare the implements of torture, then they strip the prisoner (if it be a woman, she has already been stripped by other women, upright and of good report)."

- For about four hundred years beginning in the 1400s, the Spanish Inquisition terrorized Muslim, Jewish, and nonconforming Christian peoples, consolidating power in the hands of monarchs and popes once again. In 1492, after expelling Jews and Muslims from Spain, Ferdinand II and Isabella I hired Christopher Columbus to expand their ever-expanding empire. Informed by the Inquisition, Columbus sent Ferdinand and Isabella a list of recommendations about how to manage the lands he thought he had discovered: establishment of colonies, construction of churches, allocation of gold, and "conversion of the Indians."

I wish I could undo every bit of it—the many crusades, the witch hunts, the Inquisition. It doesn't even seem possible, these six hundred-plus years of terror and then five hundred years of terror by the terrorized.

It's hard for me to say this, but since my people couldn't beat 'em in Europe, it seems as if they joined 'em overseas.

On this side of the Atlantic, it's painfully clear what it means to be settlers: to be the vanguard of the empire, to keep and advance the borders with our worldviews, our presence, our literal, physical bodies.

Today, in the everyday army of the empire, I'm tired of being a soldier. Yet every day, I find myself reenlisted.

And every day, I need to choose whether—and when—to go AWOL.

SEVEN

EVICTION AND ANOTHER WAY

Not long after the eviction of Oceti Sakowin Camp, I received an invitation, much like many people did:

> The Standing Rock Sioux Tribe and Indigenous grassroots leaders call on our allies across the United States and around the world to peacefully march on Washington, DC. We ask that you rise in solidarity with the Indigenous peoples of the world, whose rights protect Unci Maka (Grandmother Earth) for the future generations of all.

The details were still coming together, but this much was clear:

> Standing Rock and Native Nations will lead a march in prayer and action in Washington, DC, on March 10, 2017.

With Camp having been evacuated so recently, I yearned to join the march, to be present within a shared prayer space, to be a part of thousands and thousands of Water Protectors once again.

The last days of Camp had been, well, devastating . . . poignant . . . I guess I don't quite have the words.

In the final weeks, there had been many Camp pre-evacuation efforts, as people at Camp and supporters in the area did our best to arrange transportation for the thousands of people who were being evicted. At Prairie Knights Casino, in those brittle days and nights, Water Protectors set up an intricately coordinated transportation hub where volunteers like Jeff Iron Cloud would drive vanloads of people to a connecting spot in Bismarck, often the church. From there, we would get folks to a bus, a plane, or, less often, the train station about ninety miles north.

Given the nature of carpooling, folks would arrive at the church at all hours, sometimes plenty early for the next leg of their journey. With a bag or two, as well as clothing that always carried the comforting scent of the central fire, people would camp out in the church or in congregants' homes until it was time—too soon— to go.

As much as I wanted everyone to stay forever, it did my heart good to see people safely off, just as we had often welcomed them in the first place. Somebody, I may never know who, left me a hand-knit scarf with a note of encouragement, one of my favorite winter gear items today.

Meanwhile, back at Camp, I participated in work crews, some of which congregants helped to organize in order to transfer the copious stores of food and supplies to those who could use them. Ever-dedicated, Ikce Wicasa guided groups of Water Protectors to priority areas—which community tents to pack up today, where to put the canned food, how to decide what went where.

A Water Protector family from Standing Rock loaded up a horse trailer with packages of rice, beans, noodles, and more to take to families on the reservation and to others along the way, as they began a long journey to Pueblo, Colorado, more than seven hundred miles away.

A supporter from Minot, North Dakota, about 150 miles north of Camp, agreed to haul a truckload of provisions back to his hometown. We had heard that thrift stores and distribution centers in Bismarck-Mandan were no longer accepting food donations, since Water Protectors facing Camp closure had recently brought so many there.

We also did what we could to get the largest non-food items out, lest the camping gear, winter flooring, kitchen tents, and more turn into inadvertent trash. To this day, I can still hear the *tink-tink-tink* of long-handled steel ice scrapers meeting cones of ice, which had formed on the metal tent stakes at each edge of the kitchen tents.

For many Water Protectors, the plan had been to stay at Camp in spite of the oil that was soon to move beneath the great Missouri, in order to keep an eye on that very oil, that very water. A winter Camp had been planned within the larger Camp, up on higher ground. As Kandi Mossett White of the Indigenous Environmental Network has said, "Composting was in place so that we could have a garden. We were going to have greenhouses in the spring."

Briefly, I got to glimpse the plans for the new Camp within the larger Camp. There would have been wood pellet stoves, shared healing spaces, and Lakota-Dakota-led practices of community living. With every knock of my heart, I had looked more and more forward to that emerging Camp. Though I didn't count on living there myself, I felt encouraged by the possibility of such a place, such a life force, so close to home.

But an eviction was an eviction, so we sorted, hauled, and tapped at the solid ice.

Every once in a while, after an extended *tink-tink-tink, tink-tink-tink, tink-tink-tink*, a cheer would erupt, as one more tent stake was loosened at last from its icy moorings. With this cheering, this presence in the moment, those of us preparing for eviction were insisting on a way of life that stayed true to the more bountiful days of Camp.

One Saturday, a new congregant named L.T. Loar, one of many white allies who had found the church because of our solidarity with Standing Rock, drove her pickup to Camp to participate in the pre-eviction efforts. At the outskirts of Camp, her tires got wedged in the muddy ice. As she and I slogged toward the back of the truck, I said, "This is Camp. Someone will probably come by to help us soon." Sure enough, the truck was out of the mud and L.T. was back at the wheel within twenty-five minutes.

Another white ally, who had found our congregation for the same reason, rarely went anywhere without his camera in those days, even in the rasp of winter. With their permission, he interviewed Indigenous people and allies from Spain, Hawai'i, Colorado, North Dakota, Standing Rock, and beyond, who were there with ice scrapers and ready hands, giving back to this place, this community, that had offered each of us another way of life. In those recordings, Eddie, an Indigenous Water Protector from the Twin Cities, took a moment to talk about Camp, in between the unmooring of tent straps and the mutual folding of kitchen tents:

"It's really beautiful out here. It's a community."

Much like Eddie, Don Morrison, a longtime white ally from the congregation, spoke of the essence of the place, even in the final days before eviction: "This is really solidarity with human beings."

Linda Black Elk, professor at Sitting Bull College and an ethno-botanist of Korean and Mongolian cultural identities, was instrumental in the formation of the medic and healer area. As the Camps were being shut down, she said, "Standing Rock woke the world up. It helped people to see how unified we can be."

Around this time, Rita Kelly, a retired high school principal and another longtime white ally from the congregation, gave me a piece of art by Jeff MacNelly, a white cartoonist most known for the comic strip *Shoe*. In the art piece, the giant word *us* was composed of many smaller words; when you looked closely, each one spelled *them*.

Meanwhile, most local media outlets, informed by the state, still decried the so-called "massive amounts of junk" at Camp, proclaiming the place to be "less sanitary than a city landfill." One white media host even called Camp "scary," "bad," and "evil," saying he wanted to "back away from it," which was his reason for not having gone there.

Before long, the National Guard stationed themselves just outside the Camp's entrance. In fatigues and bulletproof vests, they were an intimidating, well-armed reminder of the looming eviction. Their presence interrupted our flow not only because of the military checkpoints outside of Camp but also because of the brand-new rule regarding which vehicles could enter and which could not. In the final days, we were no longer allowed to bring in vans or trucks, making removal of larger items, like the floor of the interfaith yurt, a genuine mind-bender. It was such a mind-bender, we had to leave the entire floor behind.

With a little more time to pack, we would have likely been able to bend our minds in that direction by evacuating the flooring in handy, car-sized chunks. But every request from Indigenous Camp organizers to the North Dakota governor's office and the US Army Corps of Engineers, explaining the need for an extension, was denied. When local news crews captured footage of all the so-called "toxic trash" that Water Protectors had left behind, I kept straining for a glimpse of our much-beloved floor, as well as many other markers of this nonviolent revolution.

For these reasons and more, I longed to join the events in Washington, DC, on March 10. I missed the local movement and the Camps where it had taken root, much like an aspen might miss the forest. But with many long-distance Water Protectors still stuck in Bismarck-Mandan after Camp closures and so many other Water Protectors still facing court cases in Morton County, I knew where my place was.

Then, near the end of the invitation, I read—

For those who cannot march with us, we ask that you take peaceful action at home in your tribal nations, states, cities, towns, villages, and provinces.

Peaceful action at home. Got it.

Soon I found myself in many conversations about what a peaceful action in Bismarck-Mandan could look and feel like.

Matt Lone Bear, a Hidatsa Water Protector and local musician, was one of the co-organizers and planners, as well as the designer of the poster for an action we decided to call, in plain language, the Native Nations Solidarity Event. In its first iteration, we planned to gather at the state capitol and then peacefully march toward the church, where we would join together for intercultural prayers.

Meanwhile, the states of North Dakota and South Dakota, both of which overlap the Standing Rock reservation, were among the first to pass legislation increasing penalties for protest. With great support from the majority party in the legislature, North Dakota expanded the definitions and consequences of trespassing, as well as the consequences of rioting. As many Water Protectors had begun to plan other camps to resist another pipeline—the KXL pipeline, in this case—the South Dakota legislature went even farther than North Dakota, permitting their governor to designate "public safety zones" in which protest by groups of more than twenty people would be prohibited.

Though it ultimately failed by eleven votes in the House, North Dakota was also embroiled in an effort to pass HB 1203, in which "a driver of a motor vehicle who negligently causes injury or death to an individual obstructing vehicular traffic on a public road, street, or highway may not be held liable for any damages."

In other words, if a human being, having exercised their right to protest, was injured or even killed by a motorist, the locus of responsibility would shift away from the motorist and toward the protester, making the protester's location of greater import than the motorist's actions. Had the bill passed, which many activists thought it might, the practical consequences would have been dire, granting antagonists almost-certain immunity for violence—a license to kill, some said.

Even without passage, there were distinct relational consequences.

In the midst of this legislative process, local social media was awash in posts like this:

I wonder how many #NativeNationsRise #NoDAPL protesters I could run over before I got arrested.

All Lives Splatter. Nobody cares about your protest. Moral of the story, stay off the road!!

Can I try out my new grille guard???

(As a cage-like hunk of steel that covers a pickup's front bumper, a grille guard would do more to shield the pickup than the person being struck by one.)

Early on, Matt Lone Bear anticipated such rancor. Noting the colonial pushback that Indigenous Water Protectors perpetually faced, he suggested that white allies move to the front on this one and take the heat if there was any. So our group decided that I would be the point of contact.

As March 10 neared, I had a phone call with the North Dakota Indian Affairs commissioner at the time. He explained that a major bill was soon to come before the legislature, one that could have major economic repercussions for reservation casinos. Though he was otherwise optimistic that the bill would fail, he expressed concern that a major Water Protector event at the capitol could tilt legislative public opinion away from the tribes and toward passage of the egregious bill. He asked us to alter the location.

After deliberating about the meaning of politics, leadership, and followership, our intercultural planning group decided to do as the Indian Affairs commissioner had requested. Even though we'd recently held a small gathering both to honor the Camps and mourn their closure, we discerned that a time of prayer might be just the way to begin the first public action since eviction. We opted to start the event with intercultural, interfaith prayers at the church, which was just across Divide Avenue from the capitol's backside, and then follow with a march from there.

When the time came, I loved that gathering, that circle, that reunion of sorts, as if my life depended on it. There were prayers from many sacred traditions—Lakota-Dakota prayers, Anishinaabe prayers, Hindu prayers, Catholic prayers, Protestant prayers, UU prayers, Mormon prayers, and so on. It seemed we just couldn't stop praying, couldn't stop calling on Spirit.

Much like the community suppers we would hold later on in honor of Water Protectors facing federal sentencing, this event invoked the energy of Camp in ways I had feared couldn't be done. How encouraging and reassuring it was.

In fact, the group of fifty-plus Water Protectors ended up relishing those present connections so much, we never found it in ourselves to leave the circle and march. It was almost as if we knew what was waiting outside.

But, having silenced our cell phones for the prayer time, we had no idea.

Apparently, a self-proclaimed Christian, a local white man, had stationed himself in his car just at the end of the walkway. His intention, as he watched for us at the door, was, in a manner of speaking, to try out his new grille guard. In Facebook post after Facebook post, he gave thorough accounts of who he saw, what he saw, and where he intended to greet us with his speed.

But we had prayed for too long. Hours too long.

In a heat of disgust, he had peeled away with his grille guard still intact.

Not much later, I found the words *Wigli Wiconi* pasted on the curb just outside the church, not too far from our Standing with Standing Rock banner. When I showed the words *Wigli Wiconi* to Ronya Galligo-Hoblit, she burst into a surprising peal of laughter.

I knew *Mni Wiconi* translated into English as *Water Is Life*, but I had never heard the words *Wigli Wiconi*. Apparently, the detractor had substituted *Wigli* for *Mni*, intending to proclaim *Oil Is Life*.

But traditionally, as I understand it, there is no Lakota-Dakota-Nakota word for *petroleum*. *Wigli* would translate into English more like *lard* or *grease*.

So, translated traditionally, *Wigli Wiconi* would mean *Cooking Fat Is Life*, which, in the end, may not be all wrong.

As funny as this story turned out to be, I had to wonder what would cause another human being to insist that oil, rather than water, was the very source of life. In the days of the DAPL controversy, as white settlers defended extraction the way some believers defended their God, I kept scratching my own settler head. Why would a multibillion-dollar industry need the advocacy of regular, everyday white North Dakotans? Wasn't the American extractive industry already powerful enough? Did it really need the protection of white settlers?

But of course it did! That's what we white settlers were for. That was precisely our white settler role—to be protectors of the empire, advocates for the empire, because of our role as dependents upon the empire. Especially its imperial industries. From the Plymouth Corporation to king cotton to oil and gas today.

In fact, in 2021, the Minnesota Public Utilities Commission (PUC) created an escrow account so that Enbridge, the private Canadian corporation that owns the Line 3 pipeline, could finance the public policing of its construction. Soon after Enbridge contributed over $4 million to the account, the Hubbard County attorney submitted a reimbursement request, hoping to fund his county's prosecution of Water Protectors. In an email that has since been made public, the county attorney expressed grave displeasure with the PUC when he learned that Enbridge funds were restricted to the policing and not the trying of Water Protectors.

I assume the cost to arrest them is covered, just not to prosecute them? How does that make sense?

As I faced my own Water Protector charges in that very county, none of it made sense.

Or maybe it made a terrible kind of sense. As dutiful members of a US settler colonial state, the Minnesota Public Utilities Commission, along with numerous local police departments, had put themselves in service to Enbridge Corporation. The fact that the enterprise was a Canadian one, not a US one, made the allegiance of US settlers to a powerful imperial industry even more stark. In the end, I felt almost as troubled that Minnesota residents had to fund the prosecution of Water Protectors, who were trying to protect the public from Line 3, as I was that Enbridge had bankrolled our arrest and detainment in the first place.

These connections had everything to do with the role that everyday white settlers play in boosting the power and influence of imperial power holders. But within white settler colonial spaces, almost nobody says out loud what it means to be a white settler, what specific role we play in the United States empire. Within these spaces, almost no one even calls the empire an empire.

The US has waged nearly constant wars across the planet, almost since its inception—public wars like World War I, as well as secret wars like the occupation of Nicaragua. All the while, the US continues to establish exponentially more military bases than any other country, roughly eight hundred of them in just about every possible nation, from Italy to the Philippines, from Honduras to Burkina Faso, much the way an empire sets up colonies.

Yet with all this imperial activity, how do we white settlers in the US learn our role, and how does white settler culture tell us our role, while mostly never telling us our role? White settlers might say, "These colors don't run," or, "Freedom isn't free," or even, "Wigli Wiconi." In white spaces, the meaning of these value statements seems pretty clear. Yet within these very spaces, I have rarely heard anyone (other than avowed white supremacists) directly state what consequent role we white settlers are supposed to fulfill.

When I was a child, the only white people I witnessed talking about what it means to be white were those very white supremacists whose appearances on TV made their way into my most vivid nightmares. While some white adults around me had opinions about what they thought it meant to be a person of color, whiteness was rarely a topic of discussion. Whiteness was defined through this lack of definition.

After all, as Chris Crass, a white antiracism activist and author has said in *Towards Collective Liberation*, "White supremacy has taught white people to be racially, culturally, and politically illiterate."

In this absence of literacy, if our role is not communicated through direct address, it must be communicated indirectly, situationally, contextually, as part of how we are taught to live—part of the norms and values to which we as white settlers in the US are enculturated.

As a white person with some sense of conscience, with some understanding that whiteness itself was created in order to harm Black people, Indigenous people, and people of color collectively, it isn't easy to peer into the face of white culture. But surely, for those of us who are white, dismantling imperial colonialism from within must call us, as inheritors of imperial colonialism, to have a genuine sense of what we're about—and how, psyche after psyche after psyche, we got here.

Over time, there have been plenty of critiques of whiteness, settler colonialism, and US imperialism at large. It would probably be impossible, as well as psychically overwhelming, to list them all. But here's how Vine Deloria, Jr., a Lakota historian-theologian and author of *God Is Red*, speaks about the arrival of the "first settlers," who he describes as "the psychological walking wounded": "[They] brought with them an irrational fear of the unknown that was slightly less than the fear of extinction that they had known in Europe."

In *Letter from a Region in My Mind*, James Baldwin characterizes white settlers, particularly white Christian settlers, as living in a "deep freeze," existing in a state of joylessness, "loneliness, and terror," with an "inability to renew themselves at the fountain of their own lives."

Like Vine Deloria, James Baldwin, and numerous other BIPOC leaders, antiracist white people have also wrestled with this question of whiteness. Based on cross-cultural interviews, Shelly Tochluk speaks of white culture in terms of disconnection, isolation, and emotional superficiality. After years as an antibias educator, Frances Kendall speaks of the white cultural practice of anesthetizing ourselves against confusion and guilt. Author of *White Awareness*, Judith H. Katz speaks of competitiveness, aggressiveness, rigid time schedules, and the avoidance of intimacy within white culture. In the much-quoted resource *White Supremacy Culture*, Tema Okun and collaborators speak of a fear of open conflict, posture of defensiveness, power hoarding, and an attachment to either/or thinking.

For lifelong members of white culture, that can be a lot to take in. Indeed, as Tema Okun has stated, "Culture is powerful precisely because it is so present and at the same time so very difficult to name or identify."

As I consider the common characteristics of my culture, as named and identified by many people who have come before me, I am reminded of much that I have witnessed as a counselor, minister, and human being. Taken one after the other, the common characteristics of white culture don't seem so very different from the common characteristics of trauma.

Does this mean that each and every person within white culture has experienced some kind of deep, visceral trauma? Since I don't know each and every white person, I can't make such a claim.

Instead, I am curious about a collective phenomenon, a characteristic of my larger culture. As far as I can tell, culture is a shared experience emerging over time, in which people within a culture adopt many of the characteristics of the whole. Just the way a person doesn't have to own a car in order to sense the role of automobiles in their culture, the characteristics of a culture can influence its members regardless of whether each and every person can make a one-to-one correlation between their experiences and the features of their larger culture. In this spirit, when I consider the common features of white colonial culture, I can't help noticing that they resemble the common features of trauma, almost verbatim.

According to trauma researchers—particularly Resmaa Menakem, a Black therapist, and Peter Levine, a white therapist—trauma involves a sense of dissociation and disconnection between body and soul, which can look and feel like being frozen, lack of flow, and needing to thaw. The emotional states can include numbness, terror, rage, and helplessness, being stuck in a cycle of fear, and even acting as though you are dead.

Again, I keep being drawn to the words of Vincent Harding, John Maguire, and Martin Luther King, Jr., who, in 1968, suggested that this nation, this imperial nation, was "approaching spiritual death." Indeed, if this settler colonial nation and culture weren't teetering at the edge of spiritual death, how else, as a matter of course, could we risk contaminating the very source of life? The only way this deadly preoccupation could make any sense and have any logic would be if something within us were already dying.

Based on what he terms *racialized trauma,* Resmaa Menakem offers this:

> Trauma . . . was passed from one European body to another during the Middle Ages, then imported to the New World by colonists, and then passed down by many generations of their descendants. . . . European colonists instilled it in the bodies of many Africans who were forcibly imported as indentured servants, and later as property, to the New World. . . . On this same soil, trauma

also . . . spread from the bodies of European colonists to the bodies of Native people.

This trauma-based history can sometimes be so pervasive, it's hard to grab ahold of, much like the air we breathe. As Sherman Alexie, Salish author of *The Absolutely True Diary of a Part-Time Indian*, has written in his memoir, "The abused can become abusers. It's a tragic progression."

Stated with bumper-sticker succinctness, it often goes like this: "Hurt people hurt people."

In my own life, by the time I was three years old, I knew that the hurt my body had received could readily transmute into a kind of hurt that I might then put onto somebody else's body. Shortly after a run-in with a man's belt and a man's strength in wielding it, I found a belt-like object—my jump rope—and vigorously beat the front-porch ledge. The words I mumbled at the ledge were exactly the words still ringing in my own ears.

A survivor of childhood violence himself, Sherman Alexie offers this:

> As an adult, I can look back at the violence on my reservation and logically trace it back to the horrific degradations, sexual and otherwise, committed against my tribe by generations of white American priests, nuns, soldiers, teachers, missionaries, and government officials.

Almost every Indigenous person I know has shared similar insights, spoken of similar tragedies. Real, living children, along with their real, living families, have repeatedly faced what Alexie calls these *horrific degradations*. Today, I wonder about the enactors of these degradations—all those priests, nuns, soldiers, teachers, missionaries, and government officials. As their cultural descendant, I have inherited them. Not just their aggressive actions, but the literal people, the literal aggressors, themselves.

These people are my people. They are who I come from.

In my earlier years, I couldn't begin to guess—didn't want to guess—why my people would perform such incomprehensible acts. But as Sandra Bercier once said, long before we sat at her table and spoke of the DAPL resistance, "Native kids learned abuse from teachers, nuns, and priests in the boarding schools. So those teachers, nuns, and priests must have learned it from somewhere too."

As the famous bumper sticker *almost* says, traumatized people traumatize people.

Or, as Peter Levine has said, "Trauma begets trauma and will continue to do so, eventually crossing generations and families, communities and countries until we take steps to contain its propagation."

Even the French philosopher René Descartes offers a window into the residual trauma that just might be concealed within European colonial culture. Writing in the 1600s as his country was emerging as a major imperial power, he spoke of knowing he was alive, knowing he was real, not because his body was present in the world and not because his body was in relationship with the body of the Earth, but because his mind perceived its own thoughts.

"I think, therefore I am," he revealingly said.

European colonial history has little to say about the possible hidden traumas of its philosophers, let alone its cultural philosophies. But Peg O'Connor, a white philosopher in the US whose people come from Ireland, one of the most recently colonized European countries, shares this:

> Survivors of sexual abuse often describe themselves as leaving their bodies during the abuse; they report that they are not in their bodies or do not identify with their bodies. The dualism of survivors bears an interesting resemblance to the dualism that René Descartes offered.

In a moment of receiving violence, dissociation can protect people against overwhelm. But if that trauma is not released, if that trauma becomes chronic, it almost always leads to further trauma.

Maybe it's so obvious that it doesn't need to be asked—but is my culture a culture of held trauma?

I can't help noticing the pervasive logic of trauma, the either-or logic, that is embedded within the logic of my own culture— good guys vs. evildoers, and so on.

In fact, the American Academy of Mind-Body Healing has this to say:

> Binary thinking can be a common response to trauma. Ultimately, many of us who engage in binary thinking are doing so in an effort to feel safe. . . . When we label something as "bad/wrong," we can avoid it, or spend our energy railing against it so that we feel we're still in control.

In colonialism, control is where it's at. Avoidance of chaos is where it's at.

Yet this colonial preoccupation with control, with conquering both chaos and those who are blamed for it, has led to innumerable traumas—and thus more chaos. Indeed, in this trauma-based, either/or orientation, those who aren't our friends must be our enemies; those who aren't for us must be against us.

In such a context, weapons like tanks, guns, and AK-47s can begin to look like comfort objects, defenders against external agents of evil—even against the "Axis of Evil," as former US President George W. Bush famously called Iraq, Iran, and North Korea in 2002. Within this binary, soul-splitting value system, guns, drones, and bombs themselves can become inherent agents of all things good—as long as they are detonated and wielded by the "good guys."

These days, I keep seeing weapon-inspired messages everywhere, on bumper stickers, lawn signs, and even the occasional cross-stitch pattern.

Gun sweet gun.

God, Guts, and Guns.

Babies, Guns, and Jesus.

Live. Love. Laugh. If that doesn't work—Load. Aim. Fire.

Prayer is the best way to meet the Lord. Trespassing is faster.

Each pro-gun message I encounter equates guns with goodness, even with the goodness of that mysterious presence sometimes called *God*, or *Jesus*, or *Lord*. There's even an American gun outfitter named Higher Power.

In spite of this dichotomous thinking and this pervasive presence of trauma, I certainly can't guess where the original unresolved traumas of white settler colonial people would have come from. At different points in history, maybe someone really did feel, or really did end up, jettisoned from a garden somewhere, sometime. Maybe that's why the Genesis passage about God's banishment of Adam and Eve, compared to thousands of other biblical passages, has so captured the European colonial imagination.

But Peter Levine, like other trauma specialists, would probably suggest the original source or sources of trauma don't matter so much anyway: "One of the difficulties in treating trauma has been the undue focus on the content of an event that has engendered trauma. . . . Traumatic symptoms are not caused by the 'trigger' event itself. They stem from the frozen residue of energy that has not been resolved and discharged."

As much as I have longed for one, or sometimes more than one, maybe I don't need to find the historical moment or moments in time when my people first became habituated to storing rather than discharging traumatic events and traumatized reactions. Maybe the point is that, for countless generations, this stored-up fear and subsequent rage have gone in the direction that pent-up fear and rage tend to go: toward violence.

As Ta-Nehisi Coates, a Black journalist and author of *Between the World and Me*, has said of America, violence is "its primary language."

I saw it in myself first, on the porch at age three. Resmaa Menakem might call this experience, this harm-begetting-harm, *dirty pain*: "When people respond from their most wounded parts, become cruel or violent, or physically or emotionally run away, they experience dirty pain. They also create more of it for others and themselves."

I'll never forget when I was stirring something on the stove, and a particular rerun came over the airwaves of Prairie Public Radio. The topic was human violence. The speaker was Gary Slutkin, executive director of Cure Violence and a white epidemiologist. As

I paused mid-stir, I heard him liken violence to the flu. It's like how "the flu causes more flu causes more flu," he said.

Guy Raz, host of the TED Radio Hour and a white journalist, responded, "This is amazing. I mean, you're basically saying that [violence] is not a sin or the behavior of, like, bad apples or bad people. This is like a contagious disease."

Gary Slutkin replied, "Yeah, it isn't *like* a contagious disease. It *is* a contagious disease."

Apparently, when you look at epidemiological maps, you can track the movement of violence around the planet and around regions of the planet much the way you can track the movement of other contagious diseases like the flu, meningitis, and Covid-19.

Certainly, white settler colonialism as an imperial system creates traumas and then more traumas.

But does it also transmit a disease called violence?

I hope so. As strange as that may be, I do hope so. I hope my culture has caught a disease, and I hope my people have caught an illness.

A disease calls for a remedy. A sickness can be treated. An illness can often be managed.

There are practices. There are methods. There are medicines of the soul.

In the story of my life, allyship and accompliceship have become powerfully healing practices for rejoining the circle of life.

Even as my own culture might tell me it's impossible, the circle of life is just where I long to be.

EIGHT

INCARCERATED BODIES AND MUTUAL LIBERATION

After the Dakota Access Pipeline began pumping nineteen million gallons of oil each day, I had hoped that the imperial state, written in trauma and sealed by violence, might start paying less attention. Maybe the eviction of the Water Protector Camps—and the large-scale dispersal of Water Protectors —would be enough.

But it seemed that other punishments were required.

So I used to take a trip.

Each month, behind the wheel of my 2002 Toyota, which runs better on the inside than it looks like it might from the outside, I journeyed toward the eastern sun, past teeming lakes, clustering trees, and any number of big-box stores. Two hundred and twenty-one miles later, I arrived at Sandstone prison, officially known as the Federal Correctional Institution (FCI) in Sandstone, Minnesota.

This was before the Covid-19 pandemic and the moratorium on public visitation, before Rattler's long-awaited release.

But for more than two years, Rattler lived there, along with roughly 1,155 other imprisoned men. At Oceti Sakowin Camp, Rattler had served as security—as Akicita, which, to the best of my understanding, is an honored Lakota role of protecting the people. He took the name *Rattler* in the early 1990s when he served in the Marine Corps and then used it again at Camp.

Much like Rattler, Lakota elder James "Angry Bird" White, Chumash activist Michael "Little Feather" Giron, Pueblo activist Brennon "Bravo1" Nastacio, and Pueblo activist Dion Ortiz also either served as Camp security or supported those who did. Dion, the youngest of the NoDAPL political prisoners, celebrated his twenty-first birthday in prison.

In a separate and complicated scenario, Lakota activist Red Fawn Janis (formerly Fallis) fell in love at Camp, like countless other Water Protectors. Unfortunately, her love story ended in prison time and, to quote her support committee, entrapment.

Responsive to the call from Standing Rock and the Indigenous-led Water Protector movement, Jessica Reznicek, a white activist from the Catholic Worker Movement, has also become a political prisoner of the US. After admitting that she tampered with the pipeline south of Standing Rock, in Iowa, she is also doing real time.

All told, the NoDAPL political prisoners from the Standing Rock movement here in North Dakota—Rattler, Angry Bird, Little Feather, Bravo1, Dion, and Red Fawn—are Indigenous people who were targeted by the US government for engaging in an Indigenous-led struggle to preserve Indigenous ways of life on Indigenous land.

As AIM activists often say about Leonard Peltier, an Anishinaabe-Lakota activist who was falsely convicted of murdering two FBI agents in 1973, the Indigenous political prisoners are more than political prisoners. They are *prisoners of war*, prisoners of the US government's perpetual colonial war on Indigenous peoples.

More than fifty years before Rattler and other NoDAPL prisoners of war were sent to colonial prisons, Martin Luther King, Jr., said this in his "Letter from a Birmingham Jail":

> There are two types of laws: there are just laws; and there are unjust laws. . . . Any law that uplifts human personality is just. Any law that degrades human personality is unjust. . . . An unjust law is a code that a majority inflicts on a minority that is not binding on itself.

Indeed, colonial powers tend to operate by exactly this judicial double standard, insisting that those with lesser power obey every unjust law, including those (like obstruction of a government function) that the state repurposes for the occasion. Yet here in North Dakota, the pipeline company and its vast security forces, from private to state to countless enlisted localities, were themselves never held accountable to the law, particularly not to international treaty law.

As a result, the Dakota Access Pipeline crosses all over Indigenous treaty lands.

In a more respectful way, I hope, I also crossed Indigenous lands—Lakota, Dakota, Hidatsa, Anishinaabe, and more—as I journeyed to Sandstone FCI.

Sandstone is a minimum-security facility not too far from the Kettle River and the Sandstone Ridges, which that meandering, copper river has helped to create. The prison sits just about dead center in aptly named Pine County. In the fall of 2019, I saw sandhill cranes for the first time in my life, there on the Sandstone campus.

The sandhill cranes, the river, and the rest of Pine County are separated from the men of Sandstone FCI by a double row of massive fencing and untold lengths of spiraled razor wire. The first time I visited Rattler, having just been granted visitation privileges, eight long months and three frustrating visitor applications after he was admitted, I stopped to snap a few pictures from the scrappy front patch of lawn. I was inspired by Leoyla Cowboy, Diné activist of the Bitterwater Clan, who had recently shared a selfie from the outside of USP Hazelton in West Virginia. This facility, aptly nicknamed Misery Mountain, was a maximum-security prison where Little Feather, her spouse at the time, was incarcerated as a NoDAPL Water Protector, more than 1,500 miles from home. That selfie, even with the copious razored fencing of Hazelton in the background, was strangely comforting to the rest of us, the strangers who had become loved ones through our resistance to the pipeline and our dedication to its prisoners of war.

I thought Rattler's loved ones, especially Olive "Badger" Bias, an Appalachian Water Protector we both met at Camp, might be just as comforted by a Sandstone selfie—fencing, razor wire, and sparse patches of grass notwithstanding.

But a white female guard, twice my size in muscles and bulletproof padding, burst from the solid door. "Are you a visitor?" she demanded.

I nodded, tucking my phone away.

"What are you doing? Are you taking pictures?"

As I mumbled something about the rest of Rattler's loved ones maybe wanting to see where he's living now, she interrupted, "You'd better not be taking pictures of our fence, or you'll never visit here again."

As far as harassment by armed authorities goes, this exchange was negligible. Still, if Rattler were to be isolated from a visitor on the short list of permitted visitors, he would be exponentially more isolated from life on the outside. So I chose not to speak up, keep my camera in hand, or make any gesture that could imply I was doing those things.

As harmless as this experience turned out to be, it stays with me now because of how it troubled, ever so slightly, my white settler identity—an identity which has always depended upon the consent of other white settlers to maintain. In that moment by the door, the guard had the prerogative to treat me like a quasi-prisoner, a proximal prisoner, an outsider to settler colonialism, because of my proximity to a prisoner and the imprisoned role.

Jessica Reznicek, even as a descendant of settler colonialism herself, has now become something of an outsider—incarcerated for the proximity she created between her own body and the anticolonial Water Protector movement. She switched sides, so to speak. She didn't play her settler colonial role, and now she's doing eight years with a $3 million fine.

During the summer of 2021, when I was arrested and jailed for my own proximity to the Water Protector movement and the Indigenous-led resistance to the Line 3 pipeline, I started to wonder if my own ancestors experienced this fear of punishment. If they were anything like the European immigrants of history, my Scottish, Irish, German, and Swiss ancestors, to name a few, would have fought, sometimes literally, to be admitted into whiteness and thus protected from colonialism, protected from the punishments colonialism so readily gives.

Gaining this admittance to the in-group of colonialism, they could then have been free from—or at least more free from—

injustice. But in this hoped-for state of insulation, they must rarely have felt secure against economic and existential suffering.

As I have learned from historians Theodore Allen, Nell Irvin Painter, Steven T. Newcomb, David Roediger, and others, in the 1400s, colonizers first proclaimed primacy over Indigenous peoples because of their own Christianity, using the Doctrine of Discovery as their weapon. As increasing numbers of colonized peoples adopted a Christian orientation, colonizers then proclaimed primacy because of their Anglo-Saxon identity.

Then, in the 1700s and 1800s, increasing numbers of European immigrants resisted colonial powers by joining Black people and Indigenous people in uprisings like Gabriel's Revolt, which was led by an enslaved Black man named Gabriel. Inspired by the successful revolt of enslaved peoples in Haiti, it was almost successful itself.

Because of this growing intercultural resistance, colonizers extended primacy to other European-descended groups in order to disturb affinities among the poor of many colors and, just as importantly, to find overseers for their slavery plantations and settlers for their land claims. Ironically, many English prisoners and debtors became settlers—colonizers, even—in the penal colonies of Georgia and Australia, so that the English Empire could be rid of much of its local prison population and could establish imperial territories across the oceans. It seems that prisons, in spite of their internal rigidity, have always been adaptable, mutable institutions, ready to serve an ever-expanding empire with its ever-expanding goals.

Certainly, each new wave of European immigrants to the US— Scottish, German, Irish, Polish, Italian, and more—was (and is) at first excluded from the sanctity of white identity. Their economic usefulness had (and has) to be shown.

Even after it has been established, whiteness isn't always easy to maintain.

In the 1840s, after scores of Irish immigrants escaped the Great Famine, they were originally scorned by other white settlers and immigrants, as seems to be the custom in the US. Having quickly learned the economic advantages of whiteness, a group of Irish immigrant dock workers in New York City campaigned for an "all-white waterfront," attempting to push German immigrants out of dock-working jobs by claiming Germans were a different color.

Whiteness, then and now, is a slippery device.

Whiteness, then and now, comes with a price. It's what W. E. B. Du Bois termed the *wages of whiteness.*

Once they arrived, my ancestors' economic and corporal hopes seemed to lie in ridding themselves of their histories. According to Katherine Hobson vanFossen, a white historian in my extended family, my Anabaptist ancestors in Europe had been subject to execution, my Mennonite ancestors had been subject to slavery, and my ancestors within the Dutch church had been persecuted in harsh and unconscionable ways.

In choosing to become white, it became crucial that they forget their own loss of land and culture, their own indentured servitude and slavery, and the related realities of those who could not hide behind a mask of whiteness.

To be white, my ancestors at large must have given up their own histories, covered their own losses, and shifted their historical suffering to a greater or lesser extent onto the more recently colonized peoples of Africa and this continent.

Again, I'm reminded of what Resmaa Menakem would call *dirty pain.* It seems my ancestors, the very ones who eventually gave me life, shifted their trauma, loss, and pain, in order to be safe—or at least to be in less danger.

Even today, a "safe neighborhood" is often code for a predominantly white neighborhood, regardless how much domestic violence, child abuse, and emotional suffering happens within; regardless, in fact, how unsafe a neighborhood like the Retreat at Twin Lakes might be for Trayvon Martin, a Black teenager who, in 2012, was shot to death by George Zimmerman, a white Peruvian American member of the neighborhood watch.

In my own childhood, growing up on an all-white block, a cul-de-sac shaped like an elongated button mushroom, adults in the neighborhood would have called the place safe. We kids, all of us white, could play in the cul-de-sac, dawn until dusk. My best friend Dana and I would squeeze our two wiry bodies onto her bicycle built for one, singing for all the world to hear, if they wanted to. The other kids loved to hold races from up the street by Shaun's house all the way down to Amy's. I never liked the game, but some of the kids couldn't get enough of cops and robbers. The bad guys were the robbers, of course, always getting their wrists tied up in the garage belonging to Jeff, Gregg, and their family.

When the real police drove by, that's all they did—drive by—on the bigger street, called Gettysburg Drive, which our cul-de-sac emerged from.

The only time I even remember a fire truck was a midsummer block party, the fire truck clambering with grade-school bodies that had taken a break, for a time, from bicycling, racing, and sending each other to jail. The only guns I saw on my cul-de-sac were the ones that waited side by side in my dad's bedroom closet or came out for cleaning and greasing on my parents' queen-size bed.

Mostly, out on the street, we were safe.

In the secrecy of our homes, though, where no one else could see, our bodies—too many of our bodies, anyway—faced something other than safety.

One particular cloudy evening in early spring, way past dark, not much of a moon, I bolted as if tossed by the hand of God from the front room to the front lawn. The thing I had just witnessed left me severed from my sanity. I made noise, plenty of wounded animal noise, out in public.

On that night, like other nights, I was white. Everyone involved was white. And no one came out to help me. No one checked in at our house or gave my folks a call or summoned the local police, which would have been the custom when noisy trouble was unfolding.

What must our neighbors have been thinking? What did it mean, in that moment, to live on a safe street? What did it mean to be settlers? To be white?

Somehow, I was taught, though no one ever said it out loud, that being white means we are protected. The only real danger is people who aren't white. White people do not harm us, even when they do, because that's what it means to be white.

Maybe as a child, as a descendant of settler colonialism, I longed, like my ancestors did, for the safety they came here to find. Maybe as white people, we are still afraid, still struggling to find that safety—in the very form and function of our identity.

Maybe that's what places like Sandstone FCI, USP Hazelton, and the new Burleigh-Morton Detention Center are meant to guarantee.

Maybe in 1701, in Germantown, Pennsylvania, that's what the new prison—one of the first on these lands, the one my ancestor

Arnold van Vossen's taxes helped to fund—was also meant to guarantee: safety, security, separation. Freedom from the suffering that *they*, those who belong inside the prisons, can cause.

Not *us*. We are taught that *us*-ness is the thing that makes us safe. And yet our *us*-ness doesn't save us enough. Our *us*-ness doesn't protect us enough.

My ancestors fought to be white, to be *us*, to be welcomed within colonialism, not because *us* was so loving and so welcoming, but precisely because *us* was not. By being *us*, by fighting to be white, by disavowing *them*, my ancestors sought protection, assimilation, ingratiation.

Yet the central reason white people long to be *us* is not what *they*, those with lesser might, could do to *us*. It is what *us*, by definition, do to *them*—and what suffering we would endure if we failed to be *us*.

Sometimes the gates around the communities, the walls along the borders, keep *them* out. Sometimes the razor-wire fencing around the prisons keeps *them* in. Either way, the premise is that we are safe among our kind: the settlers, the colonizers, the good ones, the people called white.

But what if our experience tells us otherwise? What if our own proximity to whiteness tells us otherwise? What if we don't stick with our own *us*-ness, our own so-called kind? Then what?

As a regular visitor at Sandstone FCI, I couldn't help noticing that the visitation room—a squat, low-ceilinged spot that felt like a deep basement—was one of the most culturally and ethnically diverse places I tended to experience in my regular North Dakota life. The only places more culturally complex, in recent memory, had been various Water Protector Camps and happenings that followed.

Certainly, I was still a descendant of settler colonialism when I was at Sandstone FCI. I didn't become Black and I didn't become Indigenous, the two most prevalent backgrounds of people I saw there, along with white. But when I arrive at any prison to visit a person imprisoned there, I am situated, for a time, on the other side of the fence. While I may not be an enemy of the empire, not a person in a cage herself, I'm also not a friend of the empire, not a person with a key, a gun, or, in those particular moments, a voice.

In those moments, I feel my whiteness slipping. While I am not *them*, I'm also not fully *us*. My proximity to prisoners disrupts the white identity that my ancestors struggled so hard—sometimes even oppressed so hard—to make for me. By fleeing Europe, my ancestors hoped to free me from such a prison, from having loved ones in exactly this kind of place.

And this is how I would arrive. These were my itchy, ancestral memories as I traveled among the cabins and lakes to Sandstone FCI.

On that first prison visit, Rattler and I sat face-to-face, hunched forward in our spots, part chair, part park bench, part locker-room seating arrangement. Except for the tan matching uniforms and the volume of talking, you would almost think we were visiting at an oversized bus depot.

In a one-gallon ziplock bag, I had brought forty dollars in quarters for the various mismatched vending machines that slumped along the exit wall. Under a sign printed on standard copy paper that read NO REFUNDS, half the machines didn't function. The other half didn't disclose the prices of their items. No meals were served in that room, except at the annual Powwow, so you had to buy lunch for your loved one. Rattler, like every person in prison, was barred from any contact with the vending machines, the microwave, or the money.

Everything prison-related seems to cost money. There's a copay to see the doctor. You have to buy soap, shoes, and phone time. Even wiring money to prisoners' commissaries costs extra money.

As Angela Y. Davis, an iconic Black leader in the prison abolition movement, has said, "Mass imprisonment generates profits as it devours social wealth, and thus it tends to reproduce the very conditions that lead people to prison."

Dion Ortiz, one of the NoDAPL prisoners of war who also did time at Sandstone, had a job in the kitchen. He made fifty cents a day. One evening on the phone, we figured he had to work fourteen days to afford one commissary pizza. In sync, we said, "It's slavery"—even though the Emancipation Proclamation was supposed to have freed enslaved peoples in 1863. Even though, in 1865, the Thirteenth Amendment abolished slavery for good.

Or so people say.

As Ava DuVernay, a Black filmmaker and director of *13th*, has made perfectly clear, there is one distinct exception to the Thirteenth Amendment: punishment for a crime.

This is section one of the Thirteenth Amendment in its entirety:

Neither slavery nor involuntary servitude, except as a punishment for crime whereof the party shall have been duly convicted, shall exist within the United States, or any place subject to their jurisdiction.

If you have been convicted of a crime, according to the US Constitution, you can be made a slave.

And it's not just the labor, the wages, or the confinement. When Little Feather and Leoyla wanted to have a legal marriage with full benefits of the certificate, they chose a few places and times. They asked if I would conduct it, as I was vested with that colonial power. Since they had been wedded in their hearts from the days of Oceti Sakowin Camp, we liked to call the event a *re-wedding*.

But the re-wedding wasn't allowed, not while he was in prison or, later, in the halfway house—because a colonial authority, not Little Feather himself, had the power to decide.

As Frederick Douglass said in 1845, "I didn't know I was a slave until I found out I couldn't do the things I wanted."

Prison is the epitome of not doing the things you want. Prison is the slavery of our age.

I will never forget seeing Little Feather in chains. Or Rattler behind the barbed-wire fences. Or Dion behind the visitation glass.

And more.

When the federal defendants from the Standing Rock movement—Red Fawn, Little Feather, Rattler, Dion, Angry Bird, and Bravo1—first received their charges, they faced possible sentences, mandatory minimums, of ten years and up. The Water Protector Legal Collective commissioned a poll, the same poll I mentioned earlier, which was meant to ascertain how likely a fair jury was.

The answer came back: not very.

As it turned out, roughly 85 percent of Bismarck-Mandan residents already believed Water Protectors were guilty, so defendants petitioned the court for a change of venue. Could their trials be relocated to Fargo, maybe, where minds weren't so made up?

The answer from the federal court came back: No.

That's when legal advisors made a difficult recommendation: Cut your losses. Take a plea. Do time, but do less.

Ultimately, NoDAPL federal defendants from the Standing Rock movement pled guilty to a lesser charge—felonious civil disorder, a category increasingly reserved for political resisters. Each plea was noncooperating, meaning defendants would not provide evidence in other cases. Red Fawn, in the most extreme example, went from possible life imprisonment to a sentence of fifty-seven months. In addition to civil disorder brought against all the defendants, Red Fawn's plea included a more significant charge related to the gun her former boyfriend, an FBI informant, had given her.

According to Daniel Hovland, a white attorney and the judge in each of these cases, 95 percent of federal defendants take plea deals. This means 95 percent of people in the federal system never have a trial, forfeit the right to appeal, and lose the chance to have their story heard.

That's one of the reasons loved ones have formed the NoDAPL Political Prisoners Support Committee, so that the story, which doesn't end there, doesn't have to end there.

Here's Red Fawn:

I stand in peace, in prayer, and in solidarity with our relatives through every struggle. Remember the strength and the lives of our ancestors. In the spirit of Tasunke Witko, protect all things sacred. Never give up, my strong heart relatives.

Here's Christina, Dion's mom:

My son had a purpose. Water is life, that's why he was there. Whatever he did to protect the water and the Water Protectors, he did out of love.

Here's Bravo1, who has gathered razor wire that was used to keep Water Protectors away from sacred sites and now makes it into dream catchers:

We figured we would take something that was negative and meant to hurt us and turn it into something positive.

Here's Angry Bird:

We need to come together as one, not as one better than the other, and to remember it's going to take us all to help fix what we're destroying. If not for us, then for our children and children's children to live.

Here's Rattler:

When I get out, quite honestly, if the fight isn't over, I'm going to jump right back in it because it's the right thing to do and it's where I belong. So when I get out, I've got your back.

Finally, here's Little Feather in words he asked me to share when he was at UCP Hazelton:

Please let our people know that I love them, and I'm honored to be where I am at for them. I want our people to know also to never give up hope on our movement. Our struggle is only the beginning, and we need to remember that what we stood for and fight for are the essence of our movement.

Though they aren't together now, Little Feather and Leoyla did have a re-wedding. We assembled down by the river, the same rolling river we had gathered to protect. Many loved ones—Little Feather, Leoyla, elders and loved ones from Standing Rock, my daughter, my grandbabies, their mom, Rattler's spouse, and more—all made our prayers that day.

In many languages.

In many ways.

Some of us touched the water. All of us touched the Earth.

We wrapped them up, Little Feather and Leoyla, in a star quilt that Lula Red Cloud, an honored Lakota elder, had donated for a raffle—and that I had bought a hundred raffle tickets to win.

Stitched with swirling threads, it was as blue as the mighty Missouri, as green as Unci Maka, Grandmother Earth.

We took pictures for the ones who couldn't join us. We said blessings for the ones who couldn't join us. We called upon the ancestors, everybody's ancestors, as complicated as our ancestors would have been to one another.

We named a difficult past. We envisioned a sacred future.

In spite of pain that came before, in spite of the pain has surely followed, maybe in that circle, in that moment with one another, we were free.

NINE

PIPELINES, CRIMES, AND EMPIRE

Though no one spoke the words out loud, I always knew I should not go to jail.

I should not bring such shame upon the family.

But in 2021, as Natali Segovia, Indigenous legal counsel for the Water Protector Legal Collective, helped me navigate the court system, she sent me the Alpha Roster Report for Minnesota's Hubbard County.

There was my name, as clear as any on the screen: Van Fossan, Karen Irene. Court Room 2. 8/27/21. 8:30 a.m.

When I spotted those anticipated letters, complete with the middle name I had inherited from Betty Irene, my grandma on my dad's side, my instinct was to lean in and cover the page. Then I remembered that my grandparents had all died more than a decade before.

For the only time in my life, I felt a rush of relief that they were gone, every single one of them. In fact, at age seventeen, after my first face-to-face interaction with police, I had waited until the trouble was all gone to tell them there had been trouble to begin with.

In 1987 or so, the whole thing started with a phone call on an early summer's day.

Bbbb-rrr-ing, went the heavy, oval-shaped phone on the kitchen wall.

My brother, recently promoted to full-fledged teenager himself, arrived at the ringing phone before I did. "It's for you," David told me. "It's the sheriff."

Somehow, he managed to infuse those four syllables with all the scorn that a younger brother who's typically on your side can muster, which was plenty.

Gingerly, I accepted the receiver as the tangled phone cord scraped across the summer-sticky linoleum. With my voice in its highest register, I said, "Hello?"

Long story short, someone had robbed a bank. Whoever she was, she hadn't performed a gun-in-hand, ski-mask type of holdup. In a less cinematic move, she had cashed a payroll check from a long-defunct business. The check had been written out to me.

And signed by . . . me?

Needless to say, I was wanted down at the station, the last place I wanted to be.

In the white settler colonial world of central Illinois, the cops were correct. Always. If they suggested that you stole a few hundred dollars, you probably did. Unlike many of my Black and Indigenous peers, who would generally have known by now that sheriffs could—and do—make violent mistakes, I had been trained to believe that the sheriff was and always would be an exemplar, even a manifester, of justice.

Schooled in the carceral logic of US imperialism, I feared that I would be punished—that I would *deserve* to be punished—by the criminal justice system and, as a result, my family system.

As my dad tussled with his tools on the driveway, perspiration streaming from his hairline, what could I say?

Steeling myself, I told him, "Dad, um, somebody stole some money from my bank, I guess. And the sheriff needs to clear it up. So he wants me to come down to the station. With a parent."

Randy Eugene Van Fossan, never one to be rushed by someone else's agenda and certainly not mine, dropped everything, including the sizable hood of the Buick, which thundered into place. He abandoned his clanging wrenches on the pavement and catapulted, grease-stained clothes and all, behind the wheel.

As he pushed through local traffic, I jostled back and forth in the passenger seat, past the Kroger's store, the Dairy Queen, and the tree-filled campus of Olivet Nazarene University, where my mother held a library job. My mom would be cataloguing new acquisitions right this minute, oblivious to the family drama hurtling by on Main Street. How I yearned to leap from the car and take up permanent residence in her tiny, book-filled office.

Soon, Dad hit the brakes at a stoplight, too blazing red to avoid. Turning to face me squarely in the eyes, Dad asked, "Did you do this? Tell me the truth."

"No, Dad."

"Are you sure?"

"Yes, Dad!" I was rolling the eyes behind my eyes, the invisible ones I didn't think parents could see.

Of course, I assumed he was on the sheriff's side. White settlers in my world were always on the sheriff's side.

Since this long-ago, high-speed drive, I have realized that his motive was to advocate for his daughter, a project that required all the relevant information—which he has since fervently confirmed. But as far as I knew at the time, he was practically the sheriff himself, and so no other side existed.

When we arrived at the station, an architectural jailhouse-mansion-bank combination, an officer took my picture facing front, left, and right. For many years afterward, when a stranger would say I looked familiar, I wondered if maybe they had spotted my face in the giant book of Kankakee County mugshots.

Before long, a heat-packing white man wearing SHERIFF on his badge told me to sit in the metal chair across from his sky-high desk, while he asked me a thousand questions.

To the best of my ability, avoiding my father's eyes, I gave my answers: Yes, I had an account at that bank. Yes, I had gone into the lobby just this week. No, I had not cashed a check from such-and-such defunct business.

At last, from a file folder, the sheriff produced the check, fully signed on the back. For a while, he kept the check angled in his direction.

I could only see the signature, *Karen I Van Fossan*, upside-down.

Wait, what? I had seen that very signature since just about the moment I learned cursive. But how could I have done this? And then how could I have forgotten I had done this? My stomach, which had been hopping around all day, plummeted to my feet. Somehow, someway, I must have robbed a bank!

Clearly, I had done wrong. I probably *was* wrong, even bad. I knew as plainly as I knew my own name, let alone my own signature, that I should not commit a crime.

No matter what.

Finally, the sheriff reached for the check. With an actor's flair, he none-too-quickly spun the check to face me.

When I saw it right-side-up, there was no question. That was not my writing. Or my signature. Or my style.

Soon, he had me sign my name on a separate sheet of paper, saying something about forensics. And then, as suddenly as we had been summoned, we could leave.

I have no memory of the car ride home, or supper that night, or what my mother said, or how long before my brother scooched back over to his regular role as my ally (but probably not very long).

In the end, forensics said my signature was not the signature in question. The bank teller said my mug was not the mug in question. The sheriff said the crime in question wasn't my crime.

As relieved as I was for myself, I wondered about the woman who had pretended to be me. At some point, the sheriff informed my family that she had been caught—and she had stolen the money *for drugs*, he said.

Though I had no way to track the story then, I'm sure she went to prison, possibly the Illinois Penitentiary for Women. In spite of the word *penitentiary*, connected to penance, forgiveness, and even healing, the chances were not great that she got therapeutic care.

Years later, the incarceration of my daughter's husband taught me that. After his arrest, the support he needed—and his family very much needed him to find—seemed nearly impossible to get.

When Rick, a young white man from the trumpet section in the high school band, fell in love with my daughter, I saw him as my second kid.

When he was sixteen, there was plenty to appreciate. He asked for my advice. He laughed at my daughter's jokes. He cried when he was sad, surely a sign of some kind of positive masculinity. When they decided to get married at eighteen years of age, I approved. Or I didn't disapprove—not out loud.

Michaela was head over heels by then. And after all the heartache in her life, I wasn't about to interrupt this joy. So I wrote them an encouraging poem for the wedding, something about rambunctious dogs, feral cats, and sweet-hearted pleasures they had in common.

But in 2016, when Rick was twenty-three, he didn't seem much older than when I had first met him. He was guileless and unsure, as if his own moral compass wasn't set yet, wasn't certain.

Or maybe there were too many magnets to follow.

As Water Protectors in the NoDAPL struggle were being arrested by the hundreds, Rick got arrested too, for a very different crime. His charge was luring a minor by computer.

A sex offense.

With his head held low, he shuffled down to the basement apartment he shared with Michaela, saying little about jail except that you don't get a pillow.

And that he was sorry.

I was sorry too, not that I came out and said it. I couldn't help feeling it was my fault somehow. I had always worried that there were influences, invitations, enticements toward toxic masculinity that I could never access, let alone ward off by myself now that I was a single parent. Ever since he had accepted me as his honorary mom, I had longed to help him find a positive male role model, a man who could take him under his wing, mentor him, or at least hang out with him and be positive toward women at the same time.

But this positive male role model kept eluding both of us.

In those days, I was still working in the child abuse prevention field, having just started serving as the minister of my church. Every day, I plotted strategies to prevent harm, including sexual harm, against minors. I felt it as my call, my hearty responsibility. Thanks to the very field I was working in, adults who injured children could face real-world consequences for their actions.

Rick's consequences went like this: Jail time and home confinement. A felony on his record. Inclusion in the public sex offender registry.

A few months after Rick's arrest, before he was sentenced, he and I went for a walk with the dogs. He talked with hardly an inhale from the moment we figured out how to turn a cargo strap into a makeshift leash to the moment I gave him a motherly see-you-soon hug. In the middle of his ruminations, he remarked that even though he had betrayed one of the most important things in the world to me (Michaela), and even though I had lost a ton (or more) of respect for him, I was still by his side.

In a bend along the wide Missouri River, that's literally where I was—by his side. But what did *by his side* even mean?

With Rick, and with Michaela, I was all about Rick's responsibility, period. Action. Consequence. End of story.

As his honorary mom, I figured this was my obligation. Too many other voices, from his biological dad to some of the men in jail, had insisted that Rick was entrapped—framed, even. Their evidence was that when Rick arrived at the Best Western to meet his victim (and her friend), he didn't encounter a girl (or two). He encountered a male police officer—a roomful of male police officers.

That's who Rick had been texting all along, one of the male police officers in that room.

Later, moments before his court appearance, Rick informed his attorney, "I want to plead not guilty." He was the victim of circumstance, he said.

I hit the proverbial roof. "If that had been a real girl," I said, "what you actually did, let alone what you went there to do, would have traumatized her for life."

Rick hadn't cared one way or another that his so-called date was ostensibly a minor. When the girl (i.e., the male police officer) had texted to say that her Craigslist ad was wrong and that she was fourteen years of age, not eighteen, Rick got no more interested— or less.

To Michaela, his disinterest in her age was both relieving and enraging. He wanted what he wanted, age and girl be damned.

Still, she wasn't a girl. And she wasn't fourteen. And she didn't have a friend. She was a male police officer running a sting, seeing how far Rick was willing to go—down to age fourteen? Add a friend? Make the friend a minor too?

To Rick, I have insisted, "On the day you were supposed to meet her, the officer gave you a chance. As he said in his statement, he stopped texting you. But you persisted. That was your way out, your chance to do the right thing or less of a wrong thing, and you didn't take it."

To my friends, I have said, "Somewhere in Bismarck, North Dakota, there was a real, live man who was opposed to male violence and who actually communicated with Rick. Why didn't he teach Rick how he should act, instead of giving him ways to do the opposite?"

What if the officer, in the midst of all that texting, had written this?

Look what you almost did. This isn't what it means to be a man. There's an intervention for you, and we're going to help you learn to do better.

What a missed opportunity to help Rick set his ever-wavering compass.

In fact, the police officer who found Rick on Craigslist didn't swoop in between Rick and an actual teenager and then rescue the girl from the conversation. He placed the ad himself. Even more, he didn't just pretend to be female or eighteen, which was fine with Rick. He pretended to be fourteen, the exact age most likely *not* to sound childlike but still be seen, by the law, to be a child.

He helped Rick create a map, a pathway, toward the kind of man he should *not* be, as if plenty of other male-driven enterprises in Rick's life hadn't already covered that.

Maybe this approach, this sting operation, makes sense if you're trying to ensure that someone who did it before doesn't do it again, that treatment is actually working, and that women and girls and other human beings are actually being protected. Maybe it makes sense if you're stopping folks like Rick before they get started—and giving them actual help.

Instead, the police officer created a hypothetical situation in which the consequences were far from hypothetical. Would Rick have kept texting with a real, live fourteen-year-old? I don't know. But now he's a registered sex offender for an action he might have done—yet for something, in real life, he never did.

Rick faced consequences and punishments that were ostensibly there to protect the most vulnerable among us. But as far as I can tell, they haven't made anyone safer—certainly not Michaela. Of all people, it seems the system should be concerned with protecting Michaela, a three-time survivor herself.

But when Rick lost his job, Michaela and our extended family lost his income. When he lost his freedom, she and our extended family lost his physical help. When he lost his friends and support-ers, she and our extended family lost a sense of belonging.

When he lost his self-respect, we lost the Rick we used to know.

After Rick pled guilty and was sentenced to home confinement, we rejoiced—in a way. It could have been so much worse. He could have been in shackles.

But suddenly, Michaela's home became a jailhouse too.

Actually, both of their homes became jailhouses—the apart-ment they got evicted from after Rick became a registered sex offender and the mobile home they rented later. Considering Rick's record, they were lucky to get that mobile home in the first place, complete with a tub that never drained, pipes that turned to ice, ants that wouldn't quit, and rent so high you'd have thought they were in a penthouse.

Rick became defined by that trailer, by joblessness, by a GPS monitor on his ankle. He wasn't easy to be around, least of all for himself.

As he told me down by the river that day, there was always more he could have done. He could have gone to support group more. He could have helped Michaela around the house more. He could have done more physical exercise at home, releasing pent-up emotions.

But through all of his mistakes, Rick was still the car fixer, the cat kisser, the wrinkly T-shirt wearer, the one who read us *Calvin and Hobbes* at holiday meals.

He was also the person who picked Michaela up and dropped her down. On purpose.

Eventually, her shoulder started healing from that unexpected injury. Eventually, she returned to full-time work. Eventually, with her heart in her hands, she left him.

And then again. And then again. And then that was that.

As a professional psychic once told me, "Michaela's going to be fine, great even. She's going to do things you can't even imagine."

This prediction has come true many times. But I have wanted the same for Rick. For his sake, as well as Micheala's, I had hoped so much would be different.

But in all the years I have known him, I have not watched Rick grow into himself. Instead, I have witnessed his unraveling, his unmaking.

Did it have to be this way? Did the system have to punish rather than teach him? Did his punishment offer anyone any genuine protection?

Immediately after his arrest, Rick tried to get help—begged to get help. But the system didn't work that way. He had to wait and wait some more until he was sentenced to treatment. Even then, he faced one complication and delay after another. The system didn't understand a self-determined willingness to heal, only treatment as a consequence.

All the while, he finally had the attention he had needed. There was a police officer, a whole roomful of police officers, as well as a judge, an assistant prosecutor, and an attorney—all male, all publicly opposed to violence against women. But Rick was deprived of connection, of relationship, with those who could have guided him the most.

Instead, Rick had to be punished.

That's when he became violent. Not just hypothetically but in real life.

This is how the empire recreates itself. From trauma to trauma, from shame to shame, this is how the empire spreads the epidemic of violence.

How, then, to *un*create an empire?

How, then, to *un*create the violence of an empire?

How, then, to *un*create an empire's violent expansion?

As I hold these larger questions, I have come to distrust the carceral system, the imperial justice system, altogether. Not long after Rick's conviction, I found myself in a public conversation that soon turned toward criminal justice. I surprised myself by blurting, "When a person goes to jail, all their loved ones go to jail too."

To my left, my daughter nodded vigorously and leaned into my embracing arm.

With that outburst, I was trying to say that the colonial concepts of individuality and, by extension, individual punishment were audacious falsehoods. The reason why nobody's free until everybody's free—as Fannie Lou Hamer, a Black civil rights leader, famously said in 1971—is that everybody's connected. Human beings are more like drops of water in a river than gadgets on an assembly line.

At the time, I wasn't thinking about my teenage exchange with the Kankakee County sheriff or anticipating any future jail stay of my own. But in 2021, I did find myself arrested.

On a powerful day, among powerful days, hundreds of people had interrupted construction of the Line 3 pipeline.

In the logic of the empire, this was a crime, and we should be punished.

While the precise moment I learned about the resistance at Standing Rock is forever fixed in my memory, much like a stone I can't help polishing with my touch, word of Line 3 crept toward my attention from the edges.

In bits and pieces, I had gathered that Line 3 would cross traditional Anishinaabe and Dakota lands, transporting tar-sands oil, which the Center for Biological Diversity calls "one of the most destructive, carbon-intensive, and toxic fuels on the planet." The ultimate beneficiary of Line 3—if anyone can truly benefit from a tar-sands pipeline—would be Energy Transfer Partners, a multinational corporation in Canada.

As wary as I was of oil pipelines, at first I didn't feel too rankled about this pipeline replacement project, which was what the Enbridge Energy Corporation called it. If Enbridge was *replacing* a dangerous pipeline, that almost seemed—could it be?—responsible.

But then Winona LaDuke, an Anishinaabe Water Protector and famed director of Honor the Earth, released this public statement:

> Think of it this way—there are six really old pipelines that they put through in northern Minnesota, shipping diluted tar sands from Alberta to Superior, Wisconsin. And one of those lines is called Line 3. It has, according to Enbridge, about nine hundred structural anomalies in it. Structural anomalies are things like small pinhole leaks, maybe some cracks. And some of those come to be big problems, like that Kalamazoo spill. That was a structural anomaly.

The Kalamazoo oil spill had happened in 2010 when an oil pipeline ruptured. About one million gallons of tar-sands oil gushed into Talmadge Creek, a tributary of the Kalamazoo. Along a thirty-mile stretch, trumpeter swans, Canada geese, muskrats, box turtles, cattails, and hundreds of other wild beings were drenched with toxic oil. Today, this Enbridge-sponsored disaster remains one of the largest onshore oil spills in history.

Winona LaDuke went on to explain that Line 3 is "a catastrophe waiting to happen. . . . Fixing these problems is very expensive, so Enbridge wants to abandon the pipeline, walk away, and build a brand-new one in a brand-new corridor. Enbridge calls this a 'replacement project' . . . They are not replacing Line 3. They are putting in a whole new corridor and doubling the size of the line."

Like DAPL, Line 3 violates the treaty rights of Indigenous peoples, particularly Ojibwe and other Anishinaabe peoples, whose access to Manoomin (wild rice) is meant to be protected in perpetuity, even according to treaties from the 1800s. Because the pipeline threatens the existence of Manoomin, which is central to Ojibwe spiritual life and relies upon healthy waters, Line 3 violates the American Indian Religious Freedoms Act—as White Earth Band of Ojibwe tribal attorney Frank Bibeau has stated many times.

When I watched a livestream of twenty-plus Water Protectors sharing intercultural prayers along the wooded pipeline route with artful masks on their faces and tufts of snow on their boots, I felt my spirit sparking with the resistance. But because of the double complexities of winter and a pandemic, people were asked to support from their own locations and not to appear on the land.

Meanwhile, Covid-19 was spreading at great speed, especially in prisons and jails. At this point, four of the NoDAPL prisoners of war—Rattler, Little Feather, Dion, and Red Fawn—were still doing time. In a tug between nagging worry and all-out panic, I joined other organizers trying to get people out.

As far as I could tell, the new federal CARES Act, which US Congress passed to reduce public health risks, would have allowed each of the still-incarcerated NoDAPL prisoners to be released, due to the nature of their charges, as well as the relatively brief length of time remaining on their sentences. But of all the people I knew or knew of in federal prisons, including those who got Covid on the inside, absolutely no one was released under the CARES Act. In 2020 and 2021, Rattler, Little Feather, Dion, and Red Fawn were each let go because their prison sentences had ended, not because the Federal Bureau of Prisons put the CARES Act into place.

Indeed, in late 2021, the Prison Policy Initiative said:

> The COVID-19 death rate in prisons is almost three times higher than among the general U.S. population, even when adjusted for age and sex. . . . State, federal, and local authorities have failed to release people from prisons and jails on a scale sufficient to protect incarcerated people's lives—and by extension, the lives of everyone in the communities where incarcerated people eventually return, and where correctional staff live and work.

As I witnessed this imperial nonchalance by the Federal Bureau of Prisons and other carceral institutions, I came to miss the up-close Water Protector movement more than ever—for its steady, embodied reverence for life. As Joseph McNeil, Jr., former Standing Rock councilmember and a Lakota community builder, once told me,

"I never experienced anything like it before, and I honestly don't know if I ever will again."

Since 2017, I have sustained a chronic ache for Oceti Sakowin Camp, a longing shared by every single NoDAPL Water Protector I know.

No doubt, there have been numerous other Water Protector Camps and Water Protector actions, from L'eau Est La Vie Camp in southern Louisiana to Camp Anishinaabek in northern Michigan.

Monisha Ríos, sister-collaborator and Boricua activist and psychologist, has joined the resistance at many such camps. She speaks of:

> The camps of Culebra and Vieques, Puerto Rico, where my people continue to struggle to protect our waters, lands, and lives from the poison of US greed, militarism, colonialism, imperialism. And the camps of the Ryukyu Nation in twice-colonized Okinawa, where their struggle against the same exact forces endures. We are all struggling for decolonization and the return to right relations with all our relatives before it is too late.

Since the closing of Oceti Sakowin Camp, even as my flight responses urged me to run from this state called North Dakota, I came to understand that my deep sense of home at Camp has been connected to my deep and complicated sense of home in this topography. I realized how deeply I am rooted here, right here where I live, thanks to my longtime relationships with people, with steadfast creatures, with this particular sweep of land, this particular stretch of space—these buttes, these prairies, these trees, these skies, these magnificent bodies of water forever on the move. How I love these rivers, as they push south like the mighty Missouri, snake north like the moseying Red—ever leaving, ever arriving, ever home.

So when Anishinaabe peoples called on Water Protectors to join them in body as well as spirit, roughly fifty miles from Fargo, no other response made sense.

By the summer of 2021, as Enbridge announced 60 percent completion of Line 3, an urgent call arose. Invitations to join the Treaty People Gathering, a weekend of activism and prayer in northern Minnesota, kept coming. This one made the rounds a lot:

> We rise together for treaties. We rise together for climate. We rise together for our water. We rise together for one another. As Enbridge builds Line 3 through Anishinaabe treaty land and the Mississippi headwaters, we continue to stand strong in our resistance.
>
> We will not stand by and watch a fossil fuel corporation line its pockets as so much is destroyed, producing oil we don't need. On June 5–8, we will gather in northern Minnesota to put our bodies on the line, to stop construction and tell the world that the days of tar sands pipelines are over.
>
> Only a major, nonviolent uprising—including direct action—will propel this issue to the top of the nation's consciousness and force Biden to act. We are rising. Join us.

Having heard the call himself, Rattler often spoke of his frustration, even his sense of futility, at not being able to join the Line 3 resistance. As a condition of probation, the NoDAPL prisoners of war had all been barred from protest actions—a movement-busting strategy if I ever heard one. Rattler and I agreed that I would go on his behalf, as well as my own.

I couldn't catch the local carpool from Fargo, since I was performing a wedding ceremony out of town. But I arrived at the large, woodsy encampment spread across three far-flung campgrounds in plenty of time for the action, prayers, and meals shared among hundreds.

Over and over, I found myself saying, "I thought I might see you here!"

That weekend, as I joined the Treaty People Gathering as well as the longer-term Line 3 resistance, I found glimpses, moments, of Camp life, stirring me to miss Oceti Sakowin Camp all the more—for being so close and yet, as the saying goes, so far away.

At the Treaty People Gathering, the prayers, along with the nonviolent direct-action training, were intended to give us strength for Monday morning. When Monday morning came, it arrived like any morning, basking in its own newness. As far as the eye could see, our purposeful caravan made the journey, one car and then another, rolling along the country roads.

Sooner than I expected, we arrived.

We disembarked at a pump station under construction, an elaborate network of jutting pipes, colossal equipment, and clear-cut, desolate space. Among hundreds of other Water Protectors, our small group of activists, both Indigenous and white, gathered at a corner of that gutted, gritty landscape. Beneath an unexpected blue awning, our group of six or so people sat side by side in front of the friends we had just made, Water Protectors who had locked themselves to pipeline-building equipment, the arm of one attached to the arm of another.

Together, we lifted our voices.

Prayerful, almost trancelike, we sang that cherished song from Sarah Dan Jones, white Southern musician and a spirited organizer herself.

Arm in arm, elbow in elbow, we sang:

When I breathe in, I breathe in peace.

When I breathe out, I breathe out love.

All day, we sang, except for when we were snacking on muffins, taking a high-noon nap, chatting with the ever-arriving media, running off to find a bathroom spot, or, in my case, sorely missing the friends who hadn't joined us.

Meanwhile, over the high metal wall of the under-construction pump station, the police kept poking their heads, one here, two here, four over there. It would have been endearing, spotting those curious faces, if hadn't been so ominous.

In the heat of the day, a helicopter circled just low enough to kick up choking storms of dirt. When I squinted, I could barely read the words US CUSTOMS AND BORDER PATROL on the door. As usual, there was activist talk, from conspiracy theories to logistical analyses, about why this particular helicopter had been deployed. All I knew was that a low-flying helicopter, whether sent or sanctioned by the state, was one reality of Oceti Sakowin Camp that I didn't care to relive.

Meanwhile, upward of three hundred Water Protectors, which included people from many different cultures, including both the hearing and Deaf communities, broadcast our intentions through chanted words and American Sign Language.

LEADER: "We are here . . ."

ALL: "We are here . . ."

LEADER: "To protect . . ."
ALL: "To protect . . ."
LEADER: "The water!"
ALL: "The water!"

Then, as the sun tilted toward the horizon, the police encroached at last, spilling from a gap in the wall. Without a word, they surged across the compound with numerous weapons and clusters of zip ties at their beltlines. Each one expressionless, each one apparently white and male, they wore four distinct uniforms from four distinct jurisdictions.

Close to the ground, still singing, we watched as a dozen officers assembled, towering just in front of us. Staring at twenty-some leather boots, I thought I would feel more afraid, more vulnerable. But as they side-eyed one another, making no other moves, I began to wonder if maybe they didn't know, like we didn't know, exactly what their plan of action would be.

Soon, in a theatrical gesture, one of them grabbed the awning from above us, tossed it to the ground, and kicked it into broken, winglike pieces. We tightened our hold, elbow to elbow. My heart picked up speed as a cluster of officers, way more than necessary, reached for our interlocking arms.

Starting from the right, the officers peeled us away—one from another, from another. As they did, we voiced our love for each person who was taken.

When my turn came, I halfway disappeared. Where I went, I couldn't say.

But now I sat among the others, all of us hunched, with zip-tied wrists, in a mismatched circle over to the side. The landscape, carved from the lavish woods in every direction, was no place for living beings.

Yet a great blue heron, with wings alight, arced above our heads.

In a flush of joy, we gasped.

For a time, everything else in the world stopped moving.

Soon, we were escorted in a not-so-straight line from the site of the arrest to the police van, from one corner of the place to its opposite. Before us, beside us, behind us, on this side of the fence and that, Water Protectors made a ruckus of sounds with hand drums and cheers, *we love you*'s, and *lililililili*'s—a sound that Tracey L. Wilkie, an Anishinaabe Water Protector, equates with honor, strength, perseverance, and matrilineal power.

Then we piled into the bright white cage on wheels, shoulder to shoulder, hip to hip.

I was the last one to enter, pressed against the door.

Even inside the stark, cramped van, there were more walls. Down the middle of the cube-shaped seating area, a metal slab divided the compartment into two long halves, making those on the other side of the wall, whoever they were, invisible to us.

Sooner than I expected, the van carried us forward, bobbling over ruts in the makeshift road, as the protest site receded beyond the window.

Still, on our side of the divider, we sang:

When I breathe in, I breathe in peace.

When I breathe out, I breathe out love.

From the other side of the wall, deep and unfamiliar voices joined our singing.

In wonder, we turned to each other with widened eyes.

As the last note drifted to silence, those unseen voices chanted the AIM song, with its steady rhythm and palpable force—the same song that had been lifted up at Wounded Knee half a century before. As best we could, we joined the singing across the wall.

About twenty minutes and four hundred breaths later, the van stopped in the Hubbard County parking lot. It stayed there, stationary, for what seemed like a thousand years. In the back of the van, I fidgeted on the metal bench, my zip-tied wrists pressed together, leg to leg with my co-arrestees.

Through the metal grate on the window, I sought the sky.

My gaze landed on a tree just beyond the parking lot. Maple? Elm? Oak? Whatever the shape of the leaves, I couldn't see.

Still, I fell in love with it.

As far as I could tell, the sun fell in love with it too, indulging each branch in a gift of purple, gold, and red.

Marking time by the slant of the sun, I figured we were held in the Hubbard County parking lot for upward of two hours. From the time the police had arrested us at the site, I figured we had been in their custody for upward of three hours.

When meetings go for three hours, flights are that late, or people are made to wait for a bathroom for that long (which was just what I was doing), sometimes they turn around and leave the place. That's exactly what I longed to do.

Hey, look! Just like that, an officer appeared, sidling past my window, heading someplace else. With my fingers wound together, I pounded on the door. But nobody opened it.

Other police vans and other Water Protectors came and went, came and went.

Even the folks on the other side of the wall, the singers of the AIM song, had been ejected.

Still, we waited.

With my breath getting shallower, I noticed the routine: A police van would arrive. Water Protectors would emerge from the van. At the edge of the Hubbard County property line, jail support folks would cheer.

But we didn't move.

Officers had come from so many jurisdictions, I figured they had forgotten us.

I didn't blame them for forgetting. People forget. The trouble was all that power, all that top-down power, over our lives and bodies. That's what got to me.

True, it didn't help that another arrestee, trying to lighten the mood, had made a joke about my name, and some other arrestees, also trying to lighten the mood, had tittered. But joke or no joke, bladder or no bladder, I wanted out.

With every cell in my body hollering, *Now!*, I confessed, "I'm about to have a panic attack."

The other arrestees, the maker of the joke included, were more than tender.

"We love you."

"You're a badass."

"LaDonna is with you."

To think that the spirit of LaDonna Brave Bull Allard, who had passed away just that year, might have been with us, with me, left me speechless.

Clumsily, awkwardly, my wrists still bound, I rummaged through the depths of my bag for an orange, a clementine I had been given at the Line 3 action.

Oh, the taste of color!

I offered wedges down the line, plenty for all. We passed slices through the needless grate, which split four of us from the other two.

"A communion," someone said.

How delicious, the scent in the air. But as I pressed the orange peel to my nose, my body still screamed, *Now!*

Soon the co-arrestees on the other side of the grate asked me a question. "Would you like us to make some noise? Try to get their attention?"

"YES!"

We hollered. We smacked the walls. We kicked the floor. We rocked the vehicle back and forth—and back and forth again.

Nothing.

So we took a deep breath. We hollered, smacked, kicked, and rocked with even greater gusto.

An officer appeared. It had worked. It actually worked!

As we descended from the steps of the van, a small cluster of jail support people raised a worn-out cheer. Rarely had I been so thankful to walk across a parking lot—or into a porta-potty.

But the evening was just getting started.

Dusk turned to night as we waited in the Hubbard County Law Enforcement Center. We each wore a canary-yellow handcuff on one wrist, attached to an indoor chain-link fence.

Eventually, though nobody explained, the officers' plan became clear:

They had arrested so many people that day that most of us would be sent to neighboring counties. Douglas County was mine. Or, more aptly, I was Douglas County's.

Zip-tied again, we were taken on a long, two-hour van ride. We got booked through the early morning in neon-orange scrubs and clunky orange-ish Crocs.

From Monday evening to Wednesday afternoon, the period we were in custody, I rarely knew what was next, or when, or where. Every sound seemed overly loud: The cell door latching behind me. The lunch tray scraping the slot. The guard's voice through the intercom. Even the staffer rounding the corner, complaining to her coworker about "those fucking bitches," which meant us.

On my first night in jail, officially named the Douglas County Jail—no euphemisms like *correctional center* or *department of rehabilitation* —I hardly had a moment of REM.

On the higher bunk, my roomie could have taken first place in the sleep-through-anything contest, if we had thought to set one up before she conked out. I tried to feel happy for her, generous rather than envious. But I was so tired!

Then, like a fussy baby who kicks until she collapses, I drifted into oblivion. As it happened, being incarcerated during the time of Covid-19 was my saving grace. Under the ever-blaring lights, I could shield my eyes with the standard-issue face mask, which was black rather than jail-orange.

But soon, way too soon, I found myself awake again, bored, discouraged, miserable.

I sat up on my cot, my roomie's mourning-dove exhales wafting above me. I said to myself, *Self, this is jail, and you are a human being. Right now, you are feeling the way your loved ones have said it feels to be in jail.*

My loved ones. That was it.

If I could stretch my attention beyond these walls, maybe I could feel the prayers, the formidable, powerful prayers—pushing at the doors, at the high, impossible windows, at the water ready to flow from the teensy metal faucet in the corner.

Meanwhile, in that place of metal and concrete, we activists were lucky. We had been trained in our rights. We had jail support to call. As complicated as our connections and periodic disconnections were, we still had one another.

As it turned out, I roomed with the kindest, most openhearted bunkie I could have hoped for: Felix Evans, a Water Protector who identifies as mixed-Korean. Felix and I scavenged tissue paper from the outside of the toilet paper roll, a treasure in that drab and windowless place. We folded miniature peace cranes from torn-off squares in mint green and ivory.

We gave them away as gifts, even though gift-giving was forbidden.

On the second day, when I finally reached my mom's cell phone, all I could do was blubber.

The conversation started like this:

ME: "I'm okay, I'm okay. It's just good to hear your voice."

MOM: "I've been wondering how you've been. I'm so proud of you."

ME: "Really?"

MOM: "Of course. Your brother is proud of you too."

ME: "Really?!"

MOM: "Yes, of course. You're so brave."

ME: "*Really?!*"

I didn't feel brave. I didn't feel anything close to bravery.

But I did feel something like . . . free. I had been loosened, at least for a time, from my long-determined role within the empire.

Since the Crusades and even before, the ever-extracting empire had always demanded loyalty from its chosen ones. Still, on June 7, 2021, I found myself saying no, something like a conscientious objector. Guided by Anishinaabe peoples and the Line 3 resistance, inspired by Lakota-Dakota peoples and the DAPL resistance, I allowed myself to be human. Not a player of a role, not a fulfiller of a function, but a person, a real, living person—made of conscience as well as flesh.

Even before I was born, my very flesh, my very skin, had been commandeered, predetermining which side I would fight for—as if sides were naturally-occurring in the first place. Born into this uniform, I was meant to collude with whiteness like a soldier of the empire. Like my former son-in-law, I was meant to learn a language of punishment, embedded within the culture of whiteness itself.

But now, as a Water Protector and Line 3 defendant, I have seen the workings of whiteness from a perspective I could not have had before. Since whiteness, a race called white, does not genetically exist, I have learned that whiteness is an orchestrated idea. This means, for us white people, that our own self-concept is unreal; our whiteness, an embodiment of an illusion.

Yet how do we white people embody an illusion? Mostly, we learn to tell ourselves that others exist *less*. We learn to tell ourselves that white people are the *most* human, the *most* real. In this imperial worldview, we attempt to add value to our own existence by trying to steal value from somebody else.

As Ijeoma Oluo, a Black scholar and author of *So You Want to Talk about Race,* has said, "This promise—that you will get more because they exist to get less—is woven throughout our entire society. . . . White Supremacy is the nation's oldest pyramid scheme."

Not only has this approach done unimaginable harm to BIPOC communities, it is also, among us white people, a pretty shaky premise for building a positive sense of self.

Or maybe *any* sense of self.

As an enlistee of the empire, I am not supposed to know myself or even *be* myself. I am supposed to stay at my station, perform my function, live as if my existence were an abstraction, a concept, a thought, not an enfleshed relationship with the Earth. From here, as fueled by this collective self-delusion, the ever-extractive empire charges along.

After all, based on a deal with the state, Enbridge got to claim ownership of the lands—in the form of imperial permits. Based on a deal with the police, Enbridge got to secure ownership of the process—in the form of imperial donations.

For me, this is the template of imperialism: Those with power control the ones with less. Those with less power control the ones with even less. And so on.

Indeed, in Christendom, the amalgamation of Empire and Christianity, God is the consummate judge, the ultimate controller, sending you up or sending you down. Even Santa Claus keeps a list, *going to find out who's naughty or nice.* On a daily basis, my bank decides, my landlord decides, the local police force decides. Even the game of Monopoly, that bastion of imperial ideology, presents the risk of jail on the corner.

In my world, this is what being white, a descendant of settler colonialism, has signified. If I comply with whiteness, if I maintain the imperial standards of whiteness, then a wide array of privileges will likely come my way. As long as I act like *us*, as long as I behave like *us*, the full force of whiteness will likely protect me from itself.

But if I don't comply, if I am unwilling or unable, I enter a not-quite-*us*-ness. That vague, diffuse threat in the distance could be realized—a banishment. A punishment. A humiliation of some kind.

Given my early indoctrination by *Perry Mason*, the Kankakee County Sheriff's Office, and the like, I used to assume that the imperial justice system, along with its punitive, carceral logic, was all about actual fairness and genuine justice. But as Michelle Alexander, a Black civil rights lawyer and author of *The New Jim Crow*, has said, "The stigma of criminality functions in much the same way that the stigma of race once did. It justifies a legal, social, and economic boundary between 'us' and 'them.'"

As far as I can tell, another incarceration, another form of prison, is not just the physical structures, the tangible doors and wires and locks; it is the belief that these structures are genuine agents of good—long-term interrupters of violence.

Since the days when Water Protectors from the NoDAPL movement were sent to jails, prisons, and halfway houses, I have been learning a language of prison abolition, yearning to disrupt the actions and assumptions of my own culture, as well as the inherited ways of thinking within my own mind.

Within me, this has been no small revolution, letting go of imperial oppositions: right versus wrong, good versus bad, lawfulness versus violence.

That conviction, at least, is one from which I've been sprung.

TEN

SACRED SUBVERSION

On a crisp, fall evening in the historical Fargo Theatre, it was time.

Rattler walked to the stage of Theatre Two, preparing to accept the 2021 Arc of Justice Award on behalf of the NoDAPL prisoners of war, most of whom lived hundreds of miles away.

Released from Sandstone FCI less than a year before, he wore a breastplate he had beaded there, featuring an American flag in the distress position. As Rattler moved, the bells at the base of the breastplate made a rousing sound. When the bells came to stillness, Rattler addressed the fond group who had assembled there in the cushioned chairs.

Lifting his voice, Rattler said, "Sometimes people call me a hero, just because I'm a political prisoner and I took a stand for the water. But I don't see myself as a hero. I'm just a flea. A flea among fleas. That's what we all are, fleas." As folks in the crowd began to imagine ourselves as tiny, wingless insects, so miniscule as to be practically invisible, he added, "But we sure can make the big dog itch!"

I loved the sudden and spontaneous laughter. Also, in spite of my longtime devotion to the canines in my extended family, I really loved the notion of making the big dog itch—of being small *together*.

That summer, during the Treaty People Gathering, I had wandered over to the awning-covered tables at Pure Bliss Ranch on the White Earth Nation, the central location of the Gathering. While visiting about the rumored menu for the evening's meal (chili and cornbread), as well as where I should take my jail support form (under the tent conveniently marked "Jail Support"), I picked up three photocopied zines.

In different ways, each spoke to the realities that Rattler evoked, of being small together. The thickest of the zines, written by Pipeline Action Network, said, "The more effective we are, the more we risk arrest and other types of repression."

True enough, most of the NoDAPL prisoners of war had been arrested for actions that had, for a time, stopped construction of DAPL. Likewise, many of the Line 3 defendants, including myself, had been arrested for actions that had led to periodic stoppage of Line 3 construction.

The zine *Everyone Calls Themselves an Ally Until It Is Time to Do Some Real Ally Shit* also takes up this point. Printed by Ancestral Pride and written by Xhopakelxhit, a Coast Salish/Nuu-Chah-Nulth/Snuneymuxw matriarch, the zine says, "Ally is a verb; it implies action. . . . Saying you are in solidarity with indigenous people and sovereignty means you accept our laws and reject the illegal laws of the military state that is actively occupying our lands."

Indeed, for this insistence on Indigenous sovereignty, Water Protectors have faced many classes of charges, from citations to misdemeanors to gross misdemeanors to felonies. The various alleged crimes have had names like *obstruction of justice, criminal trespass, fleeing a scene, rioting,* even *theft.*

The last one, theft, is a new one introduced by Minnesota's Hubbard County attorney, who charged a handful of Water Protectors with felonies for locking themselves to equipment and potentially interrupting the profit margins of Enbridge. In charges like these, where the resources of the state are finessed to maximize the resources of an extractive corporation, the inner workings of the empire become excruciatingly apparent.

After all, as John Trudell is often quoted as saying, "I'm not looking to overthrow the American government—the corporate state already has."

Borrowing many words from Xhopakelxhit, the most accurate terminology for these so-called crimes, instead of theft or trespass or rioting, might be *accepting Indigenous laws and rejecting the illegal laws of the corporatized military state that is actively occupying Indigenous lands.*

When these illegal laws are so embedded in the identity and function of the imperial state, it can be hard to imagine how a local county in the US (Hubbard County or otherwise) would even accept the primacy of Indigenous laws, until there is a collective reckoning among settlers of this land. During the summer of 2021, the sheriff of Clearwater County was widely lauded for giving Water Protectors at Fire Light Camp, which was led by Anishinaabe elders, the space to complete a weeklong prayer ceremony, instead of conducting the intimidating mass arrests that we activists faced in Hubbard County. But at the end of seven days, even he made certain all Water Protectors, including Anishinaabe and

Dakota Water Protectors, had vacated traditional Anishinaabe and Dakota lands—so that Line 3 construction could continue.

Regarding such illegal laws, the last zine I picked up at the Gathering has plenty to add.

In *Accomplices Not Allies: Abolishing the Ally Industrial Complex*, Indigenous Action Media says, "Accomplice: noun. A person who helps another commit a crime. . . . When we fight back or forward, together, becoming complicit in a struggle towards liberation, we are accomplices."

Ever since I first read those words, I find myself returning to them.

Back or forward.

Together.

Complicit.

Liberation.

Accomplices.

Whatever choices I make, I am perpetually deciding about my complicity—with collective liberation or with Empire. Which crimes do I choose? What kind of accompliceship? What kind of allegiance?

As Indigenous Action Media goes on to say, "We need to know who has our backs, or more appropriately: who is with us, at our sides?"

I hope that's where I live—together, side by side.

Still, *together* can be a complicated concept, probably for anyone who lives within the military-backed corporate state and certainly for a white person like me.

Across US history, pro-imperial white people have consistently accused anti-imperial white people of participating in the wrong togetherness, altogether. In spite of the hold of whiteness, in spite of the compelling illusion of whiteness, some white people just haven't acted white enough, colonial enough, obedient to imperial whiteness *enough*. Often, such anti-imperial white people are variously punished, justified by the label—accurate or otherwise—of anarchists, communists, socialists, abolitionists, hippies, radicals, outside agitators, and even so-called race traitors and terrorists.

In the first half of the 1900s, the US passed many Anarchist Exclusion Acts in order to target and deport immigrants, including many European immigrants, who resisted US American imperialism. These laws didn't just attack dissenters who advocated an overthrow of the US government; they also threatened immigrants who held dissenting views of other kinds—magazine editors who published dissenting thoughts, venue owners who rented space for dissenting events, and those who were misidentified as dissenters because of their associations or their profile. The risks of deportation were so great, Emma Goldman, an iconic Russian American anarchist, went underground for a time, adopting the identity E.G. Smith and ultimately being sent back to Russia.

As human beings were arrested, detained, deported, and banished to unknown locations, Goldman declared, "The rack, the thumbscrew, and the knout are still with us; so are the convict's garb and the social wrath, all conspiring against the spirit . . ."

Still, in the face of all that Goldman has described, white dissenters aren't so difficult to find, even if many of their names have been lost, especially among female and nonbinary folks.

In 1836, there was Amos Augustus Phelps, a minister and outspoken abolitionist with the American Anti-Slavery Society. In Connecticut, he was bombarded with stones and glass shards after publicly preaching against slavery. In Georgia, a newspaper offered a ten-thousand-dollar bounty for his head.

In 1915, there was Joe Hill, targeted as an organizer for the anti-racist Industrial Workers of the World (IWW). He was framed for murder and killed by firing squad in Salt Lake City, Utah. After his death, loved ones placed his ashes into hundreds of envelopes and sent them to supporters around the US and the world.

Throughout the early 1900s, there were hundreds, even thousands, of IWW members of various sexes and identities, including white, who organized extensive labor strikes and resisted the World War I draft. As they rose against the colonial state and its capitalist companions, they were routinely imprisoned, murdered, and tortured by official as well as vigilante forces. In an action that foreshadowed the unleashing of water cannons against NoDAPL Water Protectors, police sometimes sprayed strikers with icy water in the depths of winter.

In 1960, there was Paul LaPrad, who received especially violent assaults by heavy-footed white attackers during the Nashville lunch counter sit-ins. After being beaten, he pulled himself back onto the seat, covered with blood and bruises.

Shortly thereafter, in 1961, a married couple named Frances and Walter Bergman—Freedom Riders on the southbound bus—were horribly beaten by white supremacists in Anniston, Alabama, after the bus had been firebombed. Then, having boarded the next bus with Frances, Walter Bergman was again ferociously beaten at the outskirts of Birmingham. In his early sixties at the time, Bergman suffered a stroke and permanently lost the ability to walk.

Not much later, in 1965, Unitarian minister James Reeb made the journey from his home in Dorchester, Massachusetts, to Selma,

Alabama, answering the call of Martin Luther King, Jr., who had urged clergy from across the US to come. Following the murder of Jimmie Lee Jackson, a young Black civil rights worker, by a white state trooper—as well as Bloody Sunday, when white police violently attacked six hundred civil rights activists—the Selma-to-Birmingham march was meant to demand voting rights for all. After a symbolic march to the Edmund Pettis Bridge, Reeb and two other white people were attacked by a group of white supremacists outside a restaurant. Having been clubbed in the head, Reeb died two days later.

More recently, in 2020, there were Joseph Rosenbaum, Anthony Huber, and Gaige Grosskreutz, all of whom were shot by another young white man at a Black Lives Matter (BLM) rally in Kenosha, Wisconsin. The rally had been organized to honor Jacob Blake, a Black man who was partially paralyzed by a white police officer who shot him multiple times but had not been charged. In response, anti-BLM organizers summoned so-called patriots to help "protect lives and property." The gunman brought a semiautomatic rifle. In 2021, a jury found him not guilty, though Grosskreutz was wounded and Rosenbaum and Huber both died.

Again in 2021, there was Jessica Reznicek, a member of the Catholic Worker Movement, who admitted to tampering with the Dakota Access Pipeline in Iowa. Charged as a domestic terrorist, she was sentenced to many years in federal prison and an exorbitant fine. As Unicorn Riot has reported, Kelcy Warren, CEO of Energy Transfer Partners, claimed that Reznicek was "somebody who needs to be removed from the gene pool," much as eugenicists a hundred years before him might have said about immigrant dissenters. Additionally, the FBI special agent in charge sought to make an example of Reznicek, suggesting her harsh sentence would act as a "deterrent."

Finally, once again in 2021, there was Ruby Montoya, co-arrestee with Jessica Reznicek. The situation is complicated, but shortly after Reznicek's sentencing, Chase Iron Eyes, cofounder of the Lakota People's Law Project, made a statement that Ruby Montoya was "invited by an Indigenous community to protect water and help safeguard sacred lands." And then, like Jessica Reznicek, "she showed up."

Across time, there have been many people who showed up— many white people, even—both countless and uncounted, who have committed themselves to shared humanity and shared existence more than the supposed sanctity, the *us*-ness, of whiteness.

Of course, we white people don't enter the same realm of otherness that settler colonialism would reserve for BIPOC folks. While interacting with the imperial system or even its threat of punishment, I still have an escape hatch I could spring. I could still proclaim my whiteness, my allegiance to imperialism, and by disavowing my own former disobedience, I could possibly catch a break.

That's exactly what an unnamed white abolitionist did in 1835, according to the Princeton & Slavery Project, when a posse of about sixty white students from Princeton University, as well as a handful of local white residents, attempted to lynch him. After extracting the white abolitionist from a Black neighborhood, they took him captive and threatened to hang him, tar and feather him, and then some. Flooded with terror, he pleaded that he had a wife and family out of state.

For this white abolitionist, the white crowd recanted—on one condition.

He had to swear "by all that is holy," they said, to renounce abolition for the rest of his days. Fearfully, he agreed, at which point the crowd paraded him in front of Princeton Theological Seminary. There, they shouted that any abolitionist seminarians would be "served in the same manner if they caught any of them."

Today, I wonder what happens when those of us who are white, those who descend from settler colonialism, do not—or somehow cannot—spring that white escape hatch.

What is the realm between *us*-ness and otherness? In a colonial paradigm, where is the space to be fully, deeply human?

Indeed, when faced with another way to be, the considerable limits of settler colonialism often become clear. They certainly did for thousands of people, including thousands of white people like me, both at the Standing Rock Camps and in the collaborative years that have followed.

As far as I can tell, this experience is not new, this longing to find a way of life that feels more like life. According to Sebastian Junger, a journalist who comes from settler colonial culture, Benjamin Franklin often lamented that English settlers regularly left their villages to join Indigenous communities, but Indigenous people almost never left their communities to join English settlements.

Roughly three hundred years later, in spite of a much-noted tendency among white settlers to romanticize Indigenous experiences, the aggregate effects of colonial violence against Indigenous people have become very real. Maria Yellow Horse Brave Heart, a Lakota social worker and trauma researcher, has found that such violence often manifests as historical trauma, which Brave Heart defines as "cumulative emotional and psychological wounding over the lifespan and across generations, emanating from massive group trauma." As Brave Heart and many collaborators have shown, traditional spirituality can support Indigenous people and communities to transcend even the worst, most egregious imperial violence.

To the best of my understanding, many traditional Indigenous spiritualities teach that humanity is a circle. Likewise, countless BIPOC leaders, ever since they first met us white folks, have been calling on white people to act as if we're part of the circle, to understand that the freedom and healing of each human being supports and mutually depends upon the freedom and healing of the whole.

Much like I imagine LaDonna Brave Bull Allard would have wished, her funeral gave an occasion for such healing. As complicated as human events, including human memorials, can be, it was a potent coming-together, a Water Protector reunion there on the Standing Rock reservation, on the bleachers and folding chairs of the Cannonball Community Center. At the microphone and also among the bleachers, a number of people proclaimed that while the loss of her life was great, her power was greater now.

Soon, an elder from Standing Rock, whose name I wish I knew, said, "I would like all the Water Protectors to stand up."

While people around me stood here and there, I almost didn't. Being part of the white settler culture that had driven all these pipelines through in the first place, it took me years to believe that I could be called a Water Protector.

In that moment, in the invitation to stand, I wondered about my place. Was I a Water Protector? Was it even possible for me to be a Water Protector?

I could identify myself or not—the invitation was clear.

Something about the crowd, the collective presence of Water Protectors, reminded me of the early-morning voice of Guy Dull

Knife on the microphone at Oceti Sakowin Camp: *Water Protectors,
get up! You're not here to sleep! You're here to protect the water!*

Recalling this summons, this provocation, I remembered that
my body had been there at Camp, just as my body was sitting here
now on the hard wooden bleachers. Maybe, having been invited by
the movement to serve as a Water Protector, I could acknowledge
that I had answered the call.

So, to Matt Lone Bear's right and Mary Wilson's left, I rose.

After many of us waved or stood, the elder asked the rest of the
crowd to look at us, to notice. Then, as people turned their heads,
the elder said, "These Water Protectors had a dream. And now their
hearts are broken."

Yes, very much.

To be witnessed in that place, so close in space to the former
Standing Rock Camps, so close in space to each other, was a prayer.
After all, as Abraham Joshua Heschel once said, "Prayer is mean-
ingless unless it is subversive."

That is my fondest wish, to live my life as a prayer of sacred
subversion. A prayer of sacred accompliceship. Fighting back and
also forward, reaching forward and also back.

There are many ways to do so, many people doing the same. In
the months when I needed a lawyer, Natali Segovia of the Water
Protector Legal Collective helped me to find her. Before that, in the
months before I needed representation, Patricia Handlin, a white
attorney and seasoned movement lawyer, had been out there repre-
senting other activists, defending other Water Protectors.

And back and back.

And forward and forward.

In my life, this is how I strive for accompliceship.

Accompliceship doesn't just mean a white person doing some radical stuff. It's all kinds of people doing all kinds of radical stuff—from the disruptive, to the nutritious, to the absolutely tedious—for each other, for those yet to come, for the wider world, and also for ourselves. It's not a badge, like SHERIFF, that you can pin on your own shirt pocket; it's a way of showing up.

As I participate in this mutual work, it seems to me that I practice being human. In this practice, I have been taught that accompliceship means taking the lead of those most impacted by the struggle—or assuming the lead when I am among the most impacted—as a way of being true to everyone's liberation, to everyone's authentic participation in mending the circle of life.

Sometimes the circle needs lots of mending.

Sometimes we mutual allies and accomplices get pushed back, pushed down, and pushed apart, often by the culture from which we white people come.

This means that white people's relationship with whiteness is not just a matter of ancestry or even identity but also a matter of personal conscience and spiritual dignity.

Ever since I first encountered the writings of W. E. B. Du Bois, I have been stirred by his examination of whiteness. In 1946, this is what he had to say about the white worker: "He began to want, not comfort for all men, but power over other men . . . He did not love humanity." Instead, as Du Bois declared, the white worker simply hated those who were Black.

On the topic of love and hate, this admonishment by James Baldwin from *Letter from a Region in My Mind,* written in 1962, really speaks to me:

White people in this country will have quite enough to do in learning how to accept and love themselves and each other, and when
they have achieved this—which will not be tomorrow and may
very well be never—the Negro problem will no longer exist, for
it will no longer be needed.

If we human beings called white could truly love ourselves and
each other, who could we yet be?

Maybe, when we white settler colonial people stop holding the
impossible, specious line between *us* and *them*, we can remember,
together, how to be human. A way forward might emerge: returning lands, honoring treaties, making reparations, stopping pipelines, and inching ourselves back toward the circle.

Loving ourselves, loving one another, may look a lot like loving
all the world.

In this love, we might even release ourselves from the prison of
making prisons of many kinds.

Having lived on both sides of the jail walls, if for a few days so
far, I have a clearer view of my own imperial, carceral culture. I
have learned that the empire protects its favored ones, withholding
the violence by which it is sustained—as long as its people comply,
as long as its favorites behave and look like *us*.

But when *us* and *them* collude, the empire seeks to reassert dom-
inance and control, because a shared way of life, far beyond the
empire, has become possible.

Sitting in jail, I soothed myself by polishing memories of Oceti
Sakowin Camp—the voices singing late into the starstruck night,
laughing suddenly like the breeze, praying at the fire, calling out,

"Mni Wiconi!" The smell of fire smoke in my hair. The soggy dirt when the rains came down. The warm, buttery glow of the medic and healer tent. The dishes, the always-and-forever dishes. The giant cans of tomatoes, one and then another, that we opened, emptied, stirred. The people. The joining rivers. The present and healing Earth, tender beneath my feet, steady beneath my back, around me and also within me.

Maybe I will spend the rest of my life relishing these moments, holding them in the pocket of my soul, as they continue to give my being the shape of aliveness.

As Nick Estes and Jaskiran Dhillon, Indigenous scholars and editors of *Standing with Standing Rock,* have said about the Standing Rock movement, "It provided, for a brief moment in time, a collective vision of what the future could be."

That vision, that future, is how I long to live.

In freedom. In liberation. *True* freedom and liberation.

Mathew King, a Lakota Wisdomkeeper and grandchild of Crazy Horse and Sitting Bull, has often been quoted as saying, "Only one thing's sadder than remembering you once were free, and that's forgetting you once were free. That would be the saddest thing of all. That's one thing we Indians will never do."

I would like to remember that my own people once were free. I would like to remember a state of genuine freedom, a palpable, sustained state of aliveness.

Indeed, as Mathew King once told an entourage of white people who had visited him on the Pine Ridge reservation, "I know why you're here! White Man came to this country and forgot his original Instructions. We have never forgotten our Instructions. So you're here looking for the Instructions you lost."

Having lived within white colonial culture for many decades, I resonate with Mathew King's declaration that there is much we white people have forgotten. Yet there seem to be many white people who believe that we, as white people in the US (even as US citizens in general), haven't forgotten anything—not our instructions, not our purpose, not even how to be free. Popular US American slogans—"land of the free," "live free or die," "freedom isn't free"—all suggest that the settler colonial system can bring genuine freedom, can even remember how.

But there is a difference between being genuinely free and relatively free*er*, a difference between actual freedom and a lesser state of repression.

In just one example, when white people, usually female, go missing, there's little doubt that they get more attention, resources, and press than do Indigenous people, Black people, or people of color in general when they go missing. Certainly, in the white colonial system, white lives are held to be more valuable, more noteworthy than BIPOC lives.

At the same time, the white people who get kidnapped still get kidnapped, despite the gross privileges of whiteness. In an imperial system, even the lives of white people—even those with more access to power—don't end up fully valued, fully significant, or fully protected from preventable harm.

These days, as I learn more about truly human, Earth-rooted ways of being, I have come to believe that we white people, including myself, also need liberation from the empire. If imperialism in its colonial applications were a supportable, sustainable system, then we white people, as favored by this system, would pretty much have it made. If all that mattered was being stationed on a higher rung of a fast-collapsing ladder, then empire would be an excellent system for white people—or for anyone, any celebrity, capitalist, or millionaire who could get to a higher rung. Certainly, global climate change, as wrought by imperial values, might end up destroying every living being, but those on the top would know, at least, that they were the last to fall.

Somehow, all of this reminds me of the Homestead Act of 1862, which amounted to taking 270 million acres of land from Indigenous peoples. In the process, it further conceived a culture of separation and distance among homesteaders, most of whom were white. In order to get the land, homesteaders had to keep themselves remote from one another on patches of roughly one hundred and sixty acres each. Instead of clustering together in contiguous communities, which would have been more ecologically and culturally sustainable, settlers spread themselves far and wide, creating barriers from the wider world, and also from one another.

Then and now, to proclaim white settler culture—the practices and material attainments of white living—as an aspirational standard for humanity would be to collude with the empire itself. It would mean assenting to the notion that it's possible to win when so many others lose.

I keep coming back to a placard I saw in about 2000 at Pride Fest in Chicago: TARGET MARKETING ISN'T LIBERATION. Since I had never heard of anything called *target marketing* at the time, I had no idea what the placard was trying to say. But I kept chewing on the meaning. At last, I figured it out. Just because someone wants to sell us things doesn't mean we're free.

Target marketing isn't liberation.

After her legendary participation in the Stonewall rebellion, Sylvia Rivera powerfully challenged the mainstream queer liberation movement for its collusion with the white colonial paradigm, for preferencing mainstream middle-class values over essential human rights.

Much like Rivera, the person who held the sign about *target marketing* was urging us onlookers not to confuse capitalism or inclusion in the capitalist profit margin with queer liberation—not to accept the sudden inclusion of queer people in ad campaigns as the consummation of our struggles, but to insist on broader visions, to insist on being more deeply, freely human. After all, in a life-degrading system, every human being's humanity, every organism's organicity, is at stake.

In 1980, John Trudell had this to say about systems that degrade human life:

> They wish to continue to rule the world on violence and repression, and we are all the victims of that violence and repression. We as the indigenous people of the Western hemisphere have been resisting this oppression for 500 years. We know that the black people have been resisting it for at least that long. And we know that the white people have had to endure it for thousands of years.

We white people have endured it as well as sustained it. Feared it as well as protected it with our very lives.

Since my own culture was crafted to maintain what Trudell has called the American Corporate State, I have rarely felt free from it. Familiar, but not at peace. Not at home. Not at ease.

I can't help recalling how Isabel Wilkerson, in *Caste*, has described another recent empire: "Even the favored ones were diminished and driven to fear . . ." Wilkerson describes a teenage girl who took a tape measure to her face as she scrutinized herself, internalizing external judgments, desperate to belong, terrified of the consequences of not belonging. An Aryan girl living in Nazi Germany, she was perpetually afraid of not being Aryan enough, of facing the fate of non-Aryan *others*.

Whatever the threat may be in our time, we who have been capriciously claimed by the empire often sense that it could, just as capriciously, unclaim us. During the summer of 2021, we activists in the back of the police van, that roving jail on wheels, were getting the punishment that the empire, the modern-day collusion of Enbridge and Minnesota, said we deserved—even those of us who are white.

In empire, power rules. In empire, power is truth.

As Kwame Ture, a Black freedom leader best known as Stokely Carmichael, once said:

> If a white man wants to lynch me, that's his problem. If he's got the power to lynch me, that's my problem. Racism is not a question of attitude; it's a question of power. Racism gets its power from capitalism. Thus, if you're antiracist, whether you know it or not, you must be anti-capitalist. The power for racism, the power for sexism, comes from capitalism, not an attitude.

White racism as an extension of capitalism, capitalism as an extension of colonialism, and colonialism as an extension of imperialism have never been viable ways of life. Indeed, when imperial whiteness wins, everybody loses. Even we white people lose, to one extent or another.

When Energy Transfer Partners seemed to win the conflict over DAPL, and when Enbridge Energy Corporation seemed to win the conflict over Line 3, even their billionaire CEOs, much like the rest of us, lost another stretch of life—the lands, the creatures, the woods, the plants, the waters.

For generations, colonial land grabs have been part of an intricate capitalist system of land ownership and property expansion. Yet compared to the health and vitality of the Earth two hundred, let alone five hundred, years ago, even the wealthiest colonists today—with full access to jets and passports and yachts—have never experienced the fullest, most vigorous glory of this planet, something that the humblest person thousands of years ago would likely have experienced every day.

As far as I can tell, when one group of people bases its existence on taking from the rest, every living being is diminished—because stealing life doesn't guarantee life. Stealing liberty doesn't guarantee liberty. Stealing lands doesn't even guarantee access to those lands.

LaDonna Brave Bull Allard often spoke about the naming of Sacred Stone Camp.

In the story LaDonna told, a marvel would occur at the convergence of the Missouri and Cannonball Rivers, years before imperial damming. The rivers, in their turning together, created Iŋyaŋ Wakháŋagapi Othí—translated into English as *sacred stones*—shaped like spheres, often wider than a three-year-old's reach.

Over a hundred years ago, white settlers fell in love with them too.

Cannonballs, they named them.

From sacred stones to cannonballs, from reverence to weaponry. This may be the CliffsNotes of my people.

With the construction of the Oahe Dam in the 1950s, the Missouri River flooded nearly sixty-five thousand acres of land at Standing Rock and displaced nearly two hundred Indigenous families. The confluence of the rivers changed. The prosperity of the people changed. The sacred stones, the so-called cannonballs, stopped coming altogether.

Taking away the pattern of the confluence, the source of the sacred stones, didn't mean my people had them.

It meant no one did.

Today, I find myself wondering—could they return? Like the Sierra Nevada red fox, virtually extinct until it showed up in Oregon in 2012, could they come back?

What would it take?

Many times, I believe I have seen the spirit that could make such wonders possible—especially in the context of the Water Protector movement.

In 2016, I was getting overwhelmed by the Bismarck-Mandan faith community, in its apparent refusal to participate in the movement at Standing Rock. As arrests came, and blizzards came, and supplies, supplies, supplies came, tens of thousands of people kept passing through our towns. But other local congregations didn't openly engage.

Having heard about our small congregation's sense of overwhelm, my long-distance colleagues asked me what would be needed. I'll never forget the phone calls with Ashley Horan; Elizabeth Nguyen, a Vietnamese American minister; Nora Rasman, a white activist; and, later, Ian Evison, also a white minister. I could scarcely believe the question.

Soon after hearing my answer, they sent—literally sent, via airplanes, trains, and cars—an extended series of Water Protector ministers of various cultural identities who were willing to do whatever needed to be done. The ministers in residence, as we called them, hauled stuff, coordinated food deliveries, witnessed court proceedings, picked up people from jail, organized volunteer needs, helped maintain the interfaith yurt, scrubbed a roomful of children's toys, and then some. Meanwhile, people from coast to coast held actions, raised funds, and made prayers. And on. And on. And on.

This logistical ministry, this mutual accompliceship, was something Rattler has since called the humble work of fleas.

In another such moment, after Little Feather was sentenced on federal charges, those of us in the newly forming NoDAPL Political Prisoners Support Committee realized that his difficult situation would probably be the trend. The NoDAPL prisoners of war would probably do years of time in unforeseen facilities, hundreds and even thousands of miles from home.

Once again, the imperial state was treating relationships, even home itself, like a commodity to be exchanged, a product to be withheld, a reward as well as a punishment for certain kinds of behavior— as if relationships, much like water, weren't the very basis of life.

Because people from many backgrounds had been welcomed as relatives at Camp, physically onsite or spiritually from a distance, my friends and I began to wonder what it might mean for those who had been welcomed as relatives to respond as relatives if incarcerated Water Protectors arrived in their vicinities.

With guidance from the NoDAPL political prisoners, I worked with Karen Brammer, who was back in New York after her stay at Camp, to reach out to congregations and networks across the US, telling them there might be a relative doing time in their vicinity. We asked, according to the wishes of the political prisoners and families, would folks be willing to visit, write letters, raise funds, offer homestays, and provide rides for visiting loved ones?

Overwhelmingly, they did, in different ways and places: Pennsylvania. West Virginia. Minnesota. Texas. Indiana. New Mexico. And beyond.

Maybe, in the work of being accomplices with other accomplices—not just accomplices for an ideal, but directly with and for each other, in the flesh and in the spirit—that's when all kinds of people from all kinds of backgrounds can taste, touch, glimpse, and even live liberation.

Maybe wonders are possible. Maybe collective liberation is possible.

But still, there's this uneasy question of whiteness.

Leoyla Cowboy used to wear a red and white baseball cap—in a satirical response to the MAGA cap often worn by Trump supporters.

Famously, the Trump hats say MAKE AMERICA GREAT AGAIN.

With advice on how America might become great again, Leoyla's cap replies, GO BACK TO EUROPE.

The first time I saw it, my heart jumped a beat. Should *I* go back to Europe? Who would go with me? Where would I go?

Then I reasoned, *She's talking to other people, the other white people who wear those MAGA hats. Not me. Right?*

To this day, I have never asked Leoyla about her cap. It seems she has a right to express an opinion about the ubiquity of white settlers without being asked to explain. It used to itch at me, though.

As my mentor, Clyde Grubbs, has told me more than once,

"Among my Indigenous colleagues, it's often said that life would be much better if settlers would just settle."

If settlers would just get grounded, if settlers would just *be*, is how I hear it. Yet looking into the exacting face of history, with all the pain begetting pain, trauma begetting trauma, violence begetting violence, *being* can be the hardest thing to do.

As uneasy as it can make me, facing my people's history certainly feels real. Maybe being real and attending to what's real is one way of inching closer, drawing nearer, to an authentic way of life, a more human and embodied way of being.

On that topic, Adam Lawrence Dyer, an African American/ Afro Caribbean minister and friend, has implored us white people to find another way to be white.

These days, his admonition keeps calling on my heart and mind. Of the various statements I have heard white people make about what it means to be white, I have rarely aspired to a word of it, whether because it feels painfully true or painfully false. Certainly, we white folks are going to need another way to be—out of respect for the planet, for BIPOC folks, for one another, and also for our own selves. In the future, as we contend with the injustice embedded in our culture, a new word for us may become possible. In the meantime, if we take the call to accompliceship to heart, could white come to mean this?

People who used to be fake, who then got real.

People who used to be violent, who then became whole.

People who used to be takers, who then gave back—returning lands, sharing abundance, making reparations with every breath.

Later during the summer when I was arrested, I carpooled with Tracey L. Wilkie to the Shell River. We arrived just in time for a special get-together of women at Shell Camp, one of numerous Line 3 resistance camps.

Like many people who had assembled under the thick, high trees, we piled ourselves into a sturdy canoe and paddled toward the construction site. The purpose was to pray, leave flowers, and honor the otherwise desecrated land.

Somehow, we chose the trick canoe of the fleet, the one that took us to each side of the river and back again in a zig-zagging pattern of cattail-viewing splendor. Being completely unable to paddle from point A to point B and then laughing ourselves out of any kind of muscle control, we were soon at the back of the bunch.

From there, we watched the horses and riders trotting through the spray. We watched famous people visiting with not-so-famous people. We also watched lots and lots of cattails charging into view as we crisscrossed the water.

Not long after we arrived at the gathering spot, a spontaneous round dance came together, there in the clear, shallow river. There were chants. There were conversations. There were flowers laid at the site. Soon, Taysha Martineau, an Anishinaabe Water Protector and founder of Camp Migizi, spoke these words into the wading crowd, "I don't want to hear another non-Indigenous person apologize to me for their roots—or lack thereof—again. We are building a new foundation here. . . . You are the embodiment of everything good that your ancestors brought here with them."

I hope to embody my ancestors in a way that honors them and the roots they have given me. After all, since human beings are some of the newest beings on the Earth, most of the planet really is my ancestors.

What would it mean to embody that kind of truth?

A couple of months before the Shell River canoe trip, on the night I got home from jail, I took my usual walk along the meandering Red River. I greeted its curves, delighted in its tree-filled nooks. I wandered beside its overgrown banks. Before long, I found myself talking to the river. It wasn't the first time I had found myself speaking to the water. To oaks and chokecherries and cottonwoods. To the creatures in the distance. To the Spirit animating all.

On this particular day, I said, "Well, I just got out of jail. Please don't take offense, but I went there for you. And me. For all of us, you could say. Anyway, it's really good to be home."

As I wandered along, I happened upon a family group of beavers. One. Two.

Four of them, sleek and ever determined.

While I stood on the soggy bank, they allowed me to be among them as they gathered willow fronds in their teeth, swooping up to the onyx surface and then lunging down, down, down, to places unknown.

On that particular night, as the sun went pink at my shoulder, I stood there so long, I could sense the soles of my feet taking root, through weeds and sand and rock, to the living waters below, to the fire at the center of the planet.

Among the beavers, the curious deer, the willow brush at the shore, and the birds of the dusky air, I felt as if I was one of them— in a place, a living world, where I belonged.

In that moment among moments, as a creature among creatures, maybe I was.

GRATITUDE

To the Water Protector movement, thank you.

To Line 3 jail support and court support, thank you.

To the Bismarck-Mandan Unitarian Universalist Congregation, thank you.

To the members of the NoDAPL Political Prisoners Support Committee, thank you.

To my immediate family, both chosen and serendipitous—Kathy Boyens, Randy Van Fossan, David Van Fossan, Carl Boyens, Teresa Trudeau, Marta Gryglak, Michaela Miller, Raquel Campbell, Shanée Ford, Nevajeh Campbell, Brynlee Ford, Chaz Campbell, Eri Shinn, and the many loved ones of my loved ones—thank you.

To the readers who generously made this project possible at all—Laurie Baker, Peter Huff, Meg Luther Lindholm, Rattler (Michael) Markus, Tim Mathern, Joseph McNeil, Jr., Tim Mentz, Carol Kapaun Ratchenski, and Mary Wilson—thank you.

To the mentors and teachers who have guided my ministry, my writing, and my work—Aunty Bea Ballangarry, Sandra Bercier, Katie Brink, Annie Brook, Lyn Burton, Christine Caldwell, Susan Campbell Bartoletti, Paul Capetz, Amanda Cockrell, Jen Crow, Janne Eller-Isaacs, Rob Eller-Isaacs, Ian Evison, Joan Flood, Lisa Rowe Fraustino, Lisa Friedman, Alika Galloway, Lynn Gardner, Clyde Grubbs, Glen Herrington-Hall, Lola Huwe, Ryan Kennedy, Jim Lawrence, Pamela Muirhead, Bonnie Palecek, Brian Palecek, Louise M. Paré, Martha Postlethwaite, Carolyn Pressler, Marilyn Salmon, Martin Shanahan, Danny Sheehan, Lanny Sinkin, JD Stahl, Straight from the Rez Mike, CW Sullivan III, Larry Thiele, Jim Winjum, Colleen Woodley, many ministerial formation committees, many women's studies professors, and more—thank you.

To the collaborators, loved ones, and conversation partners who have inspired my dreams and visions—Juice (James) Abalos, Liz Anderson, Martin Avery, Lisa Bassett, Badger (Olive) Bias, Karen Brammer, Preston Brock, Lisa Brown, Julia Brown Wolf, Ruth Buffalo, Kathy Burek, Janis Cheney, Leoyla Cowboy, Micha Ben David, Adam Lawrence Dyer, Sandra Freeman, AJ Galazen, Ronya Galligo-Hoblit, Ann Gilmore, Little Feather (Michael) Giron, Eda Gordon, Pat Handlin, Dee Hendriks, Hannah Hafter, Ashley Horan, Barry Hoskins, Janelle Hoskins, Julie Huwe, Ikce Wicasa, Jeff Iron Cloud, Red Fawn Janis, Charles (Scorch) Jordan, Bee Kakac, Pamela Kern, Leet Killer, Judith Lane, Carol Jean Larsen, Joe Larson, Matt Lone Bear, Liz Loos, Dennis Lyon, Susan Lyon, Steve Martinez, Sheridan Seaboy-McNeil, Melanie Angel Moniz, Brennon (Bravo1) Nastacio, Elizabeth Nguyen, Barry Nelson, Karen Northcott, Mylinda Ogundipe, Victor Ogundipe, Christina Ortiz, Dion Ortiz, Gina Peltier, Nora Rasman, Tanya RedRoad,

Colleen Reinke, Darren Renville, Monisha Ríos, Tandi Rogers, Cesraea Rumpf, Wayde Schafer, Amanda Strauss, Aly Tharp, Ann Trondle-Price, Deanna Vandiver, Angry Bird (James) White, Lynnda White, Tracey L. Wilkie, Karen Wills, Paul Zondo, many friends in Gumbaynggirr country, and more—thank you.

To the UU Trauma Response Ministry who helped our Bismarck-Mandan congregation move through the intensity of the NoDAPL conflict—Bret Lortie, Rosemary Bray McNatt, and Leslie Trew (the first time), and Sally Hartman, Rita Chamblin, and Elizabeth Stephens (the second time)—thank you.

To the ministers in residence who made all the difference in the world—Karen Brammer, Terri Burnor, Marisol Caballero, Kelli Clement, Jill Cowie, Carie Johnsen, David Kraemer, Amanda Poppei, Meg Riley, Fred Small, Laura Smidzik, Julie Taylor, and Laura Thompson, as well as Jack Gaede and numerous other Water Protectors—thank you.

To the creative and justice-rooted entities that have given energy to my life—7 Medicines Collective, AIMS (African Immigrant and Minority Services), Authentic Ministry, the Bush Foundation, Chalice Lighters, Central Dakota PFLAG, Dragon Jane, Faithify, Fargo-Moorhead UU Church, Fargo-Moorhead Water Protectors, Green Sanctuary, the Group That Opened the Box, Hawkinson Foundation, International Leonard Peltier Defense Committee, Lakota People's Law Project, Minnesota UU Social Justice Alliance, MMIP Task Force, Mustard Seed Catholic Community, North Dakota Peace Coalition, Pinwheel Modern Dance Company, Sacred Stone Camp, Shell Camp, Side with Love, Spirit of Hope Catholic Community, Stories and Songs of the People, Toxic Taters, UU College of Social Justice, UU Ministry for Earth,

UUSC, Water Protector Legal Collective, Welcome Connection, and more—thank you.

To the staff at Skinner House Books—especially Mary Benard, Larisa Hohenboken, and Pierce Alquist—and their collaborators Sunshine Wolfe and Larissa Melo Pienkowski, who gave such heart to this collaboration, thank you.

To all who work for justice on behalf of future generations, thank you.

To all who have come before, thank you.

To beings of all kinds who enliven this glorious planet, thank you.

To the Spirit of Life and Love, thank you.

SUGGESTED READING

Michelle Alexander. *The New Jim Crow: Mass Incarceration in the Age of Colorblindness.* The New Press, 2011.

James Baldwin. *James Baldwin: Collected Essays.* Library of America, 1998.

Austin Channing Brown. *I'm Still Here: Black Dignity in a World Made for Whiteness.* Convergent Books, 2018.

Paul Buhle and Nicole Schulman, editors. *Wobblies! A Graphic History of the Industrial Workers of the World.* Verso, 2005.

Christine Caldwell and Lucia Bennett Leighton, editors. *Oppression and the Body: Roots, Resistance, and Resolutions.* North Atlantic Books, 2018.

Ta-Nehisi Coates. *Between the World and Me.* Spiegel & Grau, 2015.

James H Cone. *The Cross and the Lynching Tree.* Orbis Books, 2013.

Chris Crass. *Towards the "Other America": Anti-Racist Resources for White People Taking Action for Black Lives Matter.* Chalice Press, 2016.

Kimberlé Crenshaw. *On Intersectionality: Essential Writings.* The New Press, 2017.

Angela Y. Davis. *Are Prisons Obsolete?* Seven Stories Press, 2003.

Angela Y. Davis, Gina Dent, Erica R. Meiners, and Beth E. Richie. *Abolition. Feminism. Now.* Haymarket Books, 2022.

Vine Deloria Jr. *God Is Red: A Native View of Religion.* 1972. North American Press, 1993.

W. E. B. Du Bois. *The Souls of Black Folk.* 1903. Dover Thrift Editions, 2016.

Roxanne Dunbar-Ortiz. *An Indigenous Peoples' History of the United States.* Beacon Press, 2014.

Roxanne Dunbar-Ortiz and Dina Gilio-Whitaker. *"All the Real Indians Died Off" and 20 Other Myths about Native Americans.* Beacon Press, 2016.

Michael Eric Dyson. *Tears We Cannot Stop: A Sermon to White America.* St. Martin's Press, 2017.

Nick Estes. *Our History Is the Future: Standing Rock Versus the Dakota Access Pipeline, and the Long Tradition of Indigenous Resistance.* Verso, 2019.

Nick Estes and Jaskiran Dhillon, editors. *Standing with Standing Rock: Voices from the #NoDAPL Movement.* University of Minnesota Press, 2019.

Andy Fisher. *Radical Ecopsychology: Psychology in the Service of Life.* SUNY Press, 2013.

Crystal M. Fleming. *How To Be Less Stupid About Race.* Beacon Press, 2019.

Ruth Wilson Gilmore. *Abolition Geography: Essays Toward Liberation.* Verso, 2022.

Mirame Kaba. *We Do This 'Til We Free Us: Abolitionist Organizing and Transforming Justice*. Haymarket Books, 2021.

Ibram X. Kendi. *How to Be an Antiracist*. One World, 2019.

Robin Wall Kimmerer. *Braiding Sweetgrass: Indigenous Wisdom, Scientific Knowledge, and the Teachings of Plants*. Milkweed Editions, 2015.

Denise K. Lajimodiere. *Stringing Rosaries: The History, the Unforgivable, and the Healing of Northern Plains American Indian Boarding School Survivors*. NDSU Press, 2019.

Resmaa Menakem. *My Grandmother's Hands: Racialized Trauma and the Pathway to Mending Our Hearts and Bodies*. Central Recovery Press, 2017.

Steven T. Newcomb. *Pagans in the Promised Land: Decoding the Doctrine of Christian Discovery*. Fulcrum Publishing, 2008.

Ijeoma Oluo. *So You Want to Talk about Race*. Seal Press, 2018.

Nell Irvin Painter. *The History of White People*. W.W. Norton, 2010.

David Roediger. *Wages of Whiteness: Race and the Making of the American Working Class*. Verso, 2007.

Thandeka. *Learning to Be White: Money, Race, and God in America*. Continuum, 1999.

Sharon D. Welch. *After the Protests Are Heard: Enacting Civic Engagement and Social Transformation*. New York University Press, 2019.

SELECTED BIBLIOGRAPHY

13th. Directed by Ava Duvernay. Forward Movement and Kandoo Films, 2016.

Accomplices Not Allies: Abolishing the Ally Industrial Complex, an Indigenous Perspective and Provocation. 2nd ed, Indigenous Action Media, 2014.

"Addressing 400 Years of White Supremacist Colonialism: 2020 Action of Immediate Witness." *Unitarian Universalist Association,* 1 Jul. 2020, uua.org/action/statements/address-400-years-white-supremacist -colonialism.

Alexander, Michelle. *The New Jim Crow: Mass Incarceration in the Age of Colorblindness.* The New Press, 2011.

Alexie, Sherman. *You Don't Have to Say You Love Me: A Memoir.* Little, Brown and Company, 2017.

Allen, Theodore, *The Invention of the White Race.* Verso Books, 1994.

"Amen to Uprising: A Commitment and Call to Action, 2020 Action of Immediate Witness." *Unitarian Universalist Association,* 25 Jun. 2020, uua.org/files/pdf/2/20200625_aiw_amen_uprising.pdf.

Anne Braden: Southern Patriot. Directed by Anne Lewis with Mimi Pickering. Appalshop, 2012.

"Anti-Protest Bills Around the Country." *ACLU,* 23 Jun. 2017, aclu.org/ issues/free-speech/rights-protesters/anti-protest-bills-around -country.

Awake, a Dream from Standing Rock. Directed by Josh Fox, James Spione, and Myron Dewey. Bullfrog Films, 2017.

Baird, Jessie Little Doe, Ann Gilmore, and Anne Makepeace, panelists. Panel discussion. Wôpanâak Language Reclamation Project, 21 Nov. 2020, Unitarian Universalist Ministry for Earth, virtual meeting.

Baldwin, James. "Letter from a Region in My Mind." *The New Yorker,* 9 Nov. 1962, newyorker.com/magazine/1962/11/17/letter-from-a -region-in-my-mind.

Bates, Laura. "The Everyday Sexism Project." *Everyday Sexism,* everydaysexism.com.

Battle, Colette Pichon. "Religion, Race and Politics: Human Rights as a Tool to Create a Climate of Positive Change." Ministry Days, Unitarian Universalist Ministers Association, 20 Jun. 2017, Hilton Riverside, New Orleans, LA. Keynote Address.

Becker, Rachel. "Police Barricades Still Stand Between DAPL Protesters and Emergency Services." *The Verge,* 22 Dec. 2016, theverge.com/ 2016/12/22/14064412/police-barricade-oil-dapl-protest-nodapl -north-dakota-access-pipeline.

"Bismarck Residents Didn't Even Have to Fight to Re-Route the Dakota Access Pipeline." *The Takeaway,* 30 Nov. 2016, wnycstudios.org/ podcasts/takeaway/segments/bismarck-residents-concern-over -dakota-access-pipeline.

Brave Heart, Maria Yellow Horse. "The Return to the Sacred Path: Reflections on the Development of Historical Trauma Healing." *Indian Health Service,* ihs.gov/sites/telebehavioral/themes/responsive 2017/display_objects/documents/slides/historicaltrauma/htreturn sacredpatho513.pdf.

Brockell, Gillian. "Here are the Indigenous People Christopher Columbus and His Men Could Not Annihilate." *The Washington Post,* 14 Oct. 2019, washingtonpost.com/history/2019/10/14/here-are -indigenous-people-christopher-columbus-his-men-could-not -annihilate.

Brooks, Rebecca Beatrice. "History of Plymouth Colony." *History of Massachusetts Blog,* 28 Sep. 2016, historyofmassachusetts.org/ plymouth-colony-history.

Brown, Alleen. "Local Cops Said Pipeline Company Had Influence Over Government Appointment." *The Intercept*, 17 Apr. 2021, theintercept.com/2021/04/17/enbridge-line-3-minnesota-police-protest.

Ibid. "Medics Describe How Police Sprayed Standing Rock Demonstrators with Tear Gas and Water Cannons." *The Intercept*, 21 Nov. 2016, theintercept.com/2016/11/21/medics-describe-how-police-sprayed-standing-rock-demonstrators-with-tear-gas-and-water-cannons.

Brown, Brené. "Focus on Guilt Instead of Shame." *YouTube*, uploaded by 60 Minutes, 29 Mar. 2020, youtube.com/watch?v=RSrXxqKfYwI.

Buhle, Paul, and Nicole Schulman, editors. *Wobblies! A Graphic History of the Industrial Workers of the World*. Verso, 2005.

"Burgum Issues Emergency Evacuation Order." Office of the Governor, 15 Feb. 2017, governor.nd.gov/news/burgum-issues-emergency-evacuation-order.

"Bush: You Are Either with Us, or With the Terrorists—2001-09-21." *Voice of America News*, 27 Oct. 2009, voanews.com/archive/bush-you-are-either-us-or-terrorists-2001-09-21.

Caldwell, Christine, and Lucia Bennett Leighton, editors. *Oppression and the Body: Roots, Resistance, and Resolutions*. North Atlantic Books, 2018.

Capetz, Paul E. *God: A Brief History*. Augsburg Fortress Publishing, 2000.

"Changing Landscapes, Choosing Lifeways." *Early Peoples*. North Dakota Heritage Center, Bismarck, ND.

"Civil Rights Panel to Discuss Racism in Border Towns." *Indianz.com*, 8 Nov. 2007, indianz.com/News/2007/11/08/civil_rights_pa.asp.

Coates, Ta-Nehisi. *Between the World and Me*. Spiegel & Grau, 2015.

"Collectivism." *Ayn Rand Lexicon*, aynrandlexicon.com/lexicon/collectivism.html.

"Columbus's Letter to Ferdinand and Isabella of Spain, 1494." *Bill of Rights Institute*, billofrightsinstitute.org/activities/columbuss-letter-to-ferdinand-and-isabella-of-spain-1494.

"Columbusing: Discovering Things for White People." *YouTube*, uploaded by CollegeHumor, 7 Jul. 2014, youtube.com/watch?v= BWeFHddWLiY.

Cone, James H. *The Cross and the Lynching Tree.* Orbis Books, 2013.

Ibid. *God of the Oppressed.* Orbis Books, 1997.

Crass, Chris. *Towards the "Other America": Anti-Racist Resources for White People Taking Action for Black Lives Matter.* Chalice Press, 2016.

"Creating a More Just Future Through Divesting from Pipelines and Investing in Young People: Responsive Resolution, General Assembly 2021." *Unitarian Universalist Association*, Jun. 2021, uua.org/files/2021-06/Proposed_Divestment_Responsive_Resolution_Revised.pdf.

Crenshaw, Kimberlé. *On Intersectionality: Essential Writings.* The New Press, 2017.

Cushman, Philip. *Constructing the Self, Constructing America: A Cultural History of Psychotherapy.* Hachette Books, 1995.

Dalrymple, Amy. "Pipeline Route Plan First Called for Crossing North of Bismarck." *Bismarck Tribune*, 18 Aug. 2016, bismarcktribune.com/news/state-and-regional/pipeline-route-plan-first-called-for-crossing-north-of-bismarck/article_64d053e4-8a1a-5198-a1dd-498d386c933c.html.

Davis, Angela Y. *Are Prisons Obsolete?* Seven Stories Press, 2003.

Delaney, Carol. *Columbus and the Quest for Jerusalem.* Simon & Schuster, 2012.

Deloria, Barbara, Kristen Foehner, and Sam Scinta, editors. *Spirit and Reason: The Vine Deloria, Jr., Reader.* Fulcrum Publishing, 1999.

Deloria, Jr., Vine. *Custer Died for Your Sins: An Indian Manifesto.* 1969. University of Oklahoma Press, 1989.

Ibid. *God Is Red: A Native View of Religion.* 1972. North American Press, 1993.

Denton, Martha. "COVID-19 Fuels the Need for Renewable Energy in North Dakota." *Harvard Political Review*, 5 Sep. 2020, harvardpolitics.com/energy-north-dakota.

DiAngelo, Robin. *White Fragility: Why It's So Hard for White People to Talk about Racism*. Beacon, 2018.

"Donation from DAPL 'Unusual,' but a Win for ND Taxpayers, Officials Say." *Jamestown Sun*, 11 Jun. 2019, jamestownsun.com/news/4339172 -donation-dapl-company-unusual-win-nd-taxpayers-officials-say.

Douglass, Frederick. *Narrative of the Life of Frederick Douglass, an American Slave*. 1845. Ingram, 2004.

Doyle, Heather Beasley. "Unitarian Universalist Allies Cheer Standing Rock Victory." *UU World*, 12 Dec. 2016, uuworld.org/articles/ standing-rock-interfaith-day-prayer.

Du Bois, W. E. B. *Black Reconstruction in America: An Essay Toward a History of the Part Which Black Folk Played in the Attempt to Reconstruct Democracy in America, 1860–1880*. 1935. Simon & Schuster, 1999.

Ibid. *The Souls of Black Folk*. 1903. Dover Thrift Editions, 2016.

Du Mez, Kristin Kobes. *Jesus and John Wayne: How White Evangelicals Corrupted a Faith and Fractured a Nation*. Liveright, 2020.

Dunbar, Erica Armstrong. *She Came to Slay: The Life and Times of Harriet Tubman*. Simon & Schuster, 2019.

Dunbar-Ortiz, Roxanne. *An Indigenous Peoples' History of the United States*. Beacon Press, 2014.

Dunbar-Ortiz, Roxanne, and Dina Gilio-Whitaker. *"All the Real Indians Died Off" and 20 Other Myths about Native Americans*. Beacon Press, 2016.

Dyson, Michael Eric. *Tears We Cannot Stop: A Sermon to White America*. St. Martin's Press, 2017.

Eischens, Rilyn. "Law Enforcement Has Received $500,000 in Enbridge Money for Work Related to Line 3." *Minnesota Reformer*, 12 Apr. 2021, minnesotareformer.com/2021/04/12/enbridge-has-paid-law -enforcement-more-than-500000-for-work-related-to-line-3/.

Eisler, Riane. *The Chalice and the Blade: Our History, Our Future*. HarperOne, 1988.

Emerson, Blair. "Energy Transfer Partners Makes Largest Donation Ever to University of Mary Capital Project." *Bismarck Tribune*, 20 Apr.

2018, bismarcktribune.com/news/local/bismarck/energy-transfer
-partners-makes-largest-donation-ever-to-university-of-mary-capital
-project/article_c2c7f71e-03bf-5ad2-9e4d-08b45e010029.html.

End of the Line: The Women of Standing Rock. Directed by Shannon Kring.
Red Queen Media, Finnish Film Foundation, and Solar Films, 2021.

Energy Transfer Partners, commentators. Public hearing. North Dakota
Public Service Committee, 13 Nov. 2019, Emmons County Courthouse Auditorium, Linton, ND.

"Energy Transfer Partners Donates $3 Million to Mandan." *KFYR-TV,*
11 Jun. 2019, kfyrtv.com/content/news/Energy-Transfer-Partners
-511165181.html.

Escape to Alcatraz. Written and produced by Ken Miguel, performance by
Cornell Barnard, interviews with Stella Leach, Al Miller, Richard
Oakes, John Trudell, and LaNada War Jack, ABC7, 1971.

Esch, Mary. "Fracking Poses Mixed Bag for Farmers in New York." *Pitts-
burgh Post-Gazette,* 20 May 2012, post-gazette.com/business/
businessnews/2012/05/21/Fracking-poses-mixed-bag-for-farmers
-in-New-York/stories/201205210172.

Estes, Nick. *Our History Is the Future: Standing Rock Versus the Dakota
Access Pipeline, and the Long Tradition of Indigenous Resistance.* Verso,
2019.

Estes, Nick, and Jaskiran Dhillon, editors. *Standing with Standing Rock:
Voices from the #NoDAPL Movement.* University of Minnesota Press,
2019.

Eversley, Melanie. "Thousands Expected at Standing Rock Interfaith
Event Sunday." *USA Today,* 2 Dec. 2016, usatoday.com/story/
news/2016/12/02/thousands-expected-standing-rock-interfaith
-event-sunday/94839132.

Ewing, Eve. "I'm a Black Scholar Who Studies Race. Here's Why I Capitalize White." *ZORA,* 2 Jul. 2020, zora.medium.com/im-a-black
-scholar-who-studies-race-here-s-why-i-capitalize-white-f94883aa2dd3.

Farley, Jared Aaron. "Full Bibliography." *James Luther Adams Foundation,* jameslutheradams.org/full-bibliography.

Fatica, Ryan. "Ruby Montoya Case Raises Questions about Cooperation and Movement Lawyering." *Unicorn Riot,* 2 Dec. 2021, unicornriot. ninja/2021/ruby-montoya-case-raises-questions-about-cooperation -and-movement-lawyering.

Fisher, Andy. *Radical Ecopsychology: Psychology in the Service of Life.* SUNY Press, 2013.

Fleming, Crystal M. *How To Be Less Stupid About Race.* Beacon Press, 2019.

Free Leonard Peltier, International Leonard Peltier Defense Committee, 2022, whoisleonardpeltier.info.

Freire, Paulo. *Pedagogy of the Oppressed.* 1970. Translated by Myra Bergman Ramos. Bloomsbury Academic, 2012.

Friedland, Michael B. *Lift Up Your Voice Like a Trumpet: White Clergy and the Civil Rights and Antiwar Movements, 1954-1973.* University of North Carolina Press, 1998.

Gilio-Whitaker, Dina. "'Real' Indians, the Vanishing Native Myth, and the Blood Quantum Question." *Indian Country Today,* 12 Sep. 2018, indiancountrytoday.com/archive/real-indians-the-vanishing-native -myth-and-the-blood-quantum-question.

Gimbutas, Marija. *The Language of the Goddess.* 1989. Thames & Hudson, 2001.

Goldman, Emma. *Anarchism and Other Essays.* 1917. Dover Publications, 1969.

Grueskin, Caroline. "Archambault Found Innocent of Protest-Related Charge." *Bismarck Tribune,* 31 May 2017, bismarcktribune.com/ news/local/archambault-found-innocent-of-protest-related-charge/ article_4a85272b-4e04-54c7-9c72-a2d8841236b0.html.

Grueskin, Caroline, and Jessica Holdman. "Backwater Bridge Declared Structurally Sound." *Bismarck Tribune,* 12 Jan 2017, bismarck tribune. com/news/state-and-regional/backwater-bridge-declared-structurally -sound/article_41b7dddo-4404-522b-810d-05885275448c.html.

Gutiérrez, Gustavo. *A Theology of Liberation: Theology, Politics, and Salvation.* Translated by Caridad Inda and John Eagleson. Orbis Books, 1973.

Hagen, C.S. "Former DAPL Security Speaks Out, Damning TigerSwan Tactics." *High Plains Reader*, 8 Jun. 2017, hpr1.com/index.php/feature/news/former-dapl-security-speaks-out-damning-tigerswan-tactics.

Hamer, Fannie Lou. "Nobody's Free Until Everybody's Free." Founding of the National Women's Political Caucus, 10 July 1971, Washington, DC, Speech.

"The Harold Hamm Foundation Donates $10M and Continental Resources Donates $2M to the University of Mary." *University of Mary*, 1 Feb. 2022, umary.edu/about/news/all-stories/harold-hamm-foundation-donates-10m-and-continental-resources-donates-2m.

Hart, Michael. "UUs Support Standing Rock Sioux in Water Protection Action." *UUWorld*, 3 Oct. 2016, uuworld.org/articles/standing-rock.

Herr, Alexandria. "'They Criminalize Us': How Felony Charges Are Weaponized Against Pipeline Protesters." *The Guardian*, 10 Feb. 2022, theguardian.com/us-news/2022/feb/10/felony-charges-pipeline-protesters-line-3.

Heschel, Susannah, editor. *Abraham Joshua Heschel: Moral Grandeur and Spiritual Audacity*. Farrar, Straus and Giroux, 1996.

"Hess Corporation Makes Substantial $100,000 Donation to Great Plains Food Bank." *North Dakota Petroleum Foundation*, 7 Dec. 2020, ndpetroleumfoundation.org/hess-corporation-makes-substantial-100000-donation-to-great-plains-food-bank/.

"Honoring Their Lives—Jacob Blake with Brother, Pauly Jackson." *YouTube*, uploaded by Color of Change, 24 May 2021, youtube.com/watch?v=wUREk6e5c7Q.

"House Bill No. 1203." *Sixty-fifth Legislative Assembly of North Dakota*, Jan. 2017, legis.nd.gov/assembly/65-2017/documents/17-0351-01000.pdf.

Hovland, Daniel, presiding judge. Sentencing hearings. US District Court for the District of North Dakota, Bismarck, ND, 2017–2019.

Huff, Peter A. *Atheism and Agnosticism: Exploring the Issues*. ABC-CLIO, 2021.

Ibid. "Parliament of Religions on the Prairie: Standing Rock as Interreligious Event." *Southeastern Oklahoma State University*, Sept. 2019, se.edu/native-american/wp-content/uploads/sites/49/2019/09/A-NAS-2017-Proceedings-Huff.pdf.

"Include Systemic Anti-Racism in Principles: General Assembly 2021 Responsive Resolution." *Unitarian Universalist Association*, Jun. 2021, uua.org/files/2021-06/Proposed_Article_II_Responsive_Resolution.pdf.

Indigenous Peoples Law and Policy Program, University of Arizona Rogers College of Law. *Report to the Inter-Agency Commission on Human Rights.* Water Protector Legal Collective, 2019.

Iron Eyes, Chase. "DAPL Protesters Prosecuted as Terrorists." Email to Karen Van Fossan, 24 Aug. 2021.

"Jackson, Jimmie Lee." *The Martin Luther King, Jr., Research and Education Institute,* kinginstitute.stanford.edu/encyclopedia/jackson-jimmie-lee.

James, Moonanum, and Mahtowin Munro. "Thanksgiving: A National Day of Mourning for Indians." *United American Indians of New England,* uaine.org/historical.htm#ndom.

"James Reeb and the Call to Selma." *Unitarian Universalist Association,* uua.org/re/tapestry/adults/river/workshop5/175806.shtml.

Janis (Fallis), RedFawn. "Letter to the 17th Session of the United Nations Permanent Forum on Indigenous Issues." *RedFawn Support Committee,* 10 Jan. 2019, standwithredfawn.org.

Jaret, Charles. "Troubled by Newcomers: Anti-Immigrant Attitudes and Action during Two Eras of Mass Immigration to the United States." *Journal of American Ethnic History,* vol. 18, no. 3, Spring 1999.

Johnston, Angela. "North Dakota Pipeline Protest: Bismarck-Mandan Divided Over Out-of-Towners." *CBC News,* 4. Dec. 2016, cbc.ca/news/world/standing-rock-north-dakota-sunday-1.3880726.

Junger, Sebastian. *Tribe: On Homecoming and Belonging.* Grand Central Publishing, 2016.

K., Marley. "Why I'm Not Concerned about Being Nice to White People." *Marleyisms,* 22 May, 2020, medium.com/marleyisms/why-im -not-concerned-about-being-nice-to-white-people-8f2095e792b9.

Kasperkevic, Jana. "Goldman Sachs to Pay $5BN for Its Role in the 2008 Financial Crisis." *The Guardian,* 11 Apr. 2016, theguardian.com/ business/2016/apr/11/goldman-sachs-2008-financial-crisis-mortagage -backed-securities.

Katz, Judith H. *Some Aspects and Assumptions of White Culture in the United States.* Kaleel Jamison Consulting Group, 1990.

Kelly, Sharon. "For 15 Years, Energy Transfer Partners Pipelines Leaked an Average of Once Every 11 Days: Report." *DeSmog,* 17 Apr. 2018, desmog.com/2018/04/17/energy-transfer-partners-pipelines-leaked -once-every-11-days-greenpeace-report.

Kendall, Frances E., *Understanding White Privilege.* 2nd ed., Routledge, 2012.

Kendi, Ibram X. *How to Be an Antiracist.* One World, 2019.

Ibid. *Stamped from the Beginning: The Definitive History of Racist Ideas in America.* Nation Books, 2016.

Kennedy, John F. "Address of President-Elect John F. Kennedy Delivered to a Joint Convention of the General Court of the Commonwealth of Massachusetts, January 9, 1961." *John F. Kennedy Presidential Library and Museum,* jfklibrary.org/archives/other-resources/john-f-kennedy -speeches/massachusetts-general-court-19610109.

Kirgis, Frederic L. "Treaties as Binding International Obligation." *American Journal of International Law,* vol. 2, issue 4, 14 May 1997.

Kivel, Paul. *Uprooting Racism: How White People Can Work for Racial Justice,* 4th ed., New Society Publishers, 2017.

Kraft, Louis. "George Armstrong Custer: Changing Views of an American Legend." *History Net,* Jun. 2006, historynet.com/george-armstrong -custer-changing-views-of-an-american-legend.htm.

Kramer, Heinrich and Jacob Sprenger. *Malleus Maleficarum.* 1487. Translated by Montague Summers. Internet Sacred Text Archive, 2020.

Kuruvilla, Carol. "Something Extraordinary Happened at Standing Rock a Few Hours Before Victory." *Huffington Post,* 6 Dec. 2016, huffpost.

com/entry/interfaith-prayer-standing-rock_n_5845c7d0e4b055b313 98a38d.

LaDuke, Winona. "What is Line 3?" *YouTube*, uploaded by Honor the Earth, 4 Dec. 2016, youtube.com/watch?v=-S9hfiXcl_Q.

"Free the #NoDAPL Political Prisoners." *Vimeo*, uploaded by Water Protector Solidarity Now, Jun. 2020, vimeo.com/440053360.

Lajimodiere, Denise K. *Stringing Rosaries: The History, the Unforgivable, and the Healing of Northern Plains American Indian Boarding School Survivors*. NDSU Press, 2019.

Lawson, Michael L. *The Oahe Dam and the Standing Rock Sioux*. South Dakota State Historical Society, 1976.

Lee, Nathaniel. "How Police Militarization Became an Over $5 Billion Business Coveted by the Defense Industry." *CNBC*, 9 Jul. 2020, cnbc. com/2020/07/09/why-police-pay-nothing-for-military-equipment. html.

Littlebird, Leon Joseph. "Indian Wars." *YouTube*, uploaded by Leon Joseph Littlebird, 8 Feb. 2017, youtube.com/watch?v=7LjY3pKt6vU.

Levine, Peter. *Waking the Tiger: Healing Trauma*. North Atlantic Books, 1997.

Lewis, John, Andrew Aydin, and Nate Powell. *March: Book One*. Top Shelf Productions, 2013.

"The Link Between Extractive Industries and Sex Trafficking." *US Department of State Office to Monitor and Combat Trafficking in Persons*, Jun. 2017, state.gov/wp-content/uploads/2019/02/272964.pdf.

"Loved Ones of Federal Prisoners, Faith Leaders Ask New BOP Bi-Partisan Caucus to Prioritize Health and Safety of Incarcerated Persons." *UUSC*, 12 Aug. 2020, uusc.org/press/loved-ones-of-federal -prisoners-faith-leaders-ask-new-bop-bi-partisan-caucus-to-prioritize -health-and-safety-of-incarcerated-persons.

Loving. Directed by Jeff Nichols. Raindog Films and Big Beach Films, 2016.

Lux, Emma. "Four States Pass Laws Restricting Protesters." *Reporters Committee for Freedom of the Press*, 23 Oct. 2017, rcfp.org/four-states -pass-laws-restricting-protestors.

Lyla June. "Mamwlad." *YouTube*, uploaded by Lyla June, 3 May 2018, youtube.com/watch?v=TeGLDwfrvb8.

Madeson, Frances. "Federal Prison Should Not Be a Death Sentence." *The Progressive*, 28 May 2020, progressive.org/latest/federal-prison -not-death-sentence-madeson-200528.

Martineau, Taysha, speaker. Rally. Women at the Rivers, 15 Jul. 2021. Shell River, MN.

Maxouris, Christina. "Kyle Rittenhouse Was Acquitted on All Charges. Here's What We Know about the 3 Men He Shot." *CNN*, 19 Nov. 2021, cnn.com/2021/11/01/us/kyle-rittenhouse-shooting-victims -trial/index.html.

Menakem, Resmaa. *My Grandmother's Hands: Racialized Trauma and the Pathway to Mending Our Hearts and Bodies.* Central Recovery Press, 2017.

"Mental Health Disparities: Diverse Populations." *American Psychiatric Association*, 2017, psychiatry.org/psychiatrists/cultural-competency/ education/mental-health-facts.

Messerschmidt, Jim. *The Trial of Leonard Peltier.* South End Press, 1983.

Meyer, Robinson. "Trump's Dakota Access Pipeline Memo: What We Know Right Now." *The Atlantic*, 24 Jan. 2017, theatlantic.com/science/ archive/2017/01/trumps-dakota-access-pipeline-memo-what-we -know-right-now/514271.

"Might and Money Win Again." *High Plains Reader*, 17 May 2017, hpr1. com/index.php/feature/news/might-and-money-win-again.

Mitchell, Mairin. "Ferdinand Magellan: Portuguese Explorer." *Encyclopedia Britannica*, 12 Jan. 2000, britannica.com/biography/Ferdinand -Magellan.

Montagu, Ashley. *Man's Most Dangerous Myth: The Fallacy of Race.* 1942. Rowman & Littlefield, 1997.

Morales, Peter. "We Need You in Standing Rock." *Side with Love*, 27 Oct. 2016, sidewithlove.org/ourstories/we-need-you-in-standing-rock.

Morrison, Toni. *Playing in the Dark: Whiteness and the Literary Imagination.* Harvard University Press, 1992.

"Nashville Sit-Ins Begin." *Tennessee 4 Me*, tn4me.org/article.cfm/a_ id/201/minor_id/31/major_id/11/era_id/8.

Nastacio, Bravo1 (Brennon). "These Barbed Wire Dreamcatchers Help Support the Resistance at Standing Rock," by Katie Dupere. *Mashable*, 30 Jan. 2017.

Newcomb, Steven T. *Pagans in the Promised Land: Decoding the Doctrine of Christian Discovery.* Fulcrum Publishing, 2008.

Nicholson, Blake. "Gay Marriage Ban Approved in North Dakota." *The Bismarck Tribune*, 1 Nov. 2004, bismarcktribune.com/news/state -and-regional/gay-marriage-ban-approved-in-north-dakota/article_ 94bc1ce1-c5df-5dc0-b6fa-d1f2fac3b5fb.html.

Nolan, Salava. "Black and Brown People Have Been Protesting for Centuries. It's White People Who Are Responsible for What Happens Next." *TIME*, 1 Jun. 2020, time.com/5846072/black-people-protesting -white-people-responsible-what-happens-next.

Noonan, Alexander. "'What Must Be the Answer of the United States to Such a Proposition?' Anarchist Exclusion and National Security in the United States, 1887–1903." *Journal of American Studies*, vol. 50, no. 2, 2016, doi.org/10.1017/S0021875816000451.

"North Dakota Commissioner: Standing Rock Sioux Sat Out the State Process." *Morning Edition* from NPR, 2 Nov. 2016, npr.org/ 2016/11/02/500331158/north-dakota-commissioner-standing-rock -souix-sat-out-the-state-process.

"No Tar Sands." *Biological Diversity*, biologicaldiversity.org/campaigns/ no_tar_sands/index.html.

Nowatzki, Mike. "Burgum Issues Emergency Evacuation Order." *ND Response*, 15 Feb. 2017, ndresponse.gov/2016/dakota-access-pipeline/ press-releases/february-2017/burgum-issues-emergency-evacuation -order.

Obama, Barack. "University of Massachusetts at Boston Commencement." *Best Speeches of Barack Obama through His 2009 Inauguration*, 2 Jun. 2006, obamaspeeches.com/074-University-of-Massachusetts -at-Boston-Commencement-Address-Obama-Speech.htm.

O'Connor, Peg. "The Cartesian Mind in the Abused Body: Dissociation and the Mind-Body Dualism." *Dimensions of Pain*, edited by Lisa Folkmarson Käll, Routledge, 2021.

"Oil and Water Series." *The Intercept*, theintercept.com/special -investigations.

"Oil Spill." *Kalamazoo River Watershed Council*, kalamazooriver.org/ learn/what-are-the-problems/oil-spill-2.

Okun, Tema. "White Supremacy Culture." *Change Work Dismantling Racism Workbook*, n.d.

Oluo, Ijeoma. *So You Want to Talk about Race*. Seal Press, 2018.

Opper, Arianna. "Binary Thinking Can Be a Trauma Response." *YouTube*, uploaded by American Academy of Mind-Body Healing, 11 Dec. 2020, youtube.com/watch?v=XBctZP6W_hE.

Ortiz, Christina. "Dion Ortiz Reaches Noncooperating Plea." Interview by Water Protector Legal Collective, 22 Oct. 2018.

Painter, Nell Irvin. *The History of White People*. W. W. Norton, 2010.

Paré, Louise M. "A Focus on Louise M. Paré, Ph.D.—Part 2 of Women's Spirituality Then and Now, Moving Between the Worlds." *YouTube*, uploaded by Wanda Borland, 2 Oct. 2017, youtube.com/watch?v= EqNQJCOWKjc.

Pederson, Michelle. "Ministry in Residence at Standing Rock." *Unitarian Universalist Ministers Association*, 16 Feb. 2017, uuma.org/ news/329573/Ministry-in-Residence-at-Standing-Rock.htm.

Pember, Mary Annette. "Sheriff, Water Protectors Keep Peace at Enbridge Site." *Indian Country Today*, 17 Jun. 2021, indiancountrytoday.com/ news/sheriff-protesters-keep-peace-at-enbridge-site.

"Plunging Profits of Standing Rock Sioux Casino Blamed on Dakota Pipeline Protests and Frigid Winter," *Casino.org*, 27 Feb. 2017, casino. org/news/plunging-profits-of-standing-rock-sioux-casino-blamed -on-dakota-pipeline-protests.

"Poverty in North Dakota." *Welfare Info*, welfareinfo.org/poverty-rate/ north-dakota/.

Pressler, Carolyn. *Numbers*. Abingdon Old Testament Commentaries. Abingdon Press, 2017.

Protecting Our Water: Legal Strategies for Movement Activists, Book One: Pre-Action. Pipeline Legal Action Network, 2020.

Raygorodetsky, Gleb. "Indigenous Peoples Defend Earth's Biodiversity—But They're in Danger." *National Geographic*, 16 Nov. 2018, nationalgeographic.com/environment/article/can-indigenous-land -stewardship-protect-biodiversity-.

Reagan, Ronald. "President Reagan's City on a Hill." *YouTube*, uploaded by No Labels, n.d., youtube.com/watch?v=LYiOUEjzZNs.

"Religion and the Founding of the American Republic, America as a Religious Refuge: The Seventeenth Century, Part 1." *Library of Congress*, loc.gov/exhibits/religion/rel01.html.

"Rethinking Schools and Teaching for Change, 2022." *The Zinn Education Project*, zinnedproject.org.

"Rev. Karen Van Fossan on the #NODAPL Protests, and How They Shaped Her Ministry." *Prairie Public Broadcasting*, 26 Nov. 2018, news.prairiepublic.org/main-street/2018-11-26/rev-karen-van -fossan-on-the-nodapl-protests-and-how-they-shaped-her-ministry.

Ríos, Monisha. "Confronting the Militarization of Psychology in the United States of America." 2019. Saybrook University, PhD dissertation.

Roediger, David. *Wages of Whiteness: Race and the Making of the American Working Class*. Verso, 2007.

Romney, Mitt. "Watch Full Speech: Romney Calls Trump a 'Phony.'" *PBS News Hour* with Steve Peoples and Brady McCombs, 3 Mar. 2016, pbs.org/newshour/politics/romney-calling-trump-phony-urging -republicans-to-shun-him.

Roszak, Theodore, Mary E. Gomes, and Allen D. Kanner, editors. *Ecopsychology: Restoring the Earth, Healing the Mind*. Sierra Club Books, 1995.

Ruffin, Amber, and Seth Meyers. "White Savior: The Movie Trailer." *YouTube*, uploaded by Late Night with Seth Meyers, 21 Feb. 2019, youtube.com/watch?v=T_RTnuJvg6U.

"Run for Our Water." *Facebook*, uploaded by ReZpect Our Water, 18 Jul. 2016, facebook.com/ReZpectOurWater/videos/run-for-our-water/ 1158037240905236.

Schiano, Chris. "DAPL Saboteur Jessica Reznicek Sentenced to 8 Years." *Unicorn Riot*, 14 Jul. 2021, unicornriot.ninja/2021/dapl-saboteur -jessica-reznicek-sentenced-to-8-years.

Schlecht, Jenny. "Clergy Shows Solidarity with Standing Rock." *Bismarck Tribune*, 3 Nov. 2016, bismarcktribune.com/news/state-and -regional/article_31c07dd3-76fb-5ddf-aeb9-aca5c3045f6f.html.

Ibid. "Unitarian Universalist Church Plans Water Is Life Series." *Bismarck Tribune*, 23 Sept. 2016, bismarcktribune.com/lifestyles/faith -and-values/unitarian-universalist-church-plans-water-is-life-series/ article_13afe061-19ef-5ef8-adc7-3b01b8d915b6.html.

"Second Crusade." *World History*, 18 Aug. 2015, worldhistory.biz/middle -ages/23193-second-crusade-1147-1149.html.

Shin, Ian. "Violence against Asian Americans on the Rise, but Racism Isn't New" by Jared Wadley. *Michigan News*, 19 Mar. 2021, news. umich.edu/violence-against-asian-americans-on-the-rise-but-racism -isnt-new.

Sisk, Amy. "Months In, Pipeline Protest Quiets as North Dakotans Take Stock." *Inside Energy*, 2 Dec 2016, insideenergy.org/2016/12/22/ months-in-pipeline-protest-quiets-as-north-dakotans-take-stock/.

Slodysko, Brian, and Stephen Groves. "GOP Donor Pays $1M to Deploy South Dakota National Guard." *AP News*, 1 Jul. 2021, apnews.com/ article/joe-biden-south-dakota-philanthropy-immigration-government -and-politics-ea0586be65e874578ca27ffcc690dba1.

Slutkin, Gary. "Why Should We Treat Violence Like a Contagious Disease?" *TED Radio Hour*, by Guy Raz, 6 Feb. 2015.

Smedley, Audrey. *Race in North America: Origins and Evolution of a Worldview*. 1993. Westview Press, 2007.

Smith, Lillian. *Killers of the Dream*. W. W. Norton, 1949.

"SRST Council Meeting with DAPL Representatives." *Facebook*, uploaded by Standing Rock Sioux Tribe, 17 Nov. 2016, facebook.com/watch/ ?v=1437472629614336.

"Standing in Solidarity with the Standing Rock Sioux—What We Can Do." *UU College of Social Justice*, 28 Oct. 2016, uucsj.org/standing -in-solidarity-with-the-standing-rock-sioux-what-we-can-do.

"Standing Rock Sioux Akicita James 'Angry Bird' White Sentenced to Two Years of Supervised Release." *Water Protector Legal Collective*, 6 Dec. 2018, waterprotectorlegal.org/post/standing-rock-sioux -akicita-james-angry-bird-white-sentenced-to-two-years-of -supervised-release-fo.

"Standing Rock Special: Unlicensed #DAPL Guards Attacked Water Protectors with Dogs & Pepper Spray." *YouTube*, uploaded by Democracy Now!, 24 Nov. 2016.

Stanek, Roman. "Why Christopher Columbus Was the Preeminent Entrepreneur." *VentureBeat*, 11 Apr. 2013, venturebeat.com/2013/ 04/11/why-christopher-columbus-was-the-preeminent-entrepreneur.

Stone, Merlin. *When God Was a Woman*. Harcourt Brace Jovanovich, 1976.

Stout, Linda. *Bridging the Class Divide and Other Lessons for Grassroots Organizing*. Beacon Press, 1997.

Swallow, Jr., David, panelist. Panel discussion. Stories and Songs of the People, 24 Aug. 2019, Black Hills, SD.

Tatum, B. D. "Teaching White Students about Racism: The Search for White Allies and the Restoration of Hope," *Teachers College Record*, vol. 95, no. 4, 1994.

Thandeka. *Learning to Be White: Money, Race, and God in America*. Continuum, 1999.

Thompson, Becky. *A Promise and a Way of Life: White Antiracist Activism*. University of Minnesota Press, 2001.

Tochluk, Shelly. *Witnessing Whiteness: The Need to Talk about Race and How to Do It*. 2nd ed., Rowman & Littlefield Education, 2010.

"Trayvon Martin's Life Celebrated on What Would've Been His 27th Birthday." *YouTube*, uploaded by WPLG Local 10, 5 Feb. 2022, you-tube.com/watch?v=hSUokYqMK1M.

"Tribal Treaties Database." *Oklahoma State University Libraries*, treaties. okstate.edu/?fbclid=IwARormD15W3ak24kiVN9hrJYPiLA bly4PO-mvvH_eoW7vFo9bgV4wLFv63hs.

Trudell, John. "Take Back the Earth." *YouTube*, uploaded by Isten Ostora, 4 Jun. 2014, youtube.com/watch?v=q2WEVdNQAxE.

Ture, Kwame (Stokely Carmichael). *Disciples of Malcolm*, 29 Jan. 2013, disciplesofmalcolm.tumblr.com/post/41774628270.

"Unit 1: Set 2: Mapping the Land & Its People—Sitting Rabbit's Map." *State Historical Society of North Dakota*, history.nd.gov/textbook/ unit1_natworld/unit1_2_sittingrabbit.html.

Van Fossan, Karen. "Call to Standing Rock: Dec. 4th Interfaith Day of Prayer." *UU Ministry for Earth*, 23 Nov. 2016, uumfe.org/2016/11/23/ call-to-standing-rock-dec-4th-interfaith-day-of-prayer.

Ibid. "The Incarcerated Body and Mutual Liberation." *On Second Thought: The Racial Justice Issue*. Humanities North Dakota, Aug. 2020.

Ibid. "Loved Ones of Indigenous Federal Prisoners: Better Response Now to COVID-19." *UU Ministry for Earth*, 7 May 2020, uumfe. org/2020/05/07/loved-ones-of-indigenous-federal-prisoners-better -response-now-to-covid-19/.

Ibid. "Webinar September 13th—UU Solidarity with Indigenous Water Protectors." *UU Ministry for Earth*, 23 Aug. 2018, uumfe.org/2018/ 08/23/webinar-sept-13th-uu-solidarity-with-indigenous-water -protectors/.

vanFossen, Katherine Hobson. *The Van Fossen Family in America*. Columbus, Ohio, published by the author, 1952.

Vine, David. "Where in the World is the US Military?" *Politico Magazine*, Jul./Aug. 2015, politico.com/magazine/story/2015/06/us -military-bases-around-the-world-119321.

Washington, James M., editor. *A Testament of Hope: The Essential Writings and Speeches of Martin Luther King, Jr.* HarperCollins, 1997.

Waxman, Olivia B. "The First Africans in Virginia Landed in 1619. It Was a Turning Point for Slavery in American History—But Not the

Beginning." *TIME,* 20 Aug. 2019, time.com/5653369/august-1619 -jamestown-history.

"We Are All Related: Solidarity NOW with Indigenous Water Protectors: 2018 Action of Immediate Witness." *Unitarian Universalist Association,* 1 Jul. 2018, uua.org/action/statements/we-are-all-related-solidarity -now-indigenous-water-protectors.

"The Weapons of Mass Destruction." *American Experience* from PBS, 4 May 2020, pbs.org/video/george-w-bush-weapons-mass -destruction.

Welch, Sharon D. *After the Protests Are Heard: Enacting Civic Engagement and Social Transformation.* New York University Press, 2019.

West, Cornel, editor. *The Radical King.* Beacon Press, 2015.

"What Really Happened at Standing Rock?" Standing Rock Class Action, standingrockclassaction.org/?page_id=6123.

"White Populations." *Suicide Prevention Resource Center,* sprc.org/scope/ racial-ethnic-disparities/white.

Whitman, Karen. *Re-evaluating John Brown's Raid at Harper's Ferry.* State Department of Archives and History, 1972.

Wickman, Forrest. "Is Prostitution Really the World's Oldest Profession?" *Slate,* 6 Mar. 2012, slate.com/news-and-politics/2012/03/ rush-limbaugh-calls-sandra-fluke-a-prostitute-is-prostitution-really -the-worlds-oldest-profession.html.

Widra, Emily. "State Prisons and Local Jails Appear Indifferent to COVID Outbreaks, Refuse to Depopulate Dangerous Facilities." *Prison Policy Initiative,* 10 Feb. 2022, prisonpolicy.org/blog/2022/ 02/10/february2022_population.

Widra, Emily, and Tiana Herring. "States of Incarceration: The Global Context 2021." *Prison Policy Initiative,* Sep. 2021, prisonpolicy.org/ global/2021.html.

Wilkerson, Isabel. *Caste: The Origins of Our Discontents.* Random House, 2020.

Wink, Walter. *The Powers That Be: Theology for a New Millennium.* Doubleday, 1998.

Winthrop, John. "City Upon a Hill." *Digital History*, digitalhistory.
uh.edu/disp_textbook.cfm?smtID=3&psid=3918.

"Wisdomkeepers: Mathew King of the Lakota." *Beyond Words*, Beyond
Words Publishing, beyondword.com/blogs/beyond-words-blog/
wisdomkeepers-mathew-king-of-the-lakota.

Wise, Tim. *Dispatches from the Race War*. City Lights Books, 2020.

Wolff, Eric. "Obama Administration Blocks Dakota Pipeline, Angering
Trump Allies." *Politico*, 4 Dec. 2016, politico.com/story/2016/12/
us-army-corps-blocks-dakota-access-pipeline-232172.

Wong, Julia Carrie. "Dakota Access Pipeline: 300 Protesters Injured after
Police Use Water Cannons." *The Guardian*, 21 Nov. 2016, theguardian.
com/us-news/2016/nov/21/dakota-access-pipeline-water-cannon
-police-standing-rock-protest.

Woods, Daniel. "A Monument of Horizontal Proportions." *Williston
Herald*, 28 Oct. 2011, willistonherald.com/news/a-monument-of
-horizontal-proportions/article_161c2d5d-8ff0-587f-8fde-cdf3c
deb94c2.html.

Xhopakelxhit. *Everyone Calls Themselves an Ally Until It Is Time to Do
Some Real Ally Shit*. Ancestral Pride, 2015.

Yannielli, Joseph. "Princeton Students Attempt to Lynch an Abolitionist."
Princeton & Slavery Project, slavery.princeton.edu/stories/attempted
-lynching.

Yurth, Cindy, and Jan-Mikael Patterson. "Is There Racism? Depends
Whom You Ask." *Navajo Times*, 22 Jan. 2009, navajotimes.com/
news/2009/0109/012209pageside.php.

Zinn, Brad, Monique Calello, and Ayano Nagaishi. "Paving the Way:
Meet the 13 Original Freedom Riders Who Changed Travel in the
South." *Nashville Tennessean*, 1 Jun. 2021, tennessean.com/story/
news/2021/06/01/meet-13-original-freedom-riders/4882573001.